Jews & Gentiles

Werner J. Cahnman

Edited by
Judith T. Marcus
Zoltan Tarr

Jews & Gentiles

A Historical Sociology of Their Relations

Transaction Publishers
New Brunswick (U.S.A.) and London (U.K.)

This book is printed on acid-free paper that meets the American National Standard for Permanence of Paper for Printed Library Materials.

Library of Congress Catalog Number: 2003070289
ISBN: 0-7658-0212-0
Printed in Canada

Library of Congress Cataloging-in-Publication Data

Cahnman, Werner Jacob, 1902-
Jews and gentiles : a historical sociology of their relations / Werner J. Cahnman ; edited by Judith T. Marcus and Zoltán Tarr.
p. cm.
Includes bibliographical references and index.
ISBN 0-7658-0212-0 (alk. paper)
1. Jews—Social conditions. 2. Gentiles—History. 3. Jews—Relations—Christianity. 4. Christianity and other religions—Judaism. 5. Jews—History—70- 6. Antisemitism—History. I. Marcus, Judith, 1929- II. Tarr, Zoltán. III. Title.

DS112.C27 2004
305.89'4—dc21 2003070289

Contents

Introduction

Wandering in the "great maze" of Werner J. Cahnman's writings in German and English, one comes away with the understanding that his historical bent, his respect for the multitude of data, his sociological sensitivity and personal experience were all at work in order to enhance our understanding and knowledge of the past and more recent times. As his friend and mentor, Joseph B. Maier, put it: Cahnman's lifework "mirrored his fate as a wanderer between worlds and cultures and as a mediator between them."[1]

When we met in the late 1970s, I had no inkling that one day I would be asked to nurse his last unpublished manuscript on the historical relationship of Jews and Gentiles into print. Our long talks and especially the lecture of some of his published and unpublished essays were revelatory. One autobiographical essay relating his short but terrifying experience at the Dachau concentration camp dealt with "life in the Camp" and showed not only his talent to espy the sociologically significant aspect but also his analytical bent—not forsaken even in an extreme existential situation. He talks here about the morale of the Jewish prisoners with shades and grades, of course, and the fact that "on the whole, intellectuals and persons from the upper class, as well as persons from the laboring classes, stood the test better than the middle classes....The petit bourgeois simply did not understand what was happening to him.... People from the laboring classes, on the other hand, were helped by their sturdy physique and by a culture pattern which was less individualistic and more inclined toward mutual help." He attributes the strength of the "intellectuals and persons from the business elite" to "their inner resources and their keen grasp of the situation."[2] Similarly, he observes and establishes types and characteristics even among the SS overseers. As he put it: "there was a whole range of types, from the all-out bloodhound to the contemptuous sadist, and from the moral monster to the man who appeared to merely do his duty." He is aware of the dangers of generalization though, and adds that "the exception is as important as the rule."[3]

While not yet a sociologist, the young Cahnman had it in him to become the scholar who would undertake the ambitious and demanding project, to write the social history of Jews and Gentiles. Judging from several writings—published or unpublished—the intent to write a "comprehensive, yet concentrated, account of Jewish-Gentile relations" seemed to go back to the early 1930s when the unfolding social, political, and intellectual crises in Germany compelled young Cahnman to engage in political and social activities and Jewish learning. His family history, lively social life and connectedness to Munich's business, artistic, and intellectual circles, his studies at Munich University and his intense community concerns aided him greatly in this undertaking. Indeed, to know about Cahnman's early years in Germany and his life as a refugee scholar in America are important to the understanding of his life work, and, especially, his approach to this problem.

Werner Jacob Cahnman was born in Munich on September 30, 1902, the scion of an old German-Jewish family. As recounted by him, his father's village roots represented a rustic and folksy Judaism, sentimentally attached to community and family but no Jewish learning. His mother's family, on the other hand, belonged to the *haute bourgeoisie*; they were bankers, jurists, and industrialists, living in Munich and Nuremberg. They were patrons of the arts, interested in philosophy and literature; their Judaism was of a freethinking sort. As Cahnman recalled in the 1970s, his mother revered Spinoza and Mendelssohn and her religion had an ethical orientation. "The main idea of my mother," he said, "was that everybody, but especially a Jew, should promote justice in the world. She died in Piaski, in Poland, in unimaginable circumstances and in a situation of utmost injustice."[4]

Cahnman has inherited from his father the perspective of participant observer, the emotional attachment and feelings of unquestioned belongingness to a *Gemeinschaft*. He listened to his father's stories of village life told with historical enthusiasm; he interviewed older relatives and collected family-related data from them and from archives. Such early activities informed his 1974 typological study of "Village and Small-town Jews in Germany," for example. Since his parent's house was a meeting place of notables of all persuasion he encountered Zionism and socialism, and heard discussions of women's problems and present-day social problems of the Munich community. Although he was exposed to a variety of Jewish, political, and intellectual viewpoints, Cahnman claimed that on the whole, the Jews of Munich were bourgeois liberals. Already as a teenager, Cahnman became interested in demography, collected data, and read up on baptism, intermarriage, birthrates, and generally, the growth, decline or change in the make-up of Bavarian Jewish communities. He became interested in the Palestinian settlements but when the Great War broke out, his "German patriotism" was aroused, as he said, and he stayed put. His university studies in Munich and Berlin followed where he majored in economics, history, political science, and sociology, concluding with a dissertation at the University of Munich on Ricardo in 1927. There followed an absorption into Jewish learning, and Jewish political activity.

Cahnman evaluated the years of the Weimar Republic as a time when exciting things happened, teeming with intellectual and artistic fervor and controversy, but also a time when public life showed discouraging signs. In Germany, the 1920s also witnessed little hope for meaningful political action and the collectivities' inward turn. Thus, the 1920s saw a revival of Jewish consciousness and as Cahnman noted, "Jewish themes pure and simple came to the fore." The Centralverein had many new members, the Jewish Lehrhaus movement exploded, and publications abounded on the essence of Judaism. Cahnman read avidly the works of Leo Baeck, Martin Buber, Franz Rosenzweig et al., accompanied by the reading of the varied philo-Semitic as well as anti-Semitic literature of the time. He regarded Buber as his main guide and influence in the development of his own characteristic combination of elements in his work: historiography, Jewish ethnicity, romantic philosophy, and political democracy. Thus, it may also be safe to assume that *Jews and Gentiles* had been germinating ever since.

Cahnman's intellectual preoccupations were soon supplanted by varied activities which he called his "social work" period. He moved from being a research associate of the Berlin Chamber of Industry and Commerce and the Institute of World Economy to become the *Syndikus* for Bavaria's *Centralverein* (1930-1934), the major defense organization of German Jewry. He then became a teacher at the *Juedische Lehrhaus* and a member of the *Kulturbund* in Munich until his escape in 1939. In the meantime, he started work on the reasons for the rise of the Jewish national movement in Austria, centered around the person of Adolph Fischof, which he was able to finish only in the 1950s in the United States. Similarly, he started but finished only in late 1969 a study on the presence of "Three Regions of German Jewry," which was to demonstrate that a unified and uniform German Jewry never existed. Cahnman's activities included many clandestine missions on behalf of his beleaguered people, undertaken in several countries. After 1934, as a "leader of an illegal organization" he was briefly thrown into the Munich police prison, giving him a first-hand experience with the "New Order." According to Cahnman, it was his erstwhile classmate at the University of Munich, Rudolf Hess, who was instrumental in his release.[5]

After Cahnman's escape from Germany, he entered the United States in 1940 and soon after partook in a summer seminar for foreign scholars and teachers at the Brewster Free Academy in Wolfsboro, New Hampshire. Here he first encountered the sociologist Robert E. Park, of the University of Chicago, and Herbert A. Miller who evaluated Cahnman's background and designated him as a "race and cultural specialist" in sociology, with a recommendation for a visiting position at the University of Chicago. In due course, as he recalled, he became a "Chicago sociologist," in close contact with Everett Hughes, the anthropologist Robert Redfield, and, above all, Park who greatly influenced his thinking. The relationship with Louis Wirth was more complicated. In spite of their common interest in things Jewish, their perspectives differed: Cahnman had a strong survivalist perspective, meaning the survival of ethnic groups from both normative and empirical viewpoints, while Wirth maintained a strong assimilationist outlook, that is, the inevitability of the absorption of the Jews, as any other ethnic group, into the mainstream of the larger society. While trying to find his place in American academic life proved to be a long and arduous process, he was similarly not too successful in finding outlets for his earlier work. From Germany, he brought with him sets of data on Jewish life and/or emigration as well as Herzl's relation to German-Jewish communities. He was adamant not to let the German-Jewish communities go under "without a song" and constantly tried to place his studies—with more or less success. But he found his "home" in American Jewish life only when he was asked to join the editorial board of the *Reconstructionist* magazine. To the end of his life, he faithfully contributed to the journal and some of his articles reflect his brand of thinking, such as, "Intercultural Education and Jewish Content." (1948), "The Tercentenary Conference on American Jewish Sociology" (1955), "Religion in Israel" (1956), "Attitudes of German Youth" (1965), "The Interracial Jewish Children" (1967), and "New Intermarriage Studies: A Critical Survey"(1967). Interestingly, a public figure, Mario Cuomo, acknowledged Cahnman's shrewdness as participant observer and the astuteness of his analyses and called him "a sociologist friend from Forest Hills," whose insights he made use of for his 1975 book, *Forest Hills Diary—The Crisis of Low Income Housing*. In turn, Cahnman reviewed Cuomo's book and some of his comments there help to explain and evaluate his concerns and writings from the 1930s. He wrote:

I am a Forest Hills (instead of Munich) resident, a sociologist who is a race and intercultural relations specialist, and I am active in Jewish life. It goes without saying that I am aware of the complexities of urban living. I believe I know of the needs [of the newcomers] as well as the aspirations of the neighbors in the midst of whom I live.[6]

Indeed, Cahnman's choice of themes—community and family history, Jewish history, Jewish leaders and thinkers, the once-existing German-Jewish symbiosis, and last but not least, Jewish-Gentile relations—attest to his deep understanding and awareness of the complexities and problems involved in such relations. As to why he devoted a considerable part of his life and scholarly work to the examination of all aspects of these themes, Cahnman's answer was that it was the times and themes that chose him.

As Cahnman put it, he had been "finally rescued for sociology," when Joseph B. Maier, then chair of the Department of Sociology at Rutgers University's Newark Campus, brought him there in 1961; he retired from Rutgers as full professor in 1968. According to Professor Maier, Cahnman was respected but he never became part of the "inner circle" of the faculty there on account of his being too fastidious in his ideals and standards, too set in his habits, too German, too Jewish, too much himself. He was seen by others and he regarded himself to be a "stranger," and it is no accident that he devoted much time to the conceptual clarification of the term as used by Simmel, Brentano, and Toennies. Cahnman's preference was for the term "intermediary" (*Vermittler*), not meant microsociologically as in the case of Simmel but macrosociologically in the Toennisian sense, that is, as a commercial and cultural intermediary within a social structure. The macrosociological bent was more pronounced in Cahnman's last scholarly period when there emerged a systematic concern with the historical perspective in sociology. This approach resulted in the 1964 volume *Sociology and History*, which he edited with Alvin Boskoff. With his friend, Joseph B. Maier, Cahnman was instrumental in establishing a Historical Sociology Section in the American Sociological Association, which he chaired. In his essay, "Historical Sociology: What it is and What it is Not" (1976), Cahnman showed how typological devices as well as the use of comparative materials can be enormously useful in producing scholarly works which are sociologically oriented and historically relevant.

Cahnman's early practical and activist tendencies reemerged in the 1970s when he branched out from scholarship to promote intercultural relations and preservation of Jewish past. He called upon his peers to establish the Rashi Association for the Preservation of Jewish Cultural Monuments in Europe. He acted on his deeply felt conviction that after the obliteration of Jewish communities and institutions all around Europe, it was imperative that still remaining, visible testimonies of the past be saved. He singled out Germany as the first place of activity because the "aim of Hitler to obliterate all traces of Jewish life from German soul must be frustrated." It was just as important for him to salvage the sites and cultural artifacts as links to the future. Cahnman thought that the visible signs of Jewish continuity would have a significant educational and psychological impact: Gentiles in all these countries would be made to realize that Jewish history was part and parcel of their own, their country's history. Just as in his hometown back in the 1930s, for Cahnman community concerns, scholarly endeavors and Jewish activism always and everywhere went hand in hand. When I visited the first such enterprise helped along by The Rashi Association, the Martin Buber Institute at the University of Cologne, and saw there young German students engaged in learning Hebrew and writing papers on Jewish culture, I could witness how the vision of Werner Cahnman became reality.

The last, most philosophical and most elaborate essays of Cahnman, entitled "Friedrich Wilhelm Schelling and the New Thinking of Judaism," deals with an old theme of his: the German-Jewish symbiosis. As one appreciative critic, Selma Stern put it, the essay addresses the problem of "elective affinity," or the state of affairs when "the Jews achieved some sort of synthesis between Judaism and European culture."[7] As the title indicates, Cahnman goes back to the early nineteenth century, after the waning of the cabbalistic beliefs due to the collapse of the carriers: the Sabbatian and Frankist movements, and their subterranean influence. He traces its re-emergence in the "garb of romantic philosophy," as evidenced in Schelling's 1815 lectures on "Philosophy of Mythology" and the "Philosophy of Revelation," The Schellingian influence on the thinking of the representatives of the second Emancipation in Germany is thus emanated from cabbalistic sources. The line reaches the twentieth century in the persons of Franz Rosenzweig and Hermann Cohen—up to the writings of Max Horkheimer and the Frankfurt School, where Schellings *Naturphilosophie* shows through their critique of science and technology.

For years, Werner Cahnman sought to see the publication of his last full-scale work with the provisional title, "Jews and Gentiles: The Historical Sociology of Their Relations" without success. He wrote letters and sent out the synopsis of his manuscript as follows:

I have been working on a comprehensive, yet concentrated, account of Jewish-Gentile relations for a long time. I believe that a scholarly conceived yet fluidly written account of these relations is essential for the self-understanding of the present generation. The topic of the Jewish experience among the peoples in the midst of whom Jews live is not identical, although it is overlapping, with the usual history of antisemitism. If the focus is on antisemitism, Jewish history is made to appear as if it were a record of unmitigated hostility against the Jewish people and of passivity on the part of the Jews.[8]

However, as Cahnman demonstrates in his study, Jewish-Gentile relations are far more complex. There is a long history of mutual contacts, positive as well as antagonistic, even if conflict situations continue to require particular attention. He points out that the account follows a historical sequence, but it is sociological in conception. The main question addressed is whether there are recognizable patterns, common to most ages and places in which Jewish history has been enacted. At the same time, while general patterns may be recognizable, modifications and combinations of patterns are assumed to have occurred.

Cahnman's historical account runs from Roman antiquity through the Middle Ages, into the era of emancipation and the Holocaust, and finally to the present American and Israeli scene. To be sure, as far as the "present" American and Israeli scene is concerned, the account appears unfinished as well as dated. But the basic similarities and dissimilarities throughout history are laid out and analyzed. He tests the theses of classical sociology implicitly, yet unobtrusively. For example, he traces the socio-economic basis of human relations emphasized by Marx and others, and considers Jews as "strangers" and "intermediaries." He disagrees with Max Weber in that for him Jews were not "pariahs" although he finds a remarkable affinity to Weber's Protestantism-capitalism argument in the tension of Jewish-Christian relations emerging from the bitter theological argument over usury, where the antagonism between Jews and Gentiles took on a pronouncedly socio-economic rather than religious character. It is depicted how the nineteenth century added a nationalist dimension as well as the distortions of biology and race, with fateful consequences.

For Werner Cahnman, the sociological study of Jewish Gentile relations was of importance for more than one reason. For one, he held that the preservation of past history "must serve as pillars of the new Jewish consciousness which is to arise out of the memories of the past." And similarly to his promotion of intercultural relations that guided his establishment of The Rashi Association, he counted this time too on the psychological and educational impact of the examination of Jewish history that proved to be part and parcel of Gentile history. Finally, it attests to Cahnman's self-understanding as a sociologist and a student of Jewish life. On the occasion of his seventieth birthday, he was asked about his approach to Jewish history. His answer? An approach from the vantage point of the historical sociologist, and a scholar who is not chiefly concerned with "isolated phenomena but with relations between phenomena." In fact, he continued,

When I came to understand that the trader and the peasant live in symbiosis and conflict, I was relieved....The Jewish people dwells among the nations, whether in Israel or in the Diaspora, and the tensions between intimate symbiosis and bitter conflict remains a guiding theme of Jewish history.[9]

In sum, for Cahnman the primacy of Jewish-Gentile relations in all their complexity and variability seemed essential for the understanding of Jewish social and political history. While it is evident that the history of post-Emancipation German Jewry and of the Holocaust aftermath has received considerable scholarly attention, the study of Jewish life in the Diaspora, or the migrational movements has been somewhat neglected; Cahnman clearly was intent to fill the gap. His research data, his personal experiences, and historical view combined resulted in a scholarly lifework that should constitute an important element in any future large-scale historical account. Reminiscent of Martin Buber, Cahnman makes a confessional statement in this regard: "I shall try to testify… in the belief that what I have to say will stand for the truth which, while it becomes manifest only in personal experience, nevertheless transcends it."[10]

Werner Jacob Cahnman died of cancer in Forest Hills, New York, on September 27, 1980. Besides the unpublished manuscript of *Jews and Gentiles*, he left behind an even more ambitious work on "The History of Sociology." With all his other papers, they were preserved by his widow, Dr. Gisella Levi Cahnman in shared executorship with Joseph B. Maier, and later, with the editors of the present study. This volume is dedicated to the memory of Cahnman's close friend, mentor and fellow refugee scholar, Professor Joseph B. Maier, the last member of the Frankfurt School, who died on November 22, 2002.

Notes

1. In J. B. Maier and Ch. I. Waxman, eds., *Ethnicity, Identity and History. Essays in Memory of Werner J. Cahnman* (New Brunswick, NJ: Transaction Publishers, 1983), 4.
2. Werner J. Cahnman, "In the Dachau Concentration Camp: An Autobiographical Essay," in J.B. Maier, J. Marcus and Z. Tarr, eds. *German Jewry. Its History and Sociology. Selected Essays by W. J. Cahnman* (New Brunswick, NJ: Transaction Publishers, 1989), 155.
3. Ibid., 157-158.
4. Quoted in *Ethnicity, Identity and History*, 2.
5. Quoted in *German Jewry,* p. XIV. See also Cahnman, "Rudolf Hess;, or, An Introduction to the Emergence of German Geopolitics: An Autobiographical Account," in Werner J. Cahnman, *Weber and Toennies. Comparative Sociology in Historical Perspective*, ed. By J.B. Maier, J. Marcus and Z. Tarr (New Brunswick, NJ: Transaction Publishers, 1995), 319-336. There exists also a completed, unpublished manuscript entitled, "Rudolf Hess as a Symbol."
6. See Cahnman, "The Forest Hills Experience," in the *Reconstructionist*, 12, no. 2 (March 1975): 25.
7. Selma Stern's statement comes from her book, *The Court Jew*, translated by Ralph Weinman (Philadelphia: 1950), 241.
8. See Cahnman's notes published in the *Newsletter* of the Association for the Sociological Study of Jewry (1975), 20-21.

9. Quoted by Ira Eisenstein, "Werner Cahnman at Seventy," in the *Reconstructionist* (June 1973), 24-33.
10. See Cahnman, "Martin Buber: A Reminiscence," in the *Reconstructionist,* 31, no. 12 (15 October 1965): 7.

1

Approach to the Subject

The relations between Jews and Gentiles are the oldest known and thoroughly documented continuing relations between ethnically and religiously different groups of people, and they remain as problematic and intensely disturbing today as they were in antiquity. In many ways they are the prototype of intercultural relations, any place, any time. But in other respects, they are unique. The religious difference is always there, but unlike the difference between Hindus and Muslims in India, it is not a difference arising from diametrically opposed value systems, but from mutually exclusive claims to one and the same tradition. Another difference arises from the peculiar–although by no means unique–position of the Jews in the social structure, which at times appears sharply accentuated, at other times largely blurred. Linguistic differences are often present, but more frequently non-existent; and it is remarkable that even where linguistic acculturation is complete, other differences between Jews and Gentiles remain unaltered and virulent. Differences in phenotype are pronounced in some countries of Jewish settlement, but in the majority of them insignificant; yet, Jewish facial features and physical characteristics have at times been emphasized, as if they were of the essence; and racial prejudice, from the earliest times to the present moment, has assumed a *character indelibilis* of the Jews, independent of phenotype, which even conversion could not erase. All of these are elements in a comprehensive theme, the unity of which one must be able to grasp without disregarding the variety of its manifestations. One thing, though, is certain: one can hardly understand the nature of a late manifestation, such as the position of the Jews in contemporary America, if one is not aware of the pattern of history from which such a late and complex manifestation is likely derived. The occupational distribution of American Jews or the incidence of intermarriage in America is not the same as the socio-economic structure of the Jewish community in seventeenth-century Poland or the phenomenon of conversion in fourteenth century Spain, but they are variants of permanent traits. They are unique adaptations to changing circumstances; yet, if one compares them to related phenomena in the past, they testify to the durability of human intentions and institutions. To the extent that we are able to demonstrate that durability, we can say that we have provided an explication.

Our approach, then, is not historical in the sense of a conventional historical narrative; it is in the nature of a social history and even a sociological history. The historian and the sociologist share the same subject matter, but their aims and procedures are not the same. The historian, once he has chosen his topic, sets himself the goal of telling a story that may range from the earliest to the latest manifestations of a phenomenon, without much consideration for related phenomena, the recording of which is left for another story; and this story will be told by another narrator-specialist. The sociologist, on the other hand, is interested not so much in the story itself, but in the categories that it contains. In addition, he is not concerned with phenomena, but with relations between phenomena. Where the historian records and interprets materials, the sociologist compares the recorded data with and attempts to arrive at a systematic view of their relationships. If social history differs from narrative history in that it is concerned with what is typical in the social reality prevailing at a given period rather than with single occurrences connected over time, the sociological historian adds the element of comparability, both within a specific social entity and between a variety of disparate social entities. To illustrate: the social history of Jewish-Gentile relations in the European Middle Ages describes and analyzes the economic, political, social, cultural, and religious activities of Jews and Christians in that period as they relate to each other's spheres of existence. Social history becomes sociological history inasmuch as it compares events and activities observed in the Middle Ages with those that may be observed in antiquity and in the modern era and further, inasmuch as it compares Jewish-Christian–and Jewish-Moslem–relations with other minority-majority relations, especially if they are in the nature of relations between what Howard Becker has called "marginal trading peoples" and settled populations. In this way, conclusions can be drawn and even predictions may become possible.

There are various pitfalls in this procedure, as compared to others, which must be clearly stated. There are caveats for the historian, the sociologist and the sociological historian or–with a slightly different accent–for the historical sociologist. A historiographer is not a mere chronicler of events; he selects his data in accordance with a general theme, such as Heinrich Graetz's theme of Jewish history as the history of a people of "thinkers and sufferers" or Simon Dubnow's theme of Jewish history as the history of the survival of a people and its institutions. With all that, however, the historiographer remains within the boundaries of the narrative. He remains a positivist in that he aims at assembling all the available data and "letting the facts speak for themselves." One ruler's attitude toward the Jewish community differs from the attitude of another ruler, one persecution from another persecution; no conceptualization, anchored in a comparison of patterns, seems possible or is even attempted by the historian, for fear that the uniqueness of the event may be blotted out. The pitfall of the sociologist, on the other hand, is that he gets imprisoned within the categories of a preconceived "system." The data are assembled in prepared conceptual boxes, and what does not fit into a particular box, is either forced into it by hook or by crook or excluded from consideration. The color of life is likely to be lost in the generality of categories, and if specific statements are forthcoming, they are bound to be trite.

In the approach of the sociological historian, the dangers of not seeing the forest for the trees and disregarding the concreteness of phenomena in the pursuit of scientific categories, are avoided; but the danger of overextension is very real. It is plainly impossible to know all the literary sources needed for the description and analysis of a single period or specific problem, and less so the literature pertinent to several periods or problem areas or, finally, the literature informing a comparative of a variety of cultural situations. Considerations of this kind may well deter the researcher from attempting to unravel as complex a phenomenon, as Jewish-Gentile relations. Teamwork has been suggested as a remedy, but teamwork has its own pitfalls in that congenial teams of equals are hard to come by; the "Readers" that have become fashionable of late, which string together assorted fragments of approaches, are a poor substitute.

Another way of coming to grips with the problem of methodology is to adopt ideal-typical procedure. Actual life situations are of a mixed and conglomerate nature; and even if we were to succeed in catching them all in a sufficiently large net, we are not likely to gain much by enumerating the bewildering multitude of the phenomena that we encounter. If we want to achieve clarity, we are constrained to select predominant traits and train our sights on them. It must be remembered, however, that type constructs are ideal images or "things of thought," as Toennies called them, not descriptions of reality. The ideal image provides the point of departure, but modifications, transitions and exceptions may be indicated in ideal-typical analysis, but more frequently and specifically, they will have to be worked out in subsequent monographs.

Occasionally, the ideal image may assume the aspect of a symbol. Symbols are concrete or imagined signs for something that cannot be expressed directly because it defies detailed descriptions: it is either something that is feared or adored or that is too complex to be analyzed. There are positive symbols uniting people in adoration and negative symbols uniting them in fear; a complex symbol combines the aspects of both. Jewish-Gentile relations, over and over again, have been epitomized in symbols summarizing a welter of actual encounters in one single imagined encounter that contains them all. The actual encounter, which the historian or sociologist registers, approximates but never equals the imagined encounter; but the actual encounter is illuminated by the symbol under which it is subsumed. At the same time, symbolic perceptions are both summaries of past encounters or occurrences and molders of emerging attitudes. A symbol is not a stereotype. A stereotype is the generalization of traits into a *Gestalt*. A symbol resembles an ideal in that it is a product of thought, but it is not an object of selection, as a type construct would be; and it lacks the element of comparability. Instead, it partakes in the quality of enhancement, which is the essence of myth. A symbol is not a type, but it may be a sign that suggests a type construct.

To select the type construct involves more than mere perception. To be sure, the "objective" past is an illusion. If the illusion is indulged in by a historian, the process of interpretation is likely to be disregarded; if it is harbored by a sociologist, it may result in the fallacy of misplaced concreteness. There are as many pasts, recent or remote, as there are investigators and beholders of the past. But that does not mean that the individual researcher, who perceives the past from a particular vantage point in the present, holds a permit for letting his imagination run wild. To perceive the facts, one must know where to look for them; one must be ready to ask more than a single question of them; and some perceptions are more perceptive than others. The selection of the type construct, then, is a matter of trained imagination. Training involves hard work over a considerable period of time, chiefly acquainting oneself with a wide range of the pertinent literature; and imagination is kindled by the intimate acquaintance that training provides. Beyond that, there is no hard and fast rule. Fortunately, one type construct does not exclude another. the researcher is free to select and even to combine those that serve besting the circumstances. I can only hope that I have selected the constructs that illuminate the widest possible area of interest by the most economical means.

Some comments of a personal nature may be inserted at this point My first acquaintance with the literature on Jewish-Gentile relations dates back to my early youth, and I have added ever since to that initial knowledge in a variety of ways. Yet, though my present knowledge extends over a considerable segment of the literature in various languages, I am handicapped by my lack of acquaintance with works written in Hebrew and Yiddish, except where translations or, at least, partial quotations are available. I have worked from primary sources only, regarding some German, Austrian, and Hungarian materials of the nineteenth century; but I have acquired considerable knowledge concerning the contemporary Jewish scene in general and Jewish-Gentile relations in particular, as a practitioner and consultant in civic defense and social work agencies, both in Europe and America. The social scientist learns much that goes beyond the single case from participant observation. As far as history in a larger sense is concerned, in attempting to make the present state of Jewish-Gentile relations understandable from its antecedents, I am making two assumptions that arise from the nature of the data themselves. For one thing, I contend that the structural patterns that govern Jewish-Gentile relations have been consolidated in the high Middle Ages. Further, I am relying in the main on materials from the German-, French-, and English-speaking areas of central Europe. The justification for this selectivity rests with the fact that the pattern of Jewish-Gentile relations and its most powerful symbolic expressions have arisen paradigmatically in this area from the eleventh to the fourteenth century, so that what has evolved provides something akin to an ideal type construct for a wide range of subject matter.

Spain, Poland, and the modern world in Europe and America may be considered as providing modifications that are derived from the central type and are in one way or another comparable to it. What is observed in peripheral areas may then be understood as being related to the core area, and what is happening now as a variation of patterns of long standing and as a phase in an ongoing process. The combination of pattern and process means that a pattern is never erased, but perpetually modified. From century to century and from area to area, the picture becomes increasingly more complex until the modifications, as it were, threaten to outgrow the initial image; it is at this point that recalling the pattern is essential to comprehension. If these prerequisites for ordering the data are not lost sight of, some scientific quality, at least to an extent, can be imparted to the account.

Jewish-Gentile relations are not co-extensive with anti-Semitism because they involve friendly as well as antagonistic contact situations. But just as illness rather than health is the problem in medicine, so do conflict and its causes provide the focus of interest in human relations. Individual health and social equilibrium are individual constructs, but illness and conflict are actual occurrences. What is in question is the concept of conflict as well as the nature of causation. Each of these must be seen in context. If conflict were considered in isolation, the nature of the social context would be falsified because conflict is only one element of the total picture; conflict without accommodation would be destructive of social relations. Jewish-Gentile relations, like other group relations, must therefore be comprehended under the aspect of symbiosis as well as under the aspect of conflict, with both aspects conditioning each other in a variety of ways. In speaking about causation in history, we must recognize that we do not have before us isolated and unambiguously ascertainable causes which, in turn, lead to equally ascertainable consequences. The history of mankind does not resemble a laboratory in which one undertakes test-tube experiments. Rather, historical situations are distinguished by the fact that mutually dependent chains of causation, which may either reinforce or counteract each other, lead to likewise interdependent reinforcing or counteracting chains of effects, and these again grow into new causes, leading to new effects, and so forth. The bewildering multitude of cause-and-effect relations can hardly be reduced to a single general principle, but the continually changing objects of observation can be described, compared and evaluated. This means that we may have before us unity in variation: situations change over time, but if essential elements remain identifiable, the result may be that one situation, while not the exact equivalent of another, nevertheless contains an element of comparison that can serve as a guide in explanation. Within limits, comparison allows a causal interpretation to be corroborated or denied.

Among the causes of the rejection as well as the acceptance of Jews in a larger society, those of a socio-economic nature appear to be prominent. But if we search for an explication of the causes of anti-Semitism and related phenomena, we must try to ascertain in what sense we can consider causes of a socio-economic nature as a coherent chain of causation, different from other chains of causation. Economic causes of human behavior, that is, those that are connected with the need for making a living, are only partial phenomena in the totality of the societal nexus. Consequently, they can hardly be separated, except in a mental experiment, from political, legal, religious and moral causes of the behavior of members of one human group in relation to another. All these possible causations must be kept in mind, even if we pay particular attention to the socio-economic factor. We will even come to realize that the socio-economic factor is as much dependent on antecedent ideologies as it is, in turn, the causation of ideologies that arise on its foundation. In the case of the initial antagonism between the Church and the Synagogue, the ideological factor is clearly predominant; from the twelfth century onward, the socio-economic factor overshadows everything else. A multivariate analysis of sorts is called for.

However, we do not mean to scatter our considerations far and wide so as to try to uncover all the motivations of human action that may have a bearing on Jewish-Gentile relations. We will have to disregard motivations that refer to the weakness of human nature as expressed in the attitudes and behavior patterns of individual human beings. Our investigation belongs in the field of structural sociology, not because of individual psychology. This must be emphasized regarding the widely quoted modern literature about the psychological, even psychiatric, causes of group-antagonism, such as racism or anti-Semitism, for instance, the literature surrounding the concept of the "authoritarian personality." This literature deals with an entirely different chain of causation than the one we intend to scrutinize, namely one that can be considered only if and when the socio-economic chain of causation has been clarified. Leading psychologists admit that a structural element, such as economic insecurity, is required to bring to the fore one or another manifestation of group antagonism, even if the emotional predisposition for it has been present previously in certain types of individuals. In other words, the predisposition remains ineffective, if the structural conditions are not favorable for its release.

Another caveat may seem to be in order. Some authors have tried to explain away the specific causes of anti-Semitism, saying that anti-Semitism was nothing but a special case of group antagonism. A gang of youngsters at an urban playground, an association of merchants on a business street, an ethnic group that occupies a particular region or a part of town–all of these may feel that another gang, other merchants, another ethnic or racial group competes with them unfairly and that they must therefore be kept at bay or ejected from where they have already intruded. Competition leads to conflict, but not necessarily to subsequent accommodation and assimilation. Where one or the other group, the invaders or the invaded, turns out to be the weaker party in the conflagration, the outcome may be the severance of societal bonds, by means of expulsion or stark oppression: the extreme case is marked by extermination. In order to achieve that end, one starts by providing the opponent with horns and claws and proceeds to defame him as the arch-enemy of humankind, so that one do away with him with a perfectly good conscience. If the opponent is defined as no longer being human, humanitarian considerations need not be wasted on him. All this is good sociology and may be applied to Jewish-Gentile as well as to other relations among men. But this procedure does not explain wherein Jewish-Gentile relations differ from other group relations and why it was the Jews who were depicted as the Devil Incarnate. In order to understand the particular in the general, we need to be attentive to the lessons of history.

However, before we do that, we must once again make it clear that any description and analysis of Jewish-Gentile relations are bound to remain one-sided and even to miss the point, if it restricts itself to manifestations of antagonism and disregards amity altogether. The pagan prophet Balaam who, as the Bible tells us, was sent to curse but instead was moved to bless, has found many successors until this day. The words of his blessing: "How beautiful are your tents, Jacob, your dwelling-places, Israel!" have been included in the daily prayer of the Jews. Leading minds throughout the centuries have praised Jewish achievements and cultural contributions, and Jews and Gentiles have dwelled side by side as good neighbors and maintained intimate friendships at all times. If this were not so, one would have to despair of human nature. But we have observed with horror in our time or, at any rate, not so long ago, that friendship can be defamed and ostracized and finally overcome by hostility, so that it may come to pass that millions of men, women and children are humiliated, starved, executed, burned and gassed without any serious effort being made by anybody to rescue them. This shattering experience must always be before our mind's eye. We believe, therefore, that we are serving the cause of friendship if we lay bare the chains of causation that have nurtured malevolent attitudes and erupted in hostile outbreaks. For we can overcome only what we have clearly comprehended.

2

Theology as a Point of Departure

If one intends to understand the antagonism between Jews and Gentiles at its roots, one must understand its point of departure in theology. It is our initial thesis that theology comes first in the chain of causations that shape Jewish-Gentile relations as we know them today, and that the socio-economic reality that ensues bears the indelible stamp of its origin in theology. However, in this chapter we are only laying the groundwork for the main thesis. In antiquity and in the early Christian centuries until the advent of the high Middle Ages, a great many circumstances and developments had to come together to complete the plot of history. Once the major theme was established, which was not the case until the twelfth century, the newer centuries worked out the modifications. But whatever was reinforced or modified later the tale of the beginning is still evident.

In relating how it all started, one recognizes that the story has many aspects that reach far back in time. History is like a deep well in which every level of observation mirrors a deeper level beneath it. The actual depth of the well can hardly be fathomed. In the case of the Jews, one may say that Abraham came to Canaan as a migrant from beyond the Euphrates River and that the Children of Israel were "strangers in Egypt" before Moses led them out of the House of Bondage and into the Promised Land. In our context, these are matters of long ago. We begin with the statement that the antagonism between Jews and Gentiles, as we have come to know it, arises from a more immediate religious experience in Western civilization, namely the birth of Christianity out of the fusion of Judaistic and Hellenistic elements in the declining world of antiquity. We must recall that the imagination of the ancients could not grasp the idea of an invisible and universal God. To acknowledge no concrete representation of the godhead and especially to refuse recognition of the divinity of kings and emperors, which was of the essence in Judaism, appeared to the pagans to be not only absurd but contemptible. It seemed a sign of conceit, of intolerance and, to use the words of Tacitus, of an "implacable hatred of mankind," even of godlessness. When Pompey, availing himself of the prerogatives of dominion, entered the Temple in Jerusalem in 63 B.C., he found to his amazement that "inside there was no image of the gods, the place was empty, and the secrets of the sanctuary were nought." The incomprehensibility of an imageless cult, in conjunction with a rigorous culinary code that made close association with Gentiles outside of Jewish homes difficult, led some Gentiles to assume that the Jews conducted reprehensible rites in secrecy. Josephus had to go so far as to refute the accusation that human sacrifice was an essential feature of Jewish services–an ominous anticipation of the "blood accusation" of the later centuries.

More serious were the political consequences. The world of antiquity was a world of city-states that had grown into territorial states that combined a variety of tribal and local cultures under the overarching principle of divine kingship. For the Jews, however, there was no supreme authority beside the one and only God of Eternity (*melekh olam*); and although they were constrained by their leaders and teachers to conduct themselves as law-abiding subjects of legitimate authority wherever they settled, the rulers as well as the masses distinctly felt that there was a limit to the civic obedience of the Jews. This feeling was expressed on various occasions, especially in the first recorded pogrom in history, which occurred in Alexandria in Egypt in 38 B.C. At the height of the riots, the mob entered the synagogues and forcibly placed therein the statue of Emperor Caius, popularly known as Caligula, thereby desecrating the sanctuaries in the eyes of the Jews and making the Jews, who complained about the imposition, appear to the emperor to be lacking in loyalty. The placement of a statue of the emperor in the main sanctuary in Jerusalem was impeded by the Emperor's death, but the episode goes a long way to show why the religious autonomy, which the Jews alone enjoyed among the subject peoples of the Empire, remained an irritant. This autonomy has been designated by an illustrious historian of Rome as the initial cause of anti-Semitism. Theodor Mommsen's statement lifts the matter somewhat out of context. To be sure, the Jews of Alexandria and other Hellenistic cities formed a separate community or *politeuma*, with their own magistrates and institutions. They may not have enjoyed the same citizen's rights as the Greeks, but their economically favored position in addition to the special privileges they were granted by the Ptolemaic and Seleucid rulers of Egypt and Syria and later by the Romans as a religious community are likely to have aroused the envy of the native populations. Possibly, one can say that the conditions that brought about the political accommodation but not the social integration of the Jews were odious to the masses and never entirely beyond suspicion to those at the helm of the state. One may even note that beyond the special historical situation, the Jewish insistence on what might be called the exclusive divinity of a universal principle constituted a challenge to totalitarian rulers at all times, from Antiochus Epiphanes ("who appears in Divine Magnificence") of Maccabean fame and Haman in Persia (as related in the Book of Esther) to Hitler and Stalin. In this context, for the Jews to be looked upon as "international" plotters by the Nazis and "cosmopolitan" subversives by the Soviets would be but an echo reverberating from antiquity.

Max Weber, a pupil and admirer of Mommsen, puts the onus for the hostility against Jews which is found in Greek and Roman sources, not so much on the refusal of the Jews to accept the divinity of kings and emperors or–as Mommsen did–on Jewish communal autonomy, but on Jewish exclusivity. He especially had in mind the limited conviviality because of ordained food taboos. Indeed, the sharing of food and drink is a token of brotherliness. But when Max Weber further argues (at the very end of the third volume of the *Gesammelte Aufsaetze zur Religionssoziologie*, i.e., *Ancient Judaism*) that proselytism proves the absence of "racist" aversion against the Jews by the Gentiles, meaning that it was the Jews' own fault that they were segregated, he contradicts his own statement in the same passage when he talks about the three stages of becoming a proselyte to Judaism and the widely extended proselytizing activities in which the Jews were engaged. Just as the proselytes were not repelled by Judaism, the Jews did not exclude them from their ranks. What one can say is that the pagan authors, whose diatribes have been preserved, "viewed with alarm" what was going on, namely, the attraction that Judaism held for many a searching mind among their contemporaries. The spectacle was irritating for a variety of reasons, not least, as Seneca put it, because it seemed that "the vanquished (had) given laws to the victors."

One might have thought that Christianity made a difference, superseding, as it did, the gods of the heathen; but actually its original theme was reinforced and only the orchestration grew more complex. To be sure, Christianity was born as a Jewish sect. Jesus was sent "to the lost sheep of the house of Israel"; he had come "to fulfill the law and not to destroy it." The conversion of the people chosen by Providence to have witnessed the truth adumbrated in the sayings of the Prophets and embodied in the redeeming death of the Savior, whose mother was Jewish, was the goal and the hoped-for crowning triumph of the victorious Church. But many circumstances combined to overshadow this basic attitude. The apostle Paul could not hope to convert the multitude of pagans without minimizing for them "the yoke of the law" with its minute prescriptions regulating every moment of a man's waking hours, and giving them instead a visible son of God who could guide the faithful to the presence of the invisible father. For the Jews, on the other hand, the sacred law became more important as a protective shield the longer and farther they dispersed, so that the rabbis became preoccupied with erecting "fences around the Torah," hedging in every prescription with further cautionary prescriptions, in an effort to preserve the integrity of the Jewish heritage. As a result, the Jews were effectively separated from the Christians as well as from the pagans at the very same time that the conversion of the pagans to Christianity proceeded. In this context, the Jewish Christians were left out in the cold: they were ready to accept the pagan Christians under the same conditions that the Jews generally accepted proselytes, but they could not forego the special obligation that Biblical tradition generally imposed on Jews. Pauline interpretation invalidates that obligation. For the Jews, on the other hand, Christianity in either form, in view of the continuing Roman domination, was a threat to their identity and the need for closing the ranks a paramount concern. The aloofness of the Christians from the Jewish insurrections against Rome seemed therefore treasonable, quite apart from the fact that their accommodation to Hellenic concepts, such as the belief in virgin birth and in death and resurrection, entailed an abandonment of basic Judaic principles. In turn, the rejection by the Jews of the message of the Savior led Paul, who was dedicated to the task of bringing the light to the Gentiles but who personally felt himself to be a Jew, into an ambivalent interpretation of a situation that was to have fateful consequences.

"Blindness," he said, "is happening to Israel," but it can only happen "until the fulness of the Gentiles comes in"; then, when the time comes, "Israel shall be saved." And he continued: "As concerning the gospel, they are enemies for your sake; but as concerns the election, they are beloved for the fathers' sakes." As the generations passed, love drifted further and further away while enmity was ever present; it became the major theme of the people.

The claim of the Jews that they were "the people of God," and the claim of the Church that it represented "the true Israel," were indeed irreconcilable. To the Church, the Jews were blind because they rejected the Redeemer who had been born in their midst; and to the Jews the Church was impertinent, because it arrogated the inalienable inheritance of the Jewish people. But the Church became dominant when it joined forces and coalesced, as it were, with the Empire after the conversion to Christianity of Emperor Constantine while Judaism, which had been a *religio licita* under the pagan emperors, was cast in the role of an illegitimate competitor and found its adherents subjected to severe discrimination. The pagans were excused by ignorance; but if the Jews, who had prophecy at their disposal, continued to insist that the Redeemer of Israel and the whole world had not yet come and that the promise of final redemption remained unfulfilled, the only explanation in the eyes of the Church for such stubbornness was that the overwhelming pride of the Jews had caused their fall from grace and transformed the Jewish community into a "synagogue of Satan." This expression from the Revelation of St. John (2,9) had been foreshadowed in the latest of the gospels, the Gospel of St. John (8, 44-45), which said of the Jews that "because I tell you the truth, you believe me not." What this sentence means is that inasmuch as not God but the Devil is the "father" of the Jews, their devilish addiction inexorably causes them to be deaf and blind to the obvious truth. The Satanic nature of the Jews, which in effect annuls their election and ensures their condemnation, was then confirmed and elaborated by the fathers of the Church, by Chrysostom, Hilary, Ambrose, Gregory of Nyssa, Cyprian, Tertullian, and Augustine. In Chrysostom of Antiochia in Syria (ca. 350-407), the anti-Jewish invective is most unbridled; in Augustin of Hippo in North Africa (354-430), the intellectual consequences are sharply drawn. In Chrysostom, the arsenal of polemic weapons is complete; the Jew is an addict of the flesh, he is voluptuous, demonic, accursed, greedy, a slave of Mammon. The Jew is a drunkard, a fornicator, a criminal. He is a killer of prophets, of Christ, of God, a dwelling place of the Devil. All the heresies among Christians are the work of Jews. Augustine, on the other hand, must be evaluated against the background of Manichaeism, with which he was imbued and which he transmitted to Martin Luther, and to a host of dualistic thinkers and movements, religious or secular, of later centuries. According to Manichaeism, the world is the battleground between the forces of darkness and the forces of light. Manichaeism, originally an Oriental rival of Christianity, through Augustine and others, intruded into Christianity and transformed it from a message of redemption to a fighting creed. In such a creed, no accommodation is possible between angels and devils. Good and evil are irreconcilable opposites: good must triumph and evil must be crushed. In the Augustinian version, the Jew is the villain of the piece, the counter-conception to holiness.

The theology of Jewish-Christian relations was formulated by the Church fathers, but the process by which these convictions were hammered out among the people-at-large took centuries to mature. In its course, theological theory and administrative practice, otherworldly piety and societal reality interlocked and interpenetrated until the image congealed. From generation to generation, the accents were sharpened and the tone the spokesmen of the Christian faith grew from edgy controversy to bitter hostility. The brotherly name that had united Jews and Christians in their confrontation with the pagan world dimmed until it became hardly recognizable. All this had its effect in law, although here, too, the changes were gradual, frequently contested, occasionally modified, and ultimately confirmed. But the principle was established. Since the Jews were marked as outcasts and enemies of Christianity, it followed that they could not be permitted to exercise authority over Christians, as magistrates or otherwise. Neither could they be permitted to indulge in a conspicuous display of prestige, for example, through the erection of new synagogues. Even the repair of damaged or destroyed synagogues was beset with difficulties. It would lead too far afield to detail this development here; however, it is important to note that in the reign of Emperor Theodosius II (439), the Jews definitely were excluded from all governmental and municipal offices. This stipulation became of prime importance for the Jews in the Eastern as well as Western Roman Empire, when it was included in the *Codex Justinianus*. The most significant part of this collection of decisions, texts, and laws issued in the reign of Emperor Justinianus I (527-565), the *Corpus Juris Civilis,* contains the basic formulation of Roman law, as it came to be used in many European countries. Thus, the twin image of imperious Rome and enslaved Jerusalem became a corner stone of European civilization. If this assimilation of theology into law is appreciated, the symbolism in art can be properly understood. Only one small step remains before one is confronted, at the height of the Middle Ages, with the figure of the young woman, blindfolded with the broken staff of the deposed ruler in her hand, whom one can see affixed over the portals of medieval cathedrals, such as the portal of the southern transept of the Munster at Strasbourg. The veiled eyes symbolize the theological blindness, the broken staff the vanished secular power. The humiliation, which is the punishment of powerlessness, was explained and justified as a consequence of willful insensitivity. But it should also be said that the statue of the Strasbourg Synagogue has distinguished features and a dignified bearing. Even in defeat, she remains a queen. There is not yet a trace of the distorted image of the Jew that one finds in the later centuries.

Nothing was so momentous in the centuries during which antiquity changed into the Middle Ages as the fact that Jerusalem had been captured and destroyed by the Roman legions and that the Jewish religion thereby was deprived of the context of a political nationality within which it once rested. This made the Jews bitterly aware that they had been worldly sinners and prone to a mood of repentance while making the hearts of their adversaries swell with a sense that their cause was right. The destruction of the Temple and the bloody oppression of the subsequent Jewish uprisings could not fail to impress the pagan world, which was based on the glorification of physical strength and sheer power. The advancing Church, in turn, took every opportunity to make it appear that the expulsion of the Jews from the soil of their own country was a deserved punishment for the rejection of the Son of God, who had arisen in their own midst. Pagans and Christians agreed in this regard. Already Cicero, in his *Oratio pro Flacco*, had said that "even while Jerusalem was standing and the Jews were at peace with us, there was little in common between the religious customs of which their rites are examples and those which befit an empire as splendid as ours. . . .

Now, however, we can surely be less obliged to respect Jewish religious observances when the nation has demonstrated in arms what its feelings are toward Rome and has made clear how far it has enjoyed divine protection since it has been conquered, scattered, enslaved." The dependent position that the Jews occupied as *servi camerae imperatoris* in the Holy Roman Empire of the Middle Ages is derived from the impression that the conquest of Jerusalem has made on the minds of contemporary as well as succeeding generations. For instance, the *Schwabenspiegel*, one of the two great codifications of laws and usages in medieval Germany (the other was the *Sachsenspiegel)*, comments that the Jews had already been servants in Roman times, and that the German emperors had succeeded to the rights of the Roman emperors, who had disposed of the lives and possessions of the vanquished. Surely, it was not juridical fiction that brought the facts of life into being; rather, it was the stark fact that found its juridical justification in a convenient legend that the Jews stood in need of protection.

Another inheritance that Rome bequeathed to Christianity was the *Fiscus Judaicus*. Religion and nationality are closely intertwined everywhere, especially in the ancient Near East. One prays to the king of the city and the god of the fathers. But, as has already been pointed out, the Jews had elevated the god of Abraham, Isaac, and Jacob to the Lord of the Universe and were therefore unable to place him among the multitude of the gods of the Roman Pantheon. Neither could they place the statue of the divine Emperor in the Temple on Mount Zion. Hence, while the Jews enjoyed the status of Roman citizens, in matters of cult and religion, the fiction that they were strangers remained. Emperor Vespasian decreed that they should pay a special levy to *Jupiter Capitolinus* in acknowledgment of the recognition of their cult, with the receipts to flow into the imperial treasury. The assumption, therefore, is that the designation of the status of the Jews as legal strangers in the Germanic succession states of Rome is ideally derived from the institution of the *Fiscus Judaicus*, which is a prototype of juridical discrimination. What initially had been a modus vivendi between incompatible conceptions of the godhead, became in time a means of stark exploitation. The adherence of the Jews to the imperial chamber in Germany, their special taxation in France, the so-called Exchequer of the Jews in medieval England–all these may be thought of as having had their legal foundation in the *Fiscus Judaicus*. But one must note once again that the actual foundation for the special taxation of Jews was the need for protection.

Paralleling the development from brotherhood to hostility in theology and from privilege to discrimination in basic law is the similarly slow but inexorable process by which the Jews were deprived of ownership of land. The Jews had been agriculturists in ancient Palestine. Reportedly, in Mesopotamia, the first center of the Diaspora, the Jews abandoned farming only from the end of the eighth century onward. The reason was not, as Max Weber assumed, that agriculture pursuits by Jews were incompatible with feudal obligations. The land taxes imposed by the Sassanid rulers and later by the Caliphs were onerous, and Jewish owners were more heavily taxed than others. In addition, political unrest and brigandage, the brunt of which was borne by the minority populations, made the countryside insecure and drove many farmers into the cities. Similar conditions prevailed in Asia Minor and Egypt. In the countries of the western Mediterranean, the ownership of land, except for small gardens and private vineyards, depended upon the disposition of bonded servants and slaves. Jewish traders who, along with Syrians and Greeks, had connections all over the Mediterranean area and beyond, were heavily engaged in the slave trade in these early centuries. Bonded servants may have been from nearby, but slaves, as the name indicates, came mainly from the Slavic East. The Church raised no strenuous objection to the employment of slaves, whether they worked for Christians or Jews, as long as the slave was a pagan. However, in the reign of Emperors Honorius in the West and Theodosius II in the East, freedom of religion for slaves was stipulated in order to facilitate their conversion to Christianity; and if a slave became a Christian, he was encouraged to claim his liberty. Certainly, if a slave adopted Christianity, he was not permitted to remain under the dominion of a Jew. On the other hand, according to Biblical prescription, it was a matter of sacred merit (*mizwah*) for a Jew to have his slave circumcised and to make him at least a half-Jew; in the case of manumission, he became a full Jew. The conversion to Judaism was of particular importance with regard to viticulture. The employment of non-Jews in wine making as well as in wine production was to be avoided by observant Jews because of the ritual use of wine in Jewish households and its possible nefarious use in idolatrous services that would have contaminated it.

Here, then, was hot and contested ground. If the Jews could be deprived of their servants and thereby of the use of their lands and the enjoyment of their crops, and if they could be burdened with ecclesiastical fees and tithes at the same time, perhaps they would resort to the baptismal font. The pressure was primarily of an economic nature. For instance, Pope Gregory I (590-604) promised Jewish tenants who farmed on papal lands in Sicily, a reduction in rent of one-fourth or one-third, if they consented to baptism. We do not know how the Jewish tenants reacted, but we do know that they disappeared either as Jews or as tenants. More often the pressure was applied against Jews who held title to landed property than against tenants. In the case of Bishop Avitus of Clermont (576), we know that he induced about five hundred Jews, along with their children and slaves, to be baptized; the remainder left for Marseille. The alternative was clear: either the Jews abandoned agriculture and migrated to the city or they made their peace with the Church and stayed on the land. The restrictions on the use of Christian laborers by Jewish employers as well as other obstacles must have been especially persuasive to the well-to-do Jews who, at the same time, were most eagerly welcomed by the Church. As late as the eleventh century, when the process was completed, Rabbi Moses ha-Darshan of Narbonne in southern France comments that "Because of the covetousness of wealth one comes to serve other gods, as do many in the very midst of us who converted rather then lose their property." As the Narbonne rabbi indicates, economic sanctions need not have been accompanied by physical force, but the threat of it was always present. Violence was always a court of last resort. For instance, to return to an earlier era, reportedly, Bishop Severus of Magona on the island of Menorca in the fifth century first attempted to persuade the Jews of Menorca of the superiority of Christianity, then resorted to dreams and visions, wonders, and portents, all in vain. He reached his goal in the end, when monks and agitated crowds, on the verge of violence, frightened the Jews so badly that they consented to accept conversion. Seemingly insignificant ripples of this kind presage the contours of a later and larger reality.

Theology is the point of departure in Jewish-Christian relations, but the socio-economic consequences of the theological cleavage begin to appear at an early date. As a minority in dispersion, in late antiquity the Jews had become dependent on their environment. To be sure, they were engaged in a wide spectrum of occupations and not as yet legally excluded from any economic activity. However, while Jewish piety was compatible with all kinds of occupations, post-exilic rabbinical Judaism, which found its juridical fixation in the multi-volume compendium of the Talmud, preferred urban over rural settlement for a variety of reasons. The loss of political independence made a stricter religio-juridical control of conduct necessary, and such control was facilitated in densely settled centers and weakened in outlying regions. The Biblical agricultural festivals continued to be celebrated because their vale as models for an expected messianic fulfillment was inestimable; but some Biblical prescriptions, such as complete rest on the Sabbath, became onerous to observe for those engaged in agricultural pursuits. More importantly, scattered settlement among Gentile populations frequently made it difficult to form religious congregations and to maintain schools. Finally, as already mentioned, Jews in the countryside necessarily became either enmeshed in the emerging feudal institution of vassalage or, for various other reasons burdened with special fees and tithes and consequently exposed to subtle, and occasionally not so subtle, pressures for conversion. The situation was entirely different with skilled and semi-skilled workers, artisans, medical and pharmaceutical practitioners, merchants, traders, and agents of various kinds. Their dense settlement in urban areas made Jewish institutions viable. Mercantile activities, in particular, tended to provide the financial means by which schools, synagogues, and charitable institutions could be maintained within the Jewish community as well as in a larger context, merchants in general were good taxpayers and hence doubly welcome. Finally, merchants who had wide connections and knew how to make themselves useful to the powers-that-be could buy security not only for themselves, but for entire communities. To have ready cash at hand became a guarantee of survival.

Further, dispersion, while detrimental to Jewish agricultural settlement, was promoting commercial activities on a large scale. A living chain of flourishing Jewish communities extended across the entire area of Near Eastern and Mediterranean civilization, from Persia in the East to Spain in the West. In addition, numerous, if small, Jewish settlements came into being in Northern and Eastern Europe, *pari passu* with the penetration into these regions of Roman and Byzantine influence. Wherever Jewish traders went, they encountered, like the Phoenicians and Greeks before them, communities of compatriots and co-religionist, whose members offered them shelter and served as interpreters and local agents. Thus, Jewish merchants, apart from serving their own interests and advancing the material culture of their countries of residence, became powerful agents of the continuity of Jewish existence. The question that is sometimes asked, how the Jews could survive in dispersion, must therefore be answered by saying that they survived because of the specific character of their dispersion. Without the merchants, the widely scattered Jewish communities would not have been able to maintain contact with each other and thus would have lost the spiritual unity that bonded them. Scholarly merchants, along with traveling scholars and disciples of scholars who followed the trade routes, are responsible for the amazing uniformity, with only insignificant local variations, of the basic texts of Judaism and its sacred service in all the countries of the dispersion. In addition, if the need arose to change residence because of economic pressure, social unrest, religious persecution, or succession in political overlordship, it was the merchants who knew of the existence of Jewish communities in other lands where kinsmen could be expected to receive the refugees and assist them in establishing a livelihood. Heinrich Heine was right when he called the Torah a "portable fatherland," but it must be added that its carriers were merchants.

In this way, Jews grew into the role of intermediaries of material and spiritual goods, a role in which they remained throughout the centuries that followed. They made it their business to be attentive to emerging needs and budding desires, to fill economic and cultural gaps wherever they appeared, and to pioneer new ventures. They were linguists, emissaries, legal and medical advisers in addition to being merchants. As the merchant, in the words of Ferdinand Toennies, is "the first thinking and free human being to appear in the normal development of social life," so was the Jewish merchant a stimulator and innovator wherever he went. But there was a reverse side to the coin which was more obvious in the West, that is, in Europe, than in the countries of the Islamic East. In the East, urban civilization was long-standing and Greek and Arab commerce flourished. The West, however, was commercially virgin soil and its inhabitants were chiefly agriculturists. An agricultural population lives in a narrow circle and rarely meets people of a different derivation. The kin context is everything. Ethnic friction and group conflict arise only on the periphery; for the average man, this is but a tale from a distant frontier. Not so for an ethnic or religious minority. Such a minority, settling in the midst of a majority population, always lives on the periphery. The area of possible friction is larger; the chances for a disturbance to arise from marginal tension are multiplied. The smaller the minority, the greater the marginality until we arrive at the isolated individual who lives entirely at the margin. The traveling merchant or trader, who goes about his business alone or with a few companions in order to offer and exchange merchandise and services, is the prototype of a minority. He may live in a kin context of his own, but among his customers he is the "stranger" pure and simple. He is the man who is urgently needed and eagerly awaited, but with whom one does not feel entirely at ease because he does not belong to one's familiar circle. One must be on guard with him: the foreign trader or merchant makes available what the kinsman and neighbor would have offered without remuneration if he had it, but the merchant does not offer it free of charge. He sells, and because he sells, he is presumed to take advantage. In Georg Simmel's classic formulation, the merchant is a stranger, not only if he comes today and goes tomorrow, but even more so if he comes today and stays tomorrow, that is, if he lives permanently among a native population, yet belongs to a different clan and continues to serve other gods. At the same time, because the merchant-stranger is an outsider to the native clans, one can confide in him. If he stays and wherever he stays, an element of symbiosis enters into a situation of potential conflict. If the stranger becomes a neighbor, yet retains his far-flung connections so that proximity is mingled with a sense of distance, we prefer to call him the "intermediary."

Typologically, the Jew was cast in the role of the merchant, the stranger, the intermediary. To be sure, not all Jews were traders at an early stage in European history, nor were all, or even most, wholesale merchants Jews at that time. The Mediterranean countries harbored a large Jewish artisan class; an we know of Syrian, Greek, Frisian, and other traders. But the Jewish merchant was the representative of the Jewish community abroad while the Jewish artisan remained in the Jewish quarter; the Syrians, Greek, and Frisians had a home base while the Jews were a ubiquitous minority. In addition, although the Church pronounced that the Jews had been deprived of sovereignty in their own country of origin as punishment for primordial sin, they were widely recognized as the recipients of revelation. Thus, it came about that the merchant, the wanderer, the stranger, the magician from the East who was thought to hold the key to the secrets of creation, the man who is present everywhere and at home nowhere, the suspected outsider and the trusted counselor, whom we have called the "intermediary"–that all this was epitomized in the image of the Jew. This image, which takes shape at the entrance to the Middle Ages, grows denser in later centuries until it assumes mythical power and magnitude.

3

The Initial Position of the Jews in the Social Structure

In the early Middle Ages, the Jewish occupational structure was diversified and the social prestige of the Jewish community was high. This is particularly true of the Merovingian and Carolingian realms, the core area of the emerging European civilization. Gregory of Tours, in the sixth century, reports that the Jews were merchants, landowners, officials, physicians, and artisans, and that they formed an elite element in the cities where they frequently mingled with Syrians. But the Syrians were Christians, while the Jews, in the eyes of Gregory, were "liars to God," a "closed-minded, ever incredulous race," a "wicked and perfidious nation." Therein lies the difference: the Jews were religious outsiders, and the Church felt constrained to move against their allegedly pernicious influence in matters of faith. In the eighth and ninth centuries, in the reigns of Pepin the Short, Charlemagne, and Louis the Pious, numerous ecclesiastical letters and legislative directives as well as accounts of Arab travelers attest to the high social status of the Jews. They note the presence of landowners, merchants, and world-travelers who were fluent in Persian, Arabic, and Greek, in addition to European languages. Ibn Khordadbeh, postmaster of the Caliphata in Bagdad, likewise in the ninth century, refers to Jewish merchants, called Radanites, who went as far as India, trading herbs, spices, textiles, precious metals, and metalware, stimulating cultural exchange with translated fairytales (*Kalilah and Dimnah*) and "Arabic" (really Indian) numerals, along with commercial goods. At a time when Spain and Sicily were in Muslim hands and the maritime cities of Italy exposed to raids by Sarazen pirates, the international connections of the Jewish merchants were of inestimable value to the Christian rulers of Europe. It seems that the Carolingian kings even went so far as to establish in Septimania and Catalonia (roughly the region between the estuaries of the Rhône and Ebro) a Jewish princedom that was endowed with feudal prerogatives and entrusted with the guardianship of the southern frontier area against the schismatic Umayyad Caliphate in Spain. This may have been done in agreement with the Abbasid Caliphate of the East and in utilization of the Messianic expectations of the Jews which were founded on their claim that secular power had not yet been wrested from them. The Jewish Exilarchate in Babylonia and its western offshoot in Septimania may have lent credence to the assertion on the part of the Jews that they had remained "the people of God"–an assertion that was listened to attentively by king and nobles and widely accepted by the populace.

A claim of this kind, confirmed as it was by material endowment, must have been deeply irritating to the Church, since it undermined its secular position as much as it challenged the assertion that the Church was the "true Israel." It allied the Jews to the central power which was thereby strengthened administratively without being endangered politically. Consequently, Louis the Pious favored the Jews with letters of protection, safeguarding their legal status, that is, their religious autonomy, and confirming their commercial prerogatives. For instance, one royal edict prohibited the baptism of slaves and servants of Jewish masters, another transferred the fair in Lyons from Saturday to Sunday, so that the Jews could attend. The anguished protests of the spokesmen of the Church were in vain. On the other hand, the mixed Christian population, Burgundians, Aquitanians, Alemanians, along with Franks and many foreign slaves and servants, some of whom had become Christianized only recently, consisted mainly of unlettered peasants and manual workers who appreciated the employment opportunities and, on occasion, the hospitality that the Jews offered and who, in the words of the indignant Bishop Agobard of Lyons, "willingly shared with them the food of the body," not infrequently went a step farther and were "seduced by their spiritual nourishment." Some seem to have celebrated the Sabbath with the Jews instead of observing Sunday as the day of the Lord and to have preferred listening to Jewish sermons rather than to the preaching of priests and monks. Agobard goes on to complain that "laborers and peasants are inveigled in such a sea of errors that they regard the Jews as the only people of God, so that only among them is to be found the observance of a pure religion...." Under the circumstances, conversions to Judaism were not infrequent, chiefly, it would appear, of laborers and servant girls, but occasionally also of high-placed persons with whom the Jewish merchants had established contacts at court. It was, of course, these latter instances that were conspicuous. The conversion of Bodo, particularly, who was the court chamberlain of Louis the Pious, created a sensation. Bodo, of noble Alemanic descent, embraced the Jewish faith in southern France and denounced the corruption of the Church. He then went with his household to Spain, adopted the Hebrew name of Eleazar, and engaged in bitter controversy against Christianity.

The formidable anti-Jewish propaganda of Bishop Agobard paradigmatically exemplifies the Christian-Jewish antagonism of this period. The antagonism was emanating from zealous Church dignitaries, not from the nobility nor the common people. Theological considerations, including, of course, the institutional interests of the Church, were the prime motor, as far as friction between Jews and Christian is concerned. The five major letters of Agobard against the Jews, all of which have been preserved, must be evaluated against this background. Agobard makes the following suggestions: 1. Christian slaves should not be sold to Jews, and Jewish masters should not be permitted to prevent the conversion of their pagan or Jewish slaves to Christianity; 2. Jews should not be permitted to sell Christian slaves to the Saracens in Spain; 3. Jews should not be allowed to hire laborers or salaried employees for service in their homes; 4. Christians should not be permitted to work for Jews on the Sabbath, nor should they celebrate the Sabbath with Jews; 5. Christians should not have meals with Jews during Lent; 6. Christian employees of Jews should abstain from eating meat during the Lenten period; 7. Christians should not buy meat from Jews that in Jewish eyes has become impure (*trefah*): 8. Jews should not be permitted to blaspheme Christ and Christians in their religious services. The French scholar Theodore Reinach comments correctly that this list is more remarkable for what it omits than for what it mentions, especially for its omission of any accusation referring to usury, the standard accusation against Jews from the high Middle Ages onward. The reason is neither that the Church was not condemning usury at that time nor that the Jews were not engaged in the money trade. Usury did occupy clerical legislation in the Merovingian and Carolingian period, but it was chiefly directed against usury among Christians and especially by the clergy, while a specific reference to Jewish usury is lacking. The financial operations of the Jews, on the other hand, were part of their commercial activities and not yet an isolated specialty. This may have been one of the reasons why Jewish usury was not mentioned. The important observation is that the thrust of the Agobardian argument was theological and, for the sake of the faith, political in character. Agobard's concern was that the Jews should not exercise authority over Christians nor socialize with them, not so much because the Jews were the enemies of Christ and therefore theologically out of bounds, but rather because easy socializing with Christians and exercising authority over them were manifestations of a position of social prestige and political influence that tended to influence Christians to convert to Judaism, thereby frustrating the attainment of the ultimate goal of the Church, namely, the conversion of the Jews. In addition, the Jews were a pillar of support for the king and emperor, so much so that the *brachium saeculare* became impervious to the influence of Christ's Church. If, however, the Jews could be isolated socially, their way of life would not only cease to be attractive to weak Christians, whether as outright converts to Judaism or as Judaizers within the Church, but they also would find it difficult to recruit the manpower that was necessary to cultivate their landholdings. The latter point is of prime importance. Without an adequate labor force, these holdings, the major source of wealth and power in the Middle Ages, would have to be abandoned; they would be forfeited and fall into the hands of the Church. The Church, its economic and political standing secured, would appear triumphant in the eyes of the people; and the Synagogue would be humiliated. Agobard's scheme was flatly rejected by the Crown. An imperial *privilegium* affirmed the right of the Jews to block the baptism of their slaves, a right that the bishop had sought to enforce. He had to flee, to escape punishment for disobedience. His scheme came to naught in his own day, but it was realized in the course of time.

The ensuing period between the ninth and fourteenth centuries is the decisive period in the history of Jewish-Gentile relations. In these five hundred years, many events and trends changed the economic conditions of the Jews and their position in the larger society. Under Merovingian and Carolingian rule, the bitter hostility of the Church against the Synagogue was balanced by the social prestige that the

Jews enjoyed, particularly because of their close association with court and king. By the fourteenth century, the Jews had become a depressed caste, held up for contempt. In the ninth century, the elevated social position of the Jews was a challenge and an annoyance that rankled the Church. By the fourteenth century, the economic conditions of the Jews had been molded in the image of theology.

In order to trace that development, we must review a great many partial trends which, when brought together, produced the general trend that we have in mind. To start with, we must differentiate between a first and a second diaspora of the Jews. The first migratory settlement, or diaspora, extended over the Middle Eastern and Mediterranean territories to which the Jews of Palestine had migrated. To be sure, agricultural occupations receded as time progressed, but the large Jewish population occupied entire quarters of the towns, especially in the eastern part of the region, that is, in regions such as Syria, Mesopotamia, Asia Minor, and Egypt, and to a lesser degree in Greece, Italy, North Africa, and Spain. In this area, the Jews were part and parcel of a indigenous population, even though within the larger context, they formed their own structured society with an upper layer of merchants and traders and a large class of agents, artisans, and skilled laborers in the middle and lower ranges. Many rabbis of the Talmudic era were artisans who practiced their craft during the day and sat in the houses of learning at night. Jews were especially numerous among gold- and silversmiths, dyers, tanners, and silkweavers. As late as the thirteenth century in the reign of Emperor Frederick II of Swabia, the silk weavers and dyers of southern Italy and Sicily were fashioned into a state monopoly wherein the entire workforce, managers, masters, and workers, was Jewish. Still later, under the Ottoman Turks, the Jews of Salonica were entrepreneurs and agents as well as workers in the textile, armaments, and shipping industries. Jewish guilds existed throughout the Mediterranean area. Among Muslim populations, Jews were even admitted into Muslim guilds, to facilitate conversion. In some places, as in Thebes in Greece and in Lucena in Spain, as well as Salonica, Jews held a virtual monopoly of guild membership.

Quite different was the situation that evolved in the area of second settlement, or the second diaspora, which is in the countries of Western and Northern Europe. Here the Jews were outsiders, remote from their original habitat and only a small minority within a total territorial society. The community amounted to a few percent, occasionally less than one percent, of the entire population of a country and rarely more than between ten and fifty families in a particular locality. Only in a few commercial centers in this area were there more than one hundred Jewish families living in a single compact group. Under these circumstances, it stands to reason that no Jewish artisan class, organized in their own guilds and associations and working for an internal market, could be formed. At the same time, the fact that the guilds were religious brotherhoods and the native middle classes were jealous of their prerogatives combined to exclude single Jews from being admitted into the Christian guilds. Other elements in the picture were that the native populations in Northern and Western Europe were rough mannered and full of primitive superstitions; that the economy was based on barter, chiefly of grain and wine; that wealth was accumulated in land (fiefs); and that money, that is ready cash, was a rarity. Consequently, the Jews filled a need when they engaged in the import and export trade as well as in extended peddling and credit operations and therefore appeared to the peasants and manual workers of the area as a separate class of merchants. In Northern Europe, to a far larger degree than the Mediterranean countries, not only were the merchant and the stranger identical, but the Jew was the personification of both.

Another link in the chain becomes apparent at this point: the attachment of the Jews to the rulers. The stranger, the merchant, the Jew–they are all placed outside the habitual juridical system. Whenever controversy arises, the stranger is likely to be exposed to abuse, extortion, robbery and even brute force, especially if he attempts to collect debts; and consequently he stands in need of special grants and vouchsafed protection. Such grants can only be provided by the ruler, be they "letters of protection" that guarantee safe conduct or special legislation to which severe sanctions in case of violation may be attached. Hence, a complex body of rules, regulations, enactments, privileges called "Jewry-Law" arose, addressing the relations between Jews, rulers, and commoners, in distinct contrast to the customary law of the land and Jewish, that is rabbinic, law, both of which serve the needs of specific ethno-religious communities.

Further, when the foreign merchant settles down for good, he needs a separate, independent, and secure dwelling place surrounded by walls, and as close as possible to the fountainhead of protection, namely, the ruler's residence. The ruler, on the other hand, solicits the services of the merchant who provides goods that are not produced at home and disposes of the booty of warfare and the little surplus that can be extracted from local agriculture and crafts. In the early period, whatever merchandise was procured from afar was hard to get, hazardous to transport, and therefore of high value; this was another reason why only kings and nobles could be the clients of the Jews and why they felt constrained to protect them. Both secular and ecclesiastical rulers, including municipalities and monasteries, engaged in business with them. Jews were present wherever the lords of a territory created fairs, that is, places where buyers and sellers could meet. They were called in wherever cities arose to make these initially temporary meeting places permanent and secure. In the German commercial legislation of the tenth and eleventh centuries, the expression "Jews and other merchants" is used, thereby confirming that Jews were looked upon as paradigmatic merchants. The Jews were appreciated because they brought fluidity into the economy. Often quoted is the agreement that Bishop Ruediger Huozman of Speyer (1084) made with the representatives of Speyer's Jewish community. Huozman stated that he would "increase a-thousandfold the glory of the place by accepting Jews into the town." The Jews of Speyer were granted their own jurisdiction, the permission to possess land and even, contrary to canon law, to employ Christian nursemaids, male as well as female servants. The glory that the city and its overlord was to receive emanated from heightened commercial activities and increased revenue. In other words, Jews were instrumental in providing the means by which urban institutions were maintained, pubic buildings erected, and armed forces equipped. Although the Jews, in line with general medieval usage, enjoyed communal autonomy, they were considered "citizens" and called by that name. This situation continued into the thirteenth century, even though by then the commercial activities of the Jews were challenged by the growth of a native merchant class; and the pursuit of Jewish business was shaken by violent events at the onset of the Crusades. But none of these developments could have lasted if it had not been for the influence that the theological concepts, exerted of the Gentile population of Europe over the image of the Jews. At the moment the narrowly circumscribed world of the early Middle Ages was about to expand through renewed and broadened contacts with the East, when commerce flourished and wealth accumulated, the economic philosophy of the Church became more rigid than ever. The dialectic solution of the contradiction transformed Jewish-Christian relations from the level of spiritual rivalry to the level of economic antagonism.

4

The Usury Privilege

Lending money with interest is commonplace in the modern world. The economy of an industrial society is based on credit operations so much so that millions would be denied their livelihood if these operations were impeded.

The processes that ultimately led to the emergence of an industrial society, that is, the unfolding of capitalistic modes of economic activities, were already operative in the Middle Ages; but they occurred in an environment of pervasive localism and in the face of a Church doctrine that defined all interest (with certain significant omissions, which will be mentioned presently), not just an exorbitant rate of interest, as usurious, condemned in scripture and contrary to the law of nature. This idea occupied the center of medieval social thought. However, a number of variables have to be considered in order to understand the role in which the Jews were cast in the midst of these opposing movements.

The first consideration arises from the nature of social conflict in the Middle Ages compared to such a conflict in the modern era. The central conflict in an industrial society is the antagonism between employers and employees, or between capital and management on the one hand, and labor on the other. The central conflict in a largely agrarian economy is the antagonism between creditors and debtors. The social history of antiquity and the Middle Ages is replete with bitter class struggles between urban creditors and rural or otherwise depressed debtors. Typically, however, the debtors in antiquity were small rural proprietors while the bulk of the debtors in the Middle Ages, certainly from the high Middle Ages onwards, were poor artisans. What all societies, agrarian as well as industrial, have in common is that the nature of class struggles sharpens whenever the conflict of economic interests coincides with ethnic or religious differences. A few examples emphasize this point. For instance, the present worldwide propaganda against "colonialism" is nourished by the recognition that everywhere in Asia, Africa, and the Americas, white capital and colored labor confront each other, and not only whites and blacks but Europeans and natives, employers and employees. Similarly, the antagonism between Germans and Czechs in nineteenth century Bohemia or the antagonism between Magyars and Slovaks in Hungary coincidentally involved antagonism between German and Magyar agricultural and industrial employers and a Czech or Slovak labor force; significantly, the Slavs were called "servant peoples" in the old Habsburg Monarchy. An essentially different, but equally pertinent situation is illustrated by the antagonism that exists in all the countries of Southeast Asia between Chinese merchants and their native customers. In this case, the dominated group is not a majority of oppressed menial laborers, but a minority of marginal traders. This complicates matters. Colonial laboring populations are poverty-stricken but have strength of numbers at their disposal, while trading peoples are economically affluent but politically impotent. Their very affluence is a political liability. Yet, in either case, the contrasting pairs of economic position and ethno-religious designation must reinforce each other, if acute conflict is to arise. A striking illustration is offered by the Armenian massacres that occurred in Turkey during the First World War. A trading people, Armenians in the Near East, who lived outside of what is now Soviet Armenia, were and still are a commercial caste living in the midst of agrarian populations. However, in areas where they settled among Christian peoples, as in the Balkan countries and in tsarist Russia, the purely economic conflict of interest between them as creditors and their customers as debtors did not lead to social explosions, physical violence, or genocide. This happened in areas where they constituted a Christian minority among Muslims. Now, the Jews in medieval Europe were creditors of kings and nobles as well as of simple householders and artisans; in addition, they were an ethno-religious minority everywhere. It is therefore not surprising that the conflict in this instance and the hostility that arose from it were nearly universal.

The heightened antagonism between religious adversaries who were at the same time debtors and creditors was reinforced by the ecclesiastical theory about usury that was based on Aristotelian as well as Biblical notions. The Church fathers, Tertullian, Ambrose, Jerome, Augustine, and others, following Aristotle, had not been averse to the exchange of goods to satisfy needs, but they were strictly opposed to commercial activities for the sake of gain and especially to taking interest, which they regarded as an exploitation of the predicament of one's fellow man. Gregory of Nyssa reemphasized the Aristotelian position when he asserted that the taking of interest was against the law of nature because dead metal (money), being barren matter, could never be presumed to bear fruit. Still, the ancient Church had expressly forbidden the taking of interest only to the clergy. Much of Europe was then a barter economy, even a subsistence economy, and credit operations were not often needed. In the Carolingian age, money transactions seem to have become more frequent; and consequently, a general prohibition of usury is found in the Frankish capitularies. But from the eighth century on, and particularly since the twelfth century when wholesale trade, money transactions and the need for credit operations increased significantly, popes and *concilia* reiterated the old prohibitions with ever-increasing vigor. Lending money with interest by each and every Christian was considered contrary to divine and natural law and severe penalties were stipulated. Usury was recognized as a deadly sin, along with blasphemy, heresy, magic, incendiarism, patricide, and licentiousness. This position was elaborated by successive popes. Pope Alexander III declared that there would be no dispensation from the prohibition against the taking of interest (1179); Alexander IV equated the taking of interest with heresy (1257); Clement V stipulated that the mere assertion that interest was not sinful was to be considered heresy (1311); Gregory IX went so far as to forbid the advance of money in maritime trade to which a stipulation of interest was customarily attached. All these enactments were based on Biblical passages, especially Deuteronomy 23, 19-20; Exodus 22, 24; Leviticus 25, 35-37; Psalms 15,5; and Lucas 6, 35. Of these, the passages from Deuteronomy are of decisive importance, because they became the source of bitter controversy between Christians and Jews. They were at the hub of a theological argument that turned into economic antagonism and social ostracism.

The text of Deuteronomy 23, 19-20 is important enough to be quoted in full:

> "Thou shalt not lend upon interest to thy brother; usury of money, usury of victuals, usury of anything that is lent upon interest. Unto a foreigner thou mayest lend upon interest; but upon thy brother thou shalt not lend upon interest that the Lord, thy God, may bless thee in all thou settest thy hand to in the land wither thou goest to possess it.

We will not elaborate here on the tortuous controversy of this passage among the theologians, from Ambrose to the medieval popes and later canonists, since our main purpose is to show to what extent the relations between Jews and Gentiles were poisoned by it. But in order to do this, we must point out the inconsistencies and contradictions that embroiled both the churchmen and the rabbis. The Church increasingly veered toward the position that the categories of "foreigner" and "brother" had become identical in Christianity, which was considered a universal brotherhood; but this still leaves open the question whether the attribute of "brother" was meant to extend to Mohammedans and Jews. Thomas Aquinas, whose views may be considered a summary of the position of the medieval Church, however, adds other considerations which, on the one hand, reinforce the universalistic tendency, and on the other, cast aspersions upon the morality of the Jews. The universalistic tendency is strengthened by considerations of natural law that are derived from the earlier views expressed by Aristotle and the Church fathers, namely, that justice demands that the creditor must not expect more than he has contributed; that money is a good to be consumed, not used; that the creditor cannot expect advantage from what no longer belongs to him; that it is only the labor of man that adds to the value of goods, because money is barren. Concerning Deuteronomy, Thomas reiterates that, if it is forbidden to take usury from a "brother," then it is forbidden once and for all because we are all brethren, "especially in the state of the Gospel whereto all are called." Referring to the Jews, he adds: "They are permitted, however, to take usury from foreigners not as though it were lawful, but in order to avoid a greater evil, lest, to wit, through avarice to which they were prone . . . they should take usury from Jews." Consequently, Thomas advised the inquiring Duchess of Brabant that the Jews, according to scriptural as well as natural law, cannot legitimately retain what they have usuriously exacted from their debtors. This interpretation permitted the Duchess and her princely peers on the one hand to impose heavy imposts on "their" Jews for the permission to lend money with interest and, on the other hand, to confiscate what the

Jews had gained since restitution was due for what had been acquired unjustly.

In other words, both the innate depravity of the Jews and the right of a Christian sovereign to despoil them were now derived from the sacred writings of the Jews themselves. At the same time, as long as the Jews did not become Christians, their spiritual welfare was of no concern to the Church and their money lending with interest was reluctantly tolerated.

The Jewish position regarding Deuteronomy 23, 19-20 is less clear-cut. In Hebrew, the brother (*ach*) is not so much a co-religionist, but a kinsman. The term *nokhri* signifies an alien or a foreigner, that is, an outsider with whom the Israelite has merely commercial contact, as opposed to a *ger* or *toshab* who is a protected sojourner or resident stranger. The two latter terms are used either together or interchangeably. Accordingly, in the passage Leviticus 25, 35-37 (which compliments Deuteronomy 23, 19-20), the *ger-toshab*, the "stranger in your midst," is included in the concept of brotherhood. He is a neighbor, even if he is not a kinsman. It is perhaps regrettable that this line of argument was not pursued, but circumstances militated against it. In the Middle Ages, Jews were dwellers among Christians, not vice versa. Subsequently, rabbinic authorities differed as to whether taking interest from a foreigner (as well as paying interest to him) was merely permitted or was a positive commandment, while Christian authors argued that the Jews had confused the concepts of stranger and foreigner. Both these points are more of a theoretical than practical importance. The Jews had no choice but to charge interest on loans; and the concept of citizenship under a unified law, which is now familiar, was then unknown. Juridically, Jews and Christians were foreigners to each other, although, to be sure, they lived in the same localities and were subject to a common overlordship. It is more important to distinguish once again between an earlier and a later stage of development, or a first and a second diaspora, that is, between a situation in which compact masses of Jews settled among other populations, as in Babylonia, and one in which tiny Jewish communities were scattered over a wide area, as in medieval Europe. In Babylonia, where the Talmudic writings were codified, it could be maintained, on the authority of Rabh Huna, that a Jew should lend money to a non-Jew only when it was economically necessary, meaning that the Jew should avoid contact with "idolators" as much as possible, so that he may not be induced to stray from the fold and commit the sin of idolatry himself. Other caveats, such as that one should not enter into business dealings with an "idolator" on the way to his shrine and on the days preceding his holidays, serve the same purpose–to protect the purity of faith. All this was feasible since the Jews constituted a large minority with a vigorous self-government and the common people hardly had a chance to mingle with outsiders. However, in Northern Europe, where the Jews were a small minority of traders and more and more restricted to the money trade and always beholden to the princes, the Christians had to be excluded from the designation of "idolators." Contacts with Christians were not unavoidable and their goodwill had to be solicited. More importantly, the notion that business relations with Christians, including lending money with interest, ought to be conducted only when economically necessary, took on a new meaning. If trade, including credit operations, was the only means by which a Jew could make a living, the economic necessity of charging interest could not be denied. The most telling formulation of the new interpretation stems from Rabbenu Tam, a renowned rabbinic scholar of the twelfth century, "Today," he said, "people usually lend money to Gentiles, and we decide leniently . . . because we have to pay taxes to the king and the princes and everything is done so as to enable us to gain our sustenance; we live among the nations and it is impossible for us to earn a living unless we deal with them." This interpretation was accepted by the leading rabbinic authorities of the thirteenth century including the recognized head of the Jews of the Holy Roman Empire, Rabbi Meir Rothenburg. Thus, both the rabbis and the Churchmen bent theological considerations and principles of sacred law to political and economic necessities. But the rabbis yielded *expressis verbis* and, as the Hebrew expression goes, *Khedei Hayenu* ("for our lives' sake"), while the impact of ecclesiastical doctrine made itself felt in more devious ways.

The twelfth century is sharply divided on the subject of lending money. To be sure, we find already in the Carolingian period outspoken condemnations of usurious practices by ecclesiastical authorities; but they are directed chiefly against offending clerics and powerful feudal lords. It seems that traders engaged in significant numbers in large-scale loan operations only toward the end of this period. On the other hand, the loan operations of Jewish traders were but incidental to their mercantile activities, not as yet constituting a separate activity. But by the twelfth century, chiefly as a consequence of the Crusades, the concomitant extension of markets and the growth of a native class of wholesale merchants, the Jews were largely restricted to money lending while commercial activities proliferated in the general community, both in the Mediterranean cities and in Northern Europe. The canonists' theory that money was as infertile as it was indestructible and, consequently, that it should render services but not create values, clashed with the very nature of economic transactions. The idea that "dead" capital was not productive and that the capitalist was not justified in deriving monetary gain from the employment of his capital disregarded the fact that labor without capital must remain idle, thereby paying a premium for the availability of such a *conditio sine qua non*. In addition, the premium had to be high because ready cash was not easy to come by and the chance that debts were repaid was fraught with uncertainty. Whatever theory and theology might say, commercial enterprise, maritime trade, public buildings, wars, and crusades demanded capital outlay and an interest payment for its use, even if a payment of this kind occurred under a different name such as the contracted obligation to pay a "penalty" for an allegedly belated repayment, as compensation for the lost opportunity to make a profit (*damnum emergens*), or as a remuneration for "silent partnership."

Varied consequences flowed from this contradictory situation. The theologians and even more so the popular preachers, mostly friars of the mendicant orders, pressed for a radical Christian solution: they concluded that one cannot serve God and Mammon at the same time. Not unexpectedly, they met with frenetic acclaim among the craft guilds and the restless lower classes. In the process, the official ecclesiastical pronouncements grew sharper in desperation. For instance, the second Lateran Council of 1139 not only condemned the rapacity of the usurers, but deprived them of the sacrament of the Church. If this did not tame some of the hardened sinners during their lifetime, chances were that they might be cowed, by the threat of being denied a consecrated burial, into promising restitution on the deathbed, thus compensating the Church for past anguish. But, as we see in retrospect, this was in the nature of a rearguard action: the expansion of the economy could not be checked. Even more aggravating was that the Church as an institution necessarily got involved in monetary transactions in connection with the transfer of ecclesiastical dues and fees. The result was an ingenious compromise that saved theological face, yet exonerated the big financiers from the deadly sin of usury. As it turned out, the Jews were convenient scapegoats.

The researches of Benjamin Nelson have shown that the doctors of the Church differentiated between "occult" or "mental" usurers on the one hand, and "public" or "manifest" usurers on the other. The "occult" usurer derives his rewards from a seemingly legitimate contract where interest payment is merely implied. Naturally, if discovered, these people were made to pay restitution, not necessarily to individual victims (*certa*), but to the generality of the "poor," that is, preferably to the charitable institutions of the Church. The latter payments were called *incerta* because the wronged party was not clearly identifiable. The whole wrath of the theologians was directed against the "manifest" usurers. These were not the bankers and international merchants, including those who took care of the money transactions of the Holy See, nor the Fugger of Augsburg and the Medici of Florence, who took pride in their far-flung commercial activities, whereby the taking of interest, under whatever name, was merely an accessory. The "manifest" usurers were those lenders who plied their allegedly illicit traffic publicly, exclusively, and in distinctive and even notorious quarters. The term "manifest usurers" which seems to have been used first at the Third Lateran Council in 1179, was finally clarified at the Second Council of Lyons in 1274, that is, it was firmly established by the middle of the thirteenth century. Clearly, the term did not apply to glamorous native patricians and merchant princes who had masses read for them and monasteries endowed, but to tolerated strangers, moneychangers, usurers, and pawnbrokers, such as the Cahorsins and the Lombards–itinerant dealers stemming from localities in southern France and northern Italy–and especially and universally to Jews. It did not apply to the adventurous Antonio, but to the plotting Shylock. Shakespeare makes clear that the frivolous Venetian money princes knew how to extricate themselves by judicial subterfuge, exposing the Jew to the double jeopardy of spoliation and contumely. One might say that the manufactured differentiation between "occult" and "manifest" usurers bears the earmark of ideology.

The Church did not consciously select the Jews as the arch-sinners, so as to keep the Christian conscience at rest while capitalistic expansion was far from being effectively challenged. Jewish usury was vigorously condemned and the princes were repeatedly admonished to extirpate it. Nor was the scholastic dividing line between "mental" and "manifest" usurers easily observable in actual life situations. For one thing, the cleavage of internal and external morality was not a Jewish distinction. Christian creditors in Spain, Sicily, and elsewhere preferred Jewish debtors for the same reason that Jewish creditors preferred Christian debtors. Jewish communities were as heavily indebted to Christian institutions as were nobles and clergy indebted to Jews. Also, Jews took loans from Christians against the payment of interest in order to charge higher interest to Christian debtors. In addition, the prohibition against interest on loans was widely disregarded even where Jewish debtors were absent, for instance by issuing a promissory note at a higher amount than the amount of the original loan. Entire communities of Christian moneylenders, such as the Cahorsins and the Lombards and later the Florentine banking houses, replaced their Jewish competitors in wide areas of Western Europe. One would be hard put to decide what kind of usury it was that they practiced. Surely, the recklessness of their business practices was noted wherever they operated, so much that the victims wished that the Jews had never been expelled. In some instances it was obvious that the operations were of a "manifest" nature. Accordingly, they were publicly opposed, albeit not always successfully, by the ecclesiastical authorities who pressed for the expulsion of the Italian moneylenders. Frequently, the lenders were able to hide their "manifest" sins by combining usury with merchandising.

The usury monopoly of the Jews in the Middle Ages is a legend, their prominence in early capitalistic development at best a passing and partial development. Nor was it money lending, which created the image of the Jew as a monster, but rather the virulent fantasy of the demonic Jew, which the fathers of the Church had conjured up, that helped bring about the reality of the Jewish moneylender. It seems that the stigma of depravity, which was attached to publicly lending money with interest, remained fixed on the Jews. This fitted well with one of the most cherished notions of the Church, namely, that the "remnant of Israel," although in a state of abject subjection, should be preserved in precarious existence because it was a living testimony to the passion of Christ and a confirmation of the power of redemption; however, as long as the expected conversion of the sacred remnant had not occurred, the Jews were condemned to a life of anxiety and crushing servitude. Their religion was an aberration; their negation of the divinity of Christ, which they should have been able to recognize on the grounds of their own Biblical sources, a malicious denial of the laws of nature and the precepts of piety. In these circumstances, it could add little to the status of depravity into which they had sunk in any case if their usury was temporarily tolerated, even promoted against the payment of high fees, until finally countermanded by confiscation. Paradoxically, what was contrary to the nature of human nature seemed to be perfectly adapted to the nature of the Jew. This fateful theory was reinforced by economic and political trends which constricted the social function of the Jews to narrow channels.

In the early Middle Ages the Jews had been wholesale merchants, peddlers, and artisans; and their services as interpreters, translators, and medical practitioners were highly appreciated. However, the situation changed in the high Middle Ages, especially in the wake of the Crusades, when the cities, whose early growth owed much to Jewish participation, came into their own and native middle classes grew into prominence. The maritime cities of Italy imported Oriental merchandise, the merchants of upper Germany and the Netherlands transported the wares across the Alpine passes and disseminated them in Northern Europe, and the Hanseatic League monopolized trade in the countries around the North Sea and the Baltic. Fairs were instituted in which the products of many cities and of far-away countries could be exchanged. The Jews could not compete with the Christian merchants who were backed by political power. At the same time, they aroused the envy of the manual guilds and were exposed, with the onset of the Crusades, to the fanaticism of the populace. We shall have to return to consider these crosscurrents in the next chapter. At this point, we are concerned with the transformation of theology into economics and the fixation of the depressed status of the Jews in the mind of the people. This was the function of the usury privilege. Agobard of Lyons had opposed the Jews because they were proud of their heritage, enmeshed in mundane interests, and influential at court, and therefore constituted a peril to the Christian faith. Usury was not mentioned at that time; but during the second crusade (1146), when the monk Radulf, a discipline of Bernard of Clairvaux, instigated bloody pogroms in the Rhineland, the saintly Bernard, in what he intended to be a defense of the Jews, wrote to the archbishop of Mainz:

> I shall be silent about the fact that where there are no Jews, we have to deplore a worse Jewish behavior [*peius judaizare*] on the part of Christian usurers, even if it is customary to call them by the name of Christians and not designate them as baptized Jews."

In other words, usury was Jewish even if the usurer was a Christian. The term "to Judaize," which up to the twelfth century had designated something like "adherence to the notions of the Jewish faith," now took on the meaning of "being engaged in money transactions." Indeed, Christian exploiters, up to this very day, are called "white Jews," as if exploitation was an inherently Jewish kind of thing.

In the same vein, Berthol of Hegensburg, one of the most forceful and wildly popular preachers of the thirteenth century, identified the devil of avarice (*gitigkeit*) with the image of the usurer, while he depicted the Jew as the arch-usurer whose fate was bound to be shared in hell with the Christian usurer. The point that is hammered repeatedly is that when a Christian charges interest he commits a sin against his better nature that can be repented and ultimately extinguished. When a Jew did the same, it seemed to be in accordance with his nature: no good was to be expected of him. Since he was identified with one of the deadly sins, it was obvious that every perverse emotion and every imaginable criminal act could be attributed to him. As the Jewish moneylender was a notorious monster who enjoyed making barren money grow and multiply as if by invisible magic so that he could pursue his sinister ends, so was the Jewish physician a sorcerer whose sole purpose was to destroy his trusting Christian patients: at one time he would ostensibly, yet mysteriously, soothe and heal in order to be able to kill his unsuspecting victim clandestinely the next time. At any rate, if the clever healer did take care of the body–which was a Jewish, not a Christian, concern–he might do harm to the soul. In the period of the Crusades and the invasions of the Mongols, the Jew was a potential traitor in a covert league with the powerful external enemies of Christendom; at the time of the Black Death, he was suspected of surreptitiously poisoning the wells. Always and everywhere, the Jew was the evil spirit incarnate. It is impossible to understand the bitter hostility that medieval man felt towards the Jew without facing the fact that he was considered a son of Satan, a devil in man's clothing, not merely symbolically, but in stark reality. The seed that had been sown in John 2,9 f., 3,8 f., 8,44 f., where the Devil was designated as the "father" of the Jews and his house of worship as the "Synagogue of Satan," had finally borne fruit. A lost Christian might sign over his soul to the Devil; the Jew was the Devil himself. In popular imagination, he had the torso of a human being, but the horns, the legs and the beard of a lascivious goat. He was compelled to wear his master's emblems the twin-horned "Jew-hat" and the yellow ring on his cloth, making his alleged greed and avarice transparent and putting him outside the human pale. As the medieval cartoonists depicted him, Satan himself was a Jew, with a hooked nose, a goatee and a limp, hatching his evil plots while attending the services at the Synagogue: he was the animal-like, yet super-intelligent leader of the hosts of Anti-Christ. Violence against such a monstrous adversary appeared as an act of self-defense. Small wonder, then, when in turbulent times the masses of the populace believed that they were engaged in a deed that was pleasing to the Lord when they shut in many a frightened congregation of Jews in their synagogue, and burned men, women, and children to death.

5

The Revolt of the Masses

It is a common notion that the outbreak of the bloody massacres of Jews in Speyer, Worms, Mainz, Trier, Cologne, and other cities in the Rhineland, but also in northern France, came as a thunderbolt out of a blue sky and that it is attributable to a sudden eruption of religious fanaticism in connection with the First Crusade. However, this is but a half-truth. Unrest had been smoldering throughout the eleventh century. In the aftermath of the rumor that spread through the Christian world, about the demolition of the Church of the Holy Sepulcher in Jerusalem through the Fatimide Caliph Hakim (996-1021), Jews were expelled from a number of cities because they were identified with the Saracens. Sporadic popular violence against Jews is reported from some localities, especially in France, and although this violence was subdued by the territorial lords, the underlying emotions were not. When Pope Urban II issued his famous call to a Crusade to the French Knights in 1095, he unleashed these emotions and unwittingly fanned them to a consuming flame. While the Knights assiduously prepared themselves for the holy campaign, the agitation was at once taken up by popular preachers and self-appointed prophets, among whom a slight, ascetic man with a long gray beard, called Peter the Hermit, exercised a particular and irresistible fascination upon the masses of poor people. Hordes of ragged folks who gathered around him and others of his kind crossed over from France into the Rhineland and their way to the Holy Land and fell upon the unsuspecting Jewish communities along their path. While the minds were set on combating the distant enemy of the faith, it seemed utterly incongruous to spare the infidels at home who mocked Christ and stubbornly refused conversion.

But religious excitement, aroused by millenarian expectations, was only the mode of expression which offered itself for a wider and deeper tension that was present and had its roots in conditions of a socio-economic, even a demographic nature. The area from which the hordes of the popular Crusaders and the bulk of the regular armies of the knights were recruited, as well as the area where the actual outbursts occurred, was narrowly confined to northern France, Flanders, and the Rhineland; by the time of the Second and Third Crusades (1146-1190), England and large parts of southern Germany were added. This was the economically most advanced area of Europe and at the same time an area of vigorous population growth. Flourishing textile industries had been established especially in the region between the Somme and the Schelde rivers. Their products, based on imported English wool, were carried by the Norman traders across the North Sea and the Baltic to Eastern Europe and by others along the Rhine valley toward the Mediterranean shores and beyond. These early capitalistic enterprises and the urban centers where they were located exerted a powerful attraction upon the landless peasantry, especially the second and third sons of peasants who under the prevailing stem family system were excluded from inheritance. They were unable to found a family on their own account while they remained in the village, but proliferated in the towns, Although employment was precarious, misery rampant, and the death rate high, new migrants from the overcrowded countryside, wandering journeymen, and plain vagabonds who drifted from town to town quickly took the place of those who had perished. In addition, a series of floods, droughts, and famines that occurred in northeastern France and western Germany in the decade preceding the call to the First Crusade reinforced the pressure of population against resources in the towns, Consequently, in the tenth and eleventh centuries, new walls and enclosures to accommodate the inflow were built in Cologne, Liege, Verdun, Antwerp, Bruges, Ghent, Douay, Tournay, Ypres, and Regensburg, to be followed in the twelfth and thirteenth centuries by others, stretching from Brussels and Strasbourg eastward toward Nuremberg and Vienna. The masses of rootless and destitute people who filled these towns and cities were like tinder set afire by the inflaming message of the Crusade. As indicated by the documented growth of the cities, the expansion of the population, and the unrest engendered by it continued through the twelfth and thirteenth centuries and ground to a halt only after 1349, the year of the Black Death. Large parts of Europe were depopulated in that year and the excitement, which had reached a fever pitch, subsided.

The events that unfolded during the First Crusade adumbrate what was going to happen during the following Crusades and the frightening uprising of the French *pastoureux* (shepherds) up to the time of the gruesome massacres that occurred over a large part of Europe in 1348 and 1349, preceding the advent of the plague. Beyond their immediate historical significance, these events are paradigms for collective behavior within populist movements in all times and places, especially when these movements deteriorate, as they often do, in a reign of terror. The reports that have come to us from the First Crusade and that are confirmed by reports from comparable later events agree that the good and solid burghers, the patrician town counselors, and also the bishops who were the overlords of many cities, as a rule, attempted to safeguard the lives of the Jews with whom they were on good terms and from whom they derived material benefits. But their efforts were frustrated. In fact, the bloodiest riots occurred precisely in the episcopal towns where the people were at loggerheads with their ecclesiastical rulers. In attacking the Jews, who marked the point of minor resistance, the established episcopal authority was forcefully challenged. In addition, the worldly enmeshment of the Church was contrasted to a visionary egalitarian Christianity. Thus, it could happen during the First Crusade that the bishop of Trier, who pleaded with the assembled faithful for the lives of the Jews, merely aroused the indignation of his listeners and had to flee from the Church where he preached, to preserve his own life. Even a man of extraordinary reputation, like Saint Bernard of Clairvaux, was scarcely able to check the popular fury when he confronted the demagogic monk and fierce Jew-baiter Radulf of Hainaut in Mainz during the Second Crusade and ordered him, as an abbot, back to his monastery: disaster was narrowly averted at this time. Occasionally, as in Regensburg in 1348, the patricians succeeded in warding off the murderous threat without assistance from a saint, but in the majority of instances bands of armed vagabonds from out of town in the league with an agitated crowd of *menu peuple* in inside a town succeeded in cowing the authorities. They forced the gates and overwhelmed whatever feeble resistance stood in their way. Some citizens tried to protect the Jews, but others, in joining joyously or reluctantly with the intruders, tipped the scales. The pattern was repeated in town after town and century after century, whether in the Rhineland during the First Crusade (1096), in England during the

Third Crusade (1190), in France during the uprising of the *pastoureux* (1320) and in the period of the Black Death as well as intermittently all over Central Europe. Only Italy remained largely untouched.

The question arises at this point, whether a more determined stand might not have succeeded in checking the onslaught of the mob. This is not to be gainsaid, but powerful psychological mechanisms militate against that possibility. These mechanisms can take effect separately, but are more likely to be of a cumulative nature. 1. In many instances the protectors, when confronted by a famished, intoxicated and bloodthirsty crowd, are so numbed and terror-stricken that they are sorely tempted to save their skin by throwing the victims demanded by the popular fury to the wolves. 2. More important than this betrayal in the face of physical force in intimidation of a subtler kind, namely by the implicit or explicit threat of being marked as an abject traitor, even as a hireling in league with suspected criminals. The term "*Judenknecht*" comes to mind, an expression of opprobrium that the Nazis used to pillory whoever made even the slightest move that betrayed sympathy with their outlawed and harassed victims. Those who showed a modicum of human feelings were made to appear as having been ensnared by the wily Jews and ignominiously enthralled in emotional servitude or financial temptation or both. 3. Further, the process of being marked, pilloried and effectively ostracized is facilitated, if the attackers and the protectors are of the same ethnic stock, while those whose abandonment is demanded, are strangers. The invocation of blood-ties might tip the scales in a critical situation at all times. The connecting link between points 2 and 3 is provided, if the accursed strangers, at the same times, are known to be in the possession of promissory notes, precious stones and metals, and envied cash. Anyone who protects them in preference to rallying to the side of his aroused kin will be suspected as having succumbed to bribery. 4. Finally, it must be emphasized, that the full force of the murderous intentions of an aroused multitude can be unleashed only if the opponent is conceived of as being less than human. This is precisely the case with the Jews. If they are believed to be the Devil Incarnate with horns and claws and hoofs and a tail, as they are depicted by medieval cartoonists, and if they are associated in the popular imagination with unclean animals such as goats, pigs, toads, snakes, scorpions, and beaked dragons, one is persuaded that they do not belong to the human kind. Not only can they then be killed in good conscience because no violation of the canons of human behavior is involved in the slaughter, but those who wish to speak in their favor must be mortally afraid of being cast themselves in the image of monsters. This prospect paralyzes the protector's mind and arrests his arm. It adds the seal of finality to the process of abandonment: merciless extermination becomes a possibility.

These psychic mechanisms could be observed in operation again and again in the period between the First Crusade (1096) and terrifying epidemic of the Black Death (1349) – not to speak of events in recent history. One hundred and seventy years later, when the ancient Jewish community of Regensburg was driven from the city (1519), extermination had been replaced by expulsion, but abandonment was still of the essence in the process. When the fanatical preachings of Balthasar Hubmaier at the Cathedral of Regensburg had taken effect, many burghers are reported to have thought that the expulsion was unjust, but they found themselves unable or unwilling to express their opinion publicly, in view of the aggressive nature of popular sentiment. But the high mark of hysteria reached in the years 1348/49 was never surpassed. We cannot relate in detail here the events of these murderous years, when fully one-third of the population of Europe fell victim to the plague, except to say that in almost all instances where the authorities did their duty and made more or less strenuous efforts to protect the Jews, these were swept aside, as if by elementary force, by the tide of popular indignation. The exceptions were Rome and Avignon, the seats of papal power, and Regensburg, where at that time the entire patriciat, 237 leading citizens, individually and publicly, stood up against the uproar and succeeded. But the dukes of Austria and Bavaria and the town councils of Basel and Strasbourg as well as the magistrates of other cities were forced to yield when they were faced not merely with physical violence and civic disorder, but with the reproach that they would be making themselves responsible for the death of thousands upon thousands of their fellow citizens, if they attempted to protect the devilish plotters instead of rendering them innocuous before they could perpetrate their contemplated crime. The rioters demanded that the Jews be eliminated root and branch, so that the evil could not strike. That is to say the Jews were not killed because they had poisoned the wells, but because it was feared that they might poison the wells. It was not an expiating rite, but a preventive incantation when the *flagellantes* forced the gates of the towns, performed their macabre dances, tormented their own bodies, and stormed the Jewish quarters, carried along by the frenetic support of the common people. For instance, the murder of the Jews in Zurich and other places in southwest Germany occurred in September and October 1348, while the plague reached these regions only in the first half of 1349. The Jews were indeed a point of minor resistance, not only because they were a defenseless minority, but also because they were, at any rate, prime suspects whenever a misfortune of some kind befell the community. Over centuries, the Church had taught the populace that the worst could be expected from those who had killed Our Lord; now, the point was reached, where the Church's teachings turned against the Church itself. Indeed, whoever speaks of "the" Church and its role in the formation of the pattern of Jewish-Gentile relations, must know precisely what aspect of the Church he is talking about. On the one hand, we have the hierarchical aspect of the Church, that is, the Church of the popes, the prelates, the bishops, the abbots, and those, mostly men of means and their dependents, who supported them; on the other hand, we have the masses of the aroused faithful, the blessed poor and their charismatic leaders, the ascetic holy men and the fiery friar-preachers, with a suite of dissident monks and lower clerics. These lower orders had a vision of millennium, an imagined future rushed to immediate fulfillment–a paradise on earth where injustice will prevail and Christ rule in glory. Along with the Jews, the established Church was cast by the millenarians in the image of anti-Christ and the notorious corruption of the clergy was decried. However, the millenarians went further. Along with corruption, they rejected the Eucharist and all the sacraments, abolished confession and absolution, and acknowledged only the inspiration of the Holy Ghost. It was the Holy Ghost who was said to have moved the *flagellantes* and urged them to purify the world from the twin sins of *luxuria* and *avaritia*. No doubt, catchwords like these tended to attract a wide spectrum of discontents and to touch a raw nerve of the established order. But before long, the peasants and the artisans and their womenfolk, who had been the initial adherents of the movement, were replaced by a mixed multitude of vagrants and outlaws, and these, after they had disposed of the Jews, turned ferociously against the property, the institutions, and even the representatives of the Church. As it turned out, the elimination of the Jews had been but the initial skirmish; now the battle was joined against the established order itself. Consequently, Israel Abraham's statement that "unfriendliness to the Jews flows from the higher to the lower levels," that is from the clergy to the faithful, must be qualified. The statement is correct only up to the period of the high Middle Ages; with the onset of the Crusades the sequence is reversed. Fierce hatred of the Jews was now firmly implanted in the lower classes and became coupled with the spiteful rejection of the ecclesiastical hierarchy. Repressed pagan emotions surfaced again, the Christian garb in which they clothed themselves notwithstanding. One can say that the Church had sown the wind and reaped the whirlwind. Surely, when it became obvious that the very foundations of law and morality were threatened by an anarchic movement, the pope turned to the *brachium saeculare* and the secular authorities intervened. The chaotic uprising was forcibly suppressed and a semblance of order was restored. The storm had passed, but hundreds of Jewish communities had been destroyed and the dead could not be resurrected.

6

The Jews and the Society of the High Middle Ages

Max Weber has called the Jews of antiquity a *Pariah-Volk* and rabbinic Judaism a mirror of that designation. But Max Weber defines as *Pariah-Volk* a "guest people that is ritually separated from the host society." In this restricted sense, the term may be applicable to the Jewish situation, but does not carry our understanding very far. Max Weber himself realized that ritual separation, as distinguished from physical segregation, was at no time imposed on the Jews from the outside, as it was on the pariahs in India. If, however, in line with a more common understanding, we mean by pariahs a low caste population that is shunned and held in contempt by the remainder of the population, the name antedates, to say the least, the reality to which it refers by about a millennium. Far from considering themselves, or being considered by others, as persons of low caste, the Jews called themselves " the People of God" and if a Jewish trait was minded by the Gentiles, it was overweening pride rather than impotent resentment or servile submissiveness. Occupationally, the degradation of the Jews to the position of a low caste was not effectuated prior to the high Middle Ages. As has been pointed out earlier, the Jewish occupational structure remained diversified in the Mediterranean countries; in Northern Europe, where it was less diversified, the occupational role of the Jews was highly esteemed until the time of the First Crusade. In other regards, it is dubious whether the term pariah applies even to the period from the twelfth century onward. The term refers to untouchables and in a certain sense to unredeemables; redemption by means of an anticipated migration of souls in the hereafter can be disregarded in our context. In the case at hand, Jewish hospitality was eagerly sought by Gentiles and finally made impossible only by strict ecclesiastical ordinances. In the Jewish view, the Jews were ready for the coming of the Redeemer at any time; in the Christian view, they were redeemable by conversion. However, the conversion of Israel was a long way off; individual Jews converted by their own choice, others were converted under duress, but the bulk of the Jewish people preferred death at their own hands or at the hands of killers to surrender to what in *their* eyes was an inferior faith. In brief, the term pariah, if transferred from the Hindu context, has little explanatory utility.

What one can say, following Robert E. Park and Howard Becker, is that the Jews were a "marginal trading people" and, even more so, that they were "strangers." The quality of strangeness was recognized by Jews and Gentiles alike. The Jews considered themselves as living in "exile" (*galut*), waiting for a political Redeemer. The peoples in whose midst the Jews lived concurred in that they conceived of them in the image of political prisoners or, as the medieval expression has it, as "serfs of the Imperial Chamber." We will return to that concept and its consequences presently. At this point, it is important to recall that the concept has had a history. In the course of the centuries, the highborn prisoner, who was merely blinded by disbelief, was transformed into the descendant of hardened criminals. What had been a spirited discussion about the principles of faith became contorted into a mean haggling over coins. It was in consequence of that development and not because of any inherent quality of pariahs that the unrepentant Jews were relegated to the role of outcasts. In the frightening words that Abbot Petrus Venerabilis of Cluny addressed to King Louis VII of France, they "should not be exterminated, but preserved, like the fratricide Cain, for great vexations and greater turpitude and for a life worse than death. They are dependent, miserable, moaning, fearful and fugitive and shall remain that way until they are converted and saved." According to a series of papal announcements, along the line of the *Constitutio pro Judaeis* of Pope Innocent III (1199), the Jews, in spite of their vituperation of Christ and their inability to understand their own law, should be regarded as the guardians of sacred lore and should not be destroyed completely. Yet, the doctrine of "perpetual serfdom" in retribution for the alleged crime of deicide was strictly upheld. It is not amazing, then, that the agitated masses could not be restrained by a fine point of theology and that they proceeded to gruesome slaughter wherever the opportunity arose.

Sometimes the slaughter of the Jews was in the way of a massacre, as during the First Crusade; sometimes it took the shape of judicial murder, bordering on lynch justice, as in the innumerable instances where Jews were hysterically accused of the crime of the ritual murder of Christian boys and of the desecration of the Host. Entire communities were burned at the stake on this account. There are psychoanalytic interpretations of these gruesome occurrences, such as the one of Norman Cohn, who points to the fact that the presumed victims were always either boys, never girls, or the wafer who presents the martyred Christ while the Jewish persecutors are depicted as lewd elders feeding on the vitality of youth. He concludes that what was enacted there were Oedipal projections. Old men who are likened to devils are cast in the image of the "bad" father who vents his rage on youth and who, in turn, is to be consumed by the flames lit by youthful fury. Assumptions of this kind, persuasive as they may be, are in the nature of conjectures. What is certain is that, starting with William of Norwich, whose body was found on Easter Eve 1144 and supposed to have been put to death by the Jews in mockery of the passion of Christ, a long line of alleged Christian martyrs at Jewish hands makes its appearance in the popular hagiology of each and every land in Christendom. But it is also documented that popes as well as kings and emperors disapproved of the accusation and anathematized it: another example of how the teachings of the Church were carried to the extreme in the action of an aroused multitude, even to the point of distorting them. In that sense, by looking in the distorted mirror of superstition, we recognize a religiously derived chain of causation; but other causal factors that are political and economic in nature were added. They soon assumed independent virulence.

Politically, one can say that the Jews were incorporated into medieval society without being an integral part of it. In the earlier centuries, their social standing, as expressed in their privileges, was high. They were the confidants of the rulers and their relations with the general population, by and large, were of a friendly nature, or else, the Church would not have found it necessary to admonish the faithful to avoid employment and all kinds of social intercourse with Jews and especially to abstain from listening to rabbinic sermons in the synagogues. Of course, one must not apply to these times the modern principle of equality before the law; it is all the more significant that the *Sachsenspiegel*, a prime source of medieval German law, considered the Jews as free men, the special regulations and agreements under which they lived notwithstanding. During the First Crusade, the Jews of Mainz met the pogromists of Emicho of Leiningen with swords in hand, as befits the freeborn. But the small group of defenders was overwhelmed. The Jews subsequently suffered the same fate as the formerly free peasantry: it became evident that both groups stood in need of protection, but for different reasons. The peasants had to submit to bondage individually, because they could not afford to arm themselves; the Jews did not become serfs *in persona*, but they came to be considered as serfs of the Imperial Chamber communally because it was obvious that they were unable to face the attacking crusaders and their camp followers with any chance of success. In the imperial "peace of the land" (*Landfrieden*) of Emperor Henry IV (1103) and in subsequent enactments concerning the maintenance of civic peace, Jews were placed under special protection, along with clerics and women. They could avail themselves of that protection, if they renounced self-help. This was the first, if well-intentioned, step that in its consequence deprived the Jews of social honor and, as the imperial power declined, abandoned them not only to hostility but also to contempt on grounds that were other than theological in nature.

It is true, however, that the political development occurred simultaneously with the unfolding of ecclesiastical doctrine. Guido Kisch has observed that it was more than a mere coincidence that the doctrine regarding *servitus Judaeorum*, which was promulgated by Pope Gregory IX in the year 1234, was spelled out in the privilegium of the Jews of Worms, issued by Emperor Frederick II in 1236 and further in the Charter of Vienna in 1237, wherein the Jews are designated for the first time in Germanic lands (there seem to have been precedents in Sicily) as *servi camerae imperatoris speciales*. The Jews were now definitely excluded from public service (e.g., taking part in the defense of the cities) because, as the official language had it, "imperial authority in days of old has imposed upon the Jews perpetual serfdom as a punishment for their crime." In these words the adaptation of political theory to ecclesiastical doctrine is sharply expressed. A regularity became manifest which can be observed throughout Jewish history: the Jews were the pawn in a contest of power. The world of Christendom was then at the height of the struggle between Emperor and Pope and the sharper the Pope formulated the antagonism of Church and Synagogue, the more was the Emperor constrained to fall in line, so as to sustain his claim for supreme leadership. Moreover, the Emperor argued, referring to the pagan Roman Emperor whose successor he was supposed to be, that the Jews were subject to the Imperial Chamber, that is, to the secular and not to the spiritual sword. Surely, the Christian emperor could not appear less Christian than the Pope. In the present context one can say that the breathtaking hegemonic contest between the two dominant powers of the medieval world was fought on the back of the Jews.

The economic aspect is contained in the political development, because legitimate power over Jews meant disposition over sources of revenue. In the territories of his Neapolitan and Sicilian inheritance, Frederic II of Swabia, anticipating mercantilistic policies, entrusted the Jews with the receipt of the silk monopoly that comprised every stage of production from the growing of silkworms to the dyeing of silken cloth. In the Germanic lands, feudal as well as urban institutions were too far developed to permit such a direct intervention. In a first stage of development, which seems to have been well on its way of the end of the eleventh century, the growing prosperity and self-assertiveness of the cities was by no means detrimental to the Jews. The merchants who dominated the cities were interested in prying the Jews loose from the overlordship of princes and bishops because the feudal impact constituted an impairment of the city's sovereignty; feudal enmeshment provided a possible pretext for intervention and prevented the cities from taking full advantage of the Jews as a fiscal resource. To be sure, the merchants were eager to preserve the most lucrative commercial channels for themselves and also to restrict the acquisition by Jews and other outsiders of real estate, a prime source of power and influence. Further, the Jews had to reckon with a growing tendency on the part of the cities to impede their wholesaling activities, including the right to attend fairs, so that Jewish business ultimately came to be limited to credit operations. At first, the Jews were not averse to this trend because unarmed, as they were, they found themselves increasingly exposed to violence on the highroads, where they might be robbed with impunity and even be in danger of life and limb; the "peace of the land," which should have protected them, was largely ineffective. In contrast to overland trade, money transactions could be enacted in the Jew's home although, to be sure, when outstanding loans had to be collected either directly from the debtor or by means of court proceedings, the Jewish creditor remained exposed to abuse and violence. On the other hand, merchandising was not entirely impeded, inasmuch as the Jews had to be allowed to resell agricultural commodities that they had received in lieu of cash. Consequently, as long as the merchants held the reins of power in the cities, a modus vivendi was possible, especially since the ecclesiastical doctrine of usury allowed for toleration along with stigmatization of the undisguised credit operations of the Jews, thus preserving merchandising for the merchants while providing access by them to the ready cash of the Jewish moneylenders. For the cities, a source of public revenue and even a pretext for confiscatory taxation in an emergency was secured. This was the gap in the social structure into which the Jews were fitted. No sooner had the mob slain the Jews, as for instance during the Crusades and the violent turmoil accompanying the plague, than the survivors were recalled and reinstated by the returning patrician regimes.

But the conditions for readmission were less favorable than the previous arrangements had been. The fees and special imposts had a tendency to increase while the scope of the activities in which the Jews could engage was almost always markedly narrowed. Even more cumbersome was the fact that the emperor was no more in a position to protect the Jews effectively in all instances. Against pledges of support from cities and territorial lords, he might, on his part, pledge the Jews of a certain locality, that is the right to tax them, to these local powers, as he would pledge feudal fiefs or mining concessions. On account of the casuistic nature of medieval legislative enactments, the result was frequently such that several competing sovereigns contended for the right to "protect" the Jews and to exact protection money from them. Raphael Straus has classically described this process for the free city of Regensburg. The Jews could appeal to the imperial chamber against impositions of the bishop, the duke of Bavaria and the municipality of Regensburg and the frequently prevailed at the highest court, but always at the price of additional compensatory payments. The system was perfected in England, where the royal exchequer of the Jews kept the barons at bay and the Jews tightly organized for the benefit of the Crown. Although numerically insignificant, the Jews contributed one-twelfth to the total resources of the royal treasury of England. Not only were a great variety of fines and fees exacted during a man's lifetime, but upon his death his entire property reverted to the king. As in 1190 during the York massacres the deeds and charters of the Jews were destroyed, the "ordinances of Jewry" were constituted which provided an accurate register of all the money transactions of the king's Jews. In the circumstances, tax evasion was exceedingly risky. It became possible to know precisely what sums could be extorted from a particular Jew in a particular instance. If need be, incarceration would regularly yield a handsome ransom.

In the Holy Roman Empire with its splintered sovereignties, the procedure was less clear-cut than in England, but the effect was roughly the same. For instance, the Jews of Nuremberg, who by the middle of the fourteenth century comprised about 8 to 10 percent of the total population, paid more in taxes than the remainder of the citizenry. Neither the imperial chamber nor the town government could have managed their affairs without the Jewish contribution. But the golden goose was slaughtered. The higher the protective taxation, the higher would have to be the interest rate granted the Jewish moneylender, and the higher the interest rate, the higher could be the imposts. If the interest payment became oppressive to the debtors, the "Jew debts" could be canceled, the assets of the Jews confiscated, so as to indemnify the sovereign, and expel the Jews from the country. Subsequently, the re-admission and the renewal of protection was granted against the payment of an additional impost. If new needs arose, new imposts might be piled on the old. For instance, Emperor Louis the Bavarian introduced in 1342 the *goldenen Opferpfennig*, according to which every Jew and Jewess who were over twelve years of age and possessed at least twenty gilders in their fortune had to pay one gilder annually to the imperial treasury; and this in addition to the general protective tax and numerous special imposts. In the period of the Black Death hysteria, Emperor Charles IV went so far as to assign the assets of the Jews to the Burggraf of Nuremberg and the Bishop of Bamberg many months before the actual catastrophe occurred. The town council was absolved of responsibility in advance. In such fashion, a cruel mockery was made of the imperial protection. The jurists had to find the justification for all this arbitrariness. The doctrine of *servitus Judaeorum* referred to the Passion of the Lord and the conquest of Jerusalem by the Roman Emperor only in order to mask new injustice with the pretension of ancient obligations and prerogatives.

The shameless exploitation of the usury privilege by the emperor and the territorial sovereigns in the Holy Roman Empire and by the royal treasury in England and France pushed the Jews into a hopeless predicament. For sheer sustenance, they were dependent upon lending money on interest: they were permitted to dwell in a place only on condition that they devote themselves to the business of money lending and to nothing else. But the condition could not be met because some amount of merchandising was inevitably connected with credit operations, especially in the case of agricultural credit. In addition, interest rates were bound to be high because credit operations, apart from the burden of high taxation that they carried, were fraught with uncertainty. Loans were given to great lords against a grant of commercial privileges or the pledge of tolls and income from real estate, even entire villages; but either the loans proved unredeemable because the high-placed debtor defaulted on his obligation or the pledges were confiscated and the creditors despoiled as soon as they had enriched themselves. This reckless exploitation inexorably led to the impoverishment of the Jews so that, in the course of time, they could engage in credit operations only on a smaller and smaller scale. Some Jewish lenders managed to stay in business, if they worked with the money of Christian merchants who preferred taking usury directly from a Jew and only indirectly from a Christian brother. Loans of this nature, chiefly to craftsmen, were given against promissory notes and movable pledges, such as the craftsman's tools, his household goods, his coat, his wife's jewelry or bed linen, and similar items; clerics might pledge sacral objects. If the pledges could not be redeemed, they had to be sold or, as in the case of promissory notes, payment had to be secured through court proceedings. The fact that the moneylender had become a pawnbroker had further consequences. Hand in hand with pawnbroking went the right of concealment. Roman law protected the owner of stolen goods; they had to be surrendered to him and the purchaser had to see whether he could be compensated by the person from whom the purchase had been made. Newer codifications, however, which emerged in the Middle Ages and found expression in the privileges arranged with the Jews, protected the person who had acquired in good faith; he had to be compensated by the original owner, if the latter asked for return. Otherwise, nobody would have been ready to advance money on a pledge. Consequently, it was stipulated in the Vienna *privilegium* of Emperor Frederick II of 1237 and in numerous subsequent regulations and agreements that a Jew could confirm under oath the acquisition in good faith of pledges that he had taken in by daylight and with doors unlocked and which were neither wet nor bloodied nor delivered by minors or servants. Yet, in spite of the conditions with which the acquisition in good faith was hedged in, it was inevitable that the dishonest rabble of medieval towns took advantage of the situation: stolen goods did find their way to the Jewish pawnbroker. The owner who discovered them there had to buy them back. Even more unfortunate was the fact that the pawnbroker had to sell unredeemed pledges at reduced prices. Furs, shoes, coats, and other pawns were refurbished and sold at reduced prices; they found a ready market. Out of these activities developed in the later middle ages the trade in second-hand goods and the activities of Jewish peddlers and hucksters. The itinerant Jewish beggar and peddler became a ubiquitous figure, yet one that was veiled in mystery and placed, as it were, outside the human pale. The image of the itinerant Jew congealed in the legend of Ahasver, a ghost more than a man, who cannot find rest until the end of time. Occasionally, the figure of Ahasver may have been mingled by Christian homilists with the description of the Jewish people as a "New Cain," that is, a fugitive and a wanderer upon the face of the earth. Whatever the connection, the legend of the wandering Jew, which stems from the East, seems to have reached Europe in the thirteenth century, but it caught the fancy of a broad public only from the fifteenth century onward when the eternal wanderer appeared as the symbolic enhancement of what had become a familiar reality. We have here another example of how a theory preceded the facts that it helped to create.

The relegation of the Jews to the pawnbroking business, designed to keep them from competing with the guilds, nevertheless carried matters to a point of collision. The artisans were anxious to preserve the customary range of their business, especially in those cities where economic opportunities had contracted. They blamed the Jews for the declining markets and complained bitterly about the violation of the rules and regulations under which the Jews had been admitted. In Regensburg, which may be considered paradigmatic because the argument there was prolonged into the sixteenth century and because it is exceedingly well researched, the accusation of usury was kept alive by demagogic preachers, whom the Church tolerated to exert pressure on the city government. But usury plays only a subordinate role in the complaint of the artisans. They mention much more often that thievery was facilitated by the law of concealment and that the Jews were intruders and unfair competitors in the field of merchandising. Accordingly, the artisans demanded that the pawnbroking business be restricted and that merchandising by the Jews be prohibited altogether. The Jews countered that apparently the prevailing opinion was that they were able to "live off thin air" and to walk "under the ground." Somehow, they said, they had to make a living. But the municipalities lost interest in them to the extent to which their ability to pay taxes decreased. In Regensburg, a cynical attempt was made in 1476 to get rid of the Jewish presence by a trumped-up ritual murder charge and the incarceration of the wealthier members of the community. The attempt was frustrated by the intervention of the imperial court, but the Jews were unable to pay the new debts to the city incurred on this occasion as well as the customary taxes which they owed to both the city and the duke of Bavaria. Clearly, the usefulness of the Jews to the parties concerned had ceased and their expulsion in 1519, taking advantage of the interregnum after the death of Emperor Maximilian, seemed the easiest way out of a political predicament.

In conclusion, one can say that the Jews found themselves between Scylla and Charybdis in the class struggles of the Middle Ages. The theory of Wilhelm Roscher, that the rising antagonism against the Jews was due to the growth of a native mercantile class, is only partially true. The patricians weakened the bases from which the Jews operated but abandoned the Jews only when the manual classes pressed for it. In other words, the merchant elite restricted the scope of Jewish economic activities, but continued to tolerate the Jews as an asset to the municipal treasury. Consequently, when the guilds rose against the urban ruling class, as in the period of the Black Death, the Jews were considered their agents and a convenient object of attack as long as the patricians seemed too formidable an opponent to be taken on; the patricians, in turn, were sorely tempted to yield on what to them was a minor point. When in some instances, as in Strasbourg, the town council made a move to protect the Jews, the councilors were accused of having been bribed by them and they were forcibly deposed; this done, the claims of the Jews were annulled, their pledges confiscated, their cash distributed among the artisans, and the entire Jewish community burned at the stake. In this case, the alleged plot to poison the wells, which was laid at the door of the Jews, had been merely a pretext, so as to get rid of irksome creditors and to appropriate their worldly goods. "That was the poison that caused the death of the Jews" was the way the matter was put by a contemporary chronicler.

By the fifteenth century, the patrician regimes had been reinstated, but the fear of the "city mob," to use Hobsbawm's phrase, had not abated and the Jews had become expendable. Local variations notwithstanding, the outcome was amazingly uniform. While in Regensburg, the emperor attempted to uphold the right of the Jews to unhindered settlement and in Frankfurt actually succeeded in the attempt, no such attempt was made in other instances. The story of Nuremberg may stand here for many: after the Jews had been looted, some of them expelled, and the remainder burned, readmission against payment, persecution, spoliation, incarceration, ransom, renewal of privileges, and repeated cancellation of debts followed each other in dreary sequence. In the *privilegium* of Emperor Frederick III (1470) it was said that commerce and industry could not exist without credit and interest and that the Jews must consequently be retained; but three years later, the town council nevertheless insisted upon their expulsion, which was finally granted in 1498. At about the same time, the Jews were expelled from numerous other German cities and territories, starting with Mainz (1420) and ending with Brandenburg (1577). In England and France, they had been expelled and their property confiscated as early as 1290 and 1394, respectively, but in Spain and Portugal, where special conditions prevailed, the final chapter was written only in 1492 and 1506. The economic role which the Jews had performed in a variety of ways throughout the Middle Ages was played out, but the patterns of Jewish-Gentile relations were fixed for a long time to come.

7

The Judaeo-Arabic Symbiosis and the Splendor and Misery of the Jews of Spain

The dual role of the Jew as a trusted friend and a suspected outsider becomes lucidly clear, if one considers the fate of the Jews of Spain. Also, their dependence on royal power and their precariously ambiguous position within the larger societal structure are obvious. But in many other ways Spain is different. In Germany and in other Central European countries that were closely connected with Germany for a long time, such as Austria, Bohemia, Alsace, and northern Italy, the Jews were constituted as a narrowly circumscribed caste. They came to occupy this position, as we have seen, in the high Middle Ages and remained chained to it until the beginning of the nineteenth century. The Jewish settlement in Spain, on the other hand, retained until the very end the older and more diversified structure of the early Mediterranean settlement. At the same time, Spanish-Jewish history points forward because it foreshadows the role that the Jews performed in the emergence of the modern nation-state.

But Spain is different in a profounder sense. Geographically, it belongs to Europe, yet it is separated from Europe by they high wall of the Pyrenees while it is open through its many ports to influence from Africa and the countries of the Near East that lie beyond. Linguistically it is Latin, but for centuries large parts of the country were occupied by the Moors, Arabic-speaking intruders from North Africa; the prolonged *reconquista* of the Moorish-occupied areas, which reached its climax with the fall of Granada in 1492, has decisively shaped the Spanish character. The intimacy of daily contact with the Moors has suffused Spanish life with varied elements stemming from Islamic civilization while the exigencies of the military contest with the Moors have brought about the identification of Spanish national consciousness with the *Credo* of the Catholic Church. The Jews of Spain, as Americo Castro has convincingly demonstrated, acted as a third force in this development. Initially closely allied with the Moors, the Jews moved over to the Christian side in the wake of the relentless persecution of all dissenters by the fanatical Almohades, a sect of Muslim purists. Jewish refugees from the Islamic parts of Spain transmitted a subtler culture and superior organizational skills to the rough hidalgos of the north. So intimate was the integration of Moors and Jews into the total fabric of Spanish life that Spanish civilization has been defined as an intricate intermixture of Latin, Islamic, and Hebrew elements. All three aspects of Spanish civilization, the Catholic which prevailed and the Moorish and Jewish that were merged with it, in their combination, share the belief that the spirit of man rules supreme and that the material world must be serviceable to it. But in the long struggle against the Moors, the Jews were entrusted with the task of providing the material prerequisites without which the supremacy of the Christian spirit would have remained an empty aspiration. As a consequence, the role of the Jews in the Spanish environment was one of an indispensable social instrument imbued with the lofty spirit of Spain, yet as a material crutch essentially alien to it. This intimate enmeshment of contradictory elements resulted in a unique historical configuration.

Spain is East in the West, and the Jews are a link in the chain that connects the two worlds. Consideration of the position of the Jews in the social structure of Islamic countries, therefore, ought to precede consideration of the position that they came to occupy in Spanish society. Indeed, in terms of Jewish history, the Islamic countries of the Near East and of North Africa, including the contested areas of the Iberian Peninsula, of Sicily, and of Greece, are part of the larger area of the first Diaspora where the Jews were quasi-indigenous and where they settled in compact groups. In these countries, Jewish economic activities were never restricted to a single role. The Jews constituted a full-fledged sub-society that contained upper, middle, and lower classes. This regional pattern was reinforced rather than challenged by the Arab conquest that swept from the Arabian Peninsula eastward to the Indus valley and westward to Spain. The Arabs, who imposed their sovereignty upon the varied territories and flourishing cities that were heir to the civilization of Greek and Roman antiquity, were adept in desert warfare, long-distance trade, and intermittent pillage but inexperienced in the skills required by urban life. The great Tunisian sociologist Ibn Khaldun has classically analyzed the interplay between nomads and settlers as the recurrent pattern of human existence in the Near East. Consequently, the nomadic Arabs in taking possession of the territories around the Mediterranean, found themselves dependent upon the Greek or Greek-influenced indigenous population, including the numerous Jews who had settled in the same area. To be sure, in ideological terms the world of Islam falls into two sections *dar-ul-Islam*, the world of peace and devotion, and *dar-ul-harb*, the world of warfare. Muslims are believed to be obliged to engage in holy warfare until the *dar-ul-harb* progressively diminishes as more and more of it is brought under the *dar-ul-Islam*. However, partly because Islam rests on the Hebrew Bible and partly because considerations of expediency counseled tolerance, the peoples of the "Book," that is Christians and Jews, were allowed to profess their faith as well as to ply their trade, if they acquiesced in being reduced to the status of *dhimmis*, meaning that they had to renounce self-protection and instead oblige themselves to pay heavy tribute to the Muslim sovereigns. The Islamic rulers imposed special covenants upon their skilled and literate Christian and Jewish subjects and on that basis engaged their services, even in circumvention of the Koranic prescription that infidels should not be invested with authority. The position of a Jewish treasurer or diplomat who refused to convert was consequently precarious, but nevertheless influential as long as it lasted. There was even a vestige of Jewish self-government preserved in the office of the *Resh-Galuta* or Exilarch (ruler-in-exile), which, although largely ceremonial, was held in high esteem at the court of the early caliphs in Baghdad. Initially, the Jews in the Islamic countries were chiefly artisans, but starting with the eighth and ninth centuries, commercial activities expanded and flourished until about the twelfth century, especially in the far-flung wholesale trade in spices, dyestuffs, medical herbs, pearls, metals, and textiles; in addition, many Jews were engaged in the clothing business, in gold- and silversmithing, and in pharmacy; they were prominent in medicine and in banking. Their ability to master the craft of healing, to manipulate figures, and to decipher the written word was highly regarded by the rulers and held in awe by the populace. Until recently, Muslims in Algeria availed themselves of Jews as intermediaries on market days on account of their reputed knowledge of debased coinage. Their Moroccan fellows looked upon the Jews they knew with a mixture of admiration and contempt because, as they put it, "they invent new combinations all the time." One step further, the illiterate villagers in Yemen believed in the magical power of their Jewish countrymen because they could read, write, and count. In addition, the fact that the Jews had a monopoly on liquor making carried a particular meaning. For while Islamic law forbids the consumption of alcoholic beverages, a number of individual Muslims, some of them high-placed, could not do without wine and spirits which they obtained only from Jews. Alcoholic beverages thus became a means of bargaining and blackmail, almost the functional equivalent of an insurance policy.

But there were negative aspects of the Jewish-Muslim symbiosis from the start and they increased from the thirteenth century onward until they reached a nadir in the nineteenth century. If the Jews were prominent in the cultural crafts, up to the heights of statecraft, so they were numerous in the unhealthy and dirty crafts, such as tanning, dyeing, hawking, mending, and all kinds of repair work, and in the despised occupations, such as the disposition of the corpses of criminals, the sweeping of streets, the cleaning of latrines, and the like. We have already mentioned the twilight area of a forbidden craft, such as liquor making. Legally, the Jew was worse off than the Christian because no intervention on his behalf of a foreign power was to be feared–not until far into the nineteenth century. As *dhimmis*, Jews could not testify against Muslims in the courts, they could not mount horses, they were not permitted to wear shoes outside their special quarters; when encountering a Muslim in a narrow lane, they had to step aside into the gutter. There were forced conversions, the last of which occurred in Meshed in northeastern Iran in 1839 when the entire Jewish community of that town professed to embrace Islam in order to escape annihilation by a fanatical mob. In Morocco, a beautiful Jewish girl, Sol ha-Zadikah, was executed in 1834, when she refused to acknowledge a deceitful conversion to Islam. In Yemen, orphaned Jewish children were forcibly removed from Jewish custody and reared in Islam, the idea being that only filial piety could justify their persistence in the state of infidelity. The proliferation of these negative features had much to do with the decline in external power of the caliphate and of the various emirates, imam-ates, and sultanates of the Muslim world. Religious fanaticism increased with the pauperization of the masses of the population and allied itself not infrequently with the love of loot, especially in the interregnum between the death of a ruler-protector and the initiation of his successor. In such instances, the mob had free rein to enter the Jewish quarter and to pillage and rape until new authority was established. It was only occasionally that a particular favorite rose to dazzling heights at court until he fell victim to palace intrigues; in which case, he was summarily executed. With all that, there was more intimate contact between Jews and Muslims when things were quiet. In Eugene Delacroix's painting, "A Jewish Wedding," one sees Jewish and Muslim guests and onlookers peacefully intermingled–a scene that could hardly have occurred in Russia at the same time. In spite of the endemic insecurity, the Muslim countries, unlike the Christian kingdoms, knew only a few massacres and no expulsions. To the contrary, emigration of an Islamic sovereign's Jewish subjects, as a rule, was prohibited. The exception was Islamic Spain.

The Moorish kingdoms in Spain were the most tolerant of all Islamic societies until the intrusion of the zealous Almoravides and Almohades who crossed over from North Africa in the eleventh and twelfth centuries. From that time onward, the most capable, educated, and resolute members of the Jewish communities in Andalusia migrated to the territories of Castile and Aragon, whenever the opportunity offered itself. In the thirteenth century, large parts of Moorish Spain were conquered by the Christian knights, and entire cities with large and flourishing Jewish communities, such as Seville and Valencia, changed hands. These Andalusian Jews carried over from Islamic civilization into Christian Spain the learned and at the same time applied arts of medicine, pharmacology, astronomy, and cartography, along with specialized skills, such as the construction of nautical, chirurgical and other instruments, and the manufacture of jewelry, textiles, and leatherware. Jews were the translators of the philosophical and scientific literature in the Arabic language that was largely derived from the classical literature of the Greeks; they were knowledgeable in comparative linguistics and in administration, especially in the fields of taxation and public finance. Besides, Jews were active in the crafts; they were especially numerous among bookbinders, embroiderers and goldsmiths, weavers, tailors, and tanners. Although the lending of money on interest was not lacking among Jewish activities, as the story of Racquel and Vidas from the romance of the Cid shows, this was only part of a broad canvas: the bulk of the urban middle classes of the nascent Spanish nation was Jewish. This coincidence of religio-ethnicity and position in the occupational structure, to the extent that ethnicity takes the place of what otherwise would be designated as social class, is one of the indications of the essentially middle-eastern character of Spanish society.

The Jews became indispensable to the crown and to the Spanish nation in arms. They enabled the knights and their peasant armies to devote themselves unswervingly to combating the Moorish enemy while they took care of procurement and logistics. The alliance of the Jews and the kings was nowhere more solidly anchored and seemingly unshakable than in Spain. The usefulness of the Jews extended from the heights of science down to the lowly crafts. The mariners of Spain sailed the seas with the help of nautical instruments made by Jews. One Abraham Crescas of Majorca drew for King John I his celebrated "map of the world." Alfonso X assembled around his court an entire assemblage of savants whom he supported as a scholarly foundation does in our days: Isaac ibn Cid and Don Judah ben Moses Ha-Kohen drew up the Alfonsine astronomical tables, Samuel Ha-Levi invented an ingenious water clock, others worked as astrologers, mathematicians, physicians, and translators. The kings and the courtiers entrusted their health to Jewish physicians and their diplomatic representation to Jewish linguists while both physicians and linguists were at the same time learned rabbis; and they entrusted their financial administration to Jewish tax farmers. From the administrative point of view, the Jews were doubly indispensable; on the one hand, the taxes paid by the Jewish subjects of the king through the intervention of the Jewish communities were the backbone of public finance, on the other hand, the Jewish financial agents; organized as business firms, collected taxes and tithes from the general population. The Jewish financial agents lent to the royal treasury as well as to the knights and the prelates the sums that were requested by them and they recovered these sums, in addition to a profit for themselves, from the peasantry by way of the public auction of agricultural produce. Not infrequently, as documentary evidence indicates, the auction took place inside a church. The Arabic word *almondea* for auction provides proof that public sales were an affair of the Moors and the Jews. As elsewhere in Europe, many Jewish communities were financially ruined by the burden of taxation, but contrary to what happened in other countries, the king was so beholden to the Jewish courtiers and tax collectors that he granted them tax exemption in return for their services. This was a cause of bitter contention within the Jewish communities where these courtiers were domiciled as well as a cause of equally bitter complaints in the *Cortes*. More seriously, the activities of the Jewish financial agents were a challenge to the Church because they placed the enemies of Christ in a position where they were bound to exercise authority over Christians. The laboring classes contrasted their depressed status with the wealth of the royal agents, the knights and the burghers compared their inability to climb out of burdensome debts with the ostentatiousness of the Jewish favorites of the Crown. The problems of the Jewish working classes and of the hard-pressed Jewish communities were overlooked. As a matter of fact, the role which the Jews played in Spain was illegal from the point of view of the ecclesiastical order of the Middle Ages. Motives of a socio-economic nature as well as considerations of Church doctrine co-mingled, when the local *Cortes*, over and over again, pointed out to the king the impropriety of the position which the Jewish courtiers occupied; they petitioned for remedial action which would be consonant with the spirit and the letter of canonical law and the papal encyclica.

But this could not change the fact that not only the public finances, but the entire economy of Christian Spain was largely dependent on the Jews and to some extent on the Moors. The lofty ideal of a Christian society rested on the solid base of alien organizational efforts. But the material base did not decide the outcome. Rather, the blatant contradiction between the substructure and the superstructure created a tragic rift in the Spanish mind as well as in the mind of the Spanish Jews. Within the Church, the idea arose to bridge the gap between imagination and reality by providing the spiritual authority of the Church with access to the mundane armament of brute coercion. The outcome was the sacred institution of the Inquisition, a tribunal established in 1478 to extirpate heresy and other crimes against the faith. The procedures of the Inquisition were directed not only against words and actions but also against thoughts and intentions, real or imaginary. Its sessions were secret, but its sentences—

mostly death sentences–were proclaimed publicly. The sacred tribunal's terrible power was thus employed to secure a spiritual truth. The contrast is glaringly highlighted in the story told by Dostoevski (in *The Brothers Karamazov*) of the meeting between the Grand Inquisitor of Spain and his prisoner, who is none else but Jesus Christ himself. Immediately, however, the power of the tribunal was aimed chiefly at baptized and presumably backsliding Jews after other attempts to attract them unequivocally to Christianity had met only with partial success. We have in mind especially the religious disputations of Barcelona (1236) and Tortosa (1413-14) between Dominican monks who were baptized Jews and learned rabbis, staged amidst the splendor of the royal and/or papal presence. In these disputations, the truth of the Church that Jesus was the Redeemer who had been foretold in the Hebrew Scriptures was to be confirmed once and for all in spiritual combat. But the staging was such that the Church was to emerge victorious irrespective of the arguments used. The Jewish scholars were intimidated by a show of overwhelming force, but the outcome was nevertheless inconclusive. However, the cleavage in the mind of the Jews, which the disputations thinly veiled, was no less profound than the cleavage affecting the Church. The rabbis defended as best they could the Jewish conception of sacred history, but the imagined security of the Jewish community in Spain rested, as everybody knew, not on the brilliance of their defense but on the assumption of the indispensability of the services that the Jews rendered to the Crown and thereby to the economy of Spain. As Spaniards, then, the Jews could not help but contrast the material base of Jewish existence, which was lacking in power, with the power-backed authority of eternal truth that was represented by the Church. In this light, the sensible rabbinic argument that the Redeemer was to be a king of flesh and blood, who could establish a realm of peace in the world, took on the color of materialistic thinking in comparison with the idea that Christ had come to redeem every individual sinner's soul, even in the midst of misery and this-worldly corruption. The messianic ideal of the rabbis looked like an empty hunt after a remote worldly goal while the crying need for individual redemption was close at hand. Conversions to Christianity among the Jewish intelligentsia increased as a consequence. Later, when conversion became a mass phenomenon, the attempt to reach the heights of the pure spirituality of an ideally conceived Christian faith became enmeshed–always under the watchful eyes of the Inquisition–with the remorse of having forsaken the ancestral inheritance which, in spite of its acknowledged ancient nobility, was viewed with contempt by the "old Christians," but was all the more eagerly embraced in thought by the "new Christians," because its material base had vanished. The desperate attempt of these truly marginal men and women to combine the uncombinable produced the ascetic poetry of Fernando de Rojas and Luis Vives and the otherworldly ecstasies of another descendant of Jews, Santa Teresa de Avila. Thus, Spanish mysticism assumed a Jewish flavor after Judaism in the flesh had disappeared from the Spanish scene.

However, all these attempts could not resolve the dilemma of the Crown. The bonds that tied in a most solid fashion the fortunes of Castile and Aragon to the activities of the Jews could not be severed, or even loosened, without courting great peril to the long drawn-out and costly crusade against the Muslim intruders upon the soil of Spain. Consequently, King Ferdinand III of Castile succeeded in having some of the decrees of the Fourth Lateran Council of 1215 that were utterly obnoxious to his Jewish subjects, such as the wearing of the "yellow badge" on the outer garments, suspended, the justification being that the larger part of the royal revenues were derived from Jewish sources. Likewise, his successors, especially Pedro IV, Alfonso VI, and Alfonso VIII, preferred to provoke severe papal rebukes rather that to dispense with the services of their Jewish *almoxarifes* (tax-gatheres) and *alfaquims* (scribes, scholars, physicians). Alfonso X, as we have seen, surrounded himself with prominent Jews in the sciences, in finance, and in government, although his famous law code, *Las Siete Partidas*, incorporated–in principle–the canonical conception of the depressed status of the Jews. Alfonso's son, Sancho IV, surrendered in 1287 to Abraham el Barchillon the most extensive rights over the revenues of the kingdom. They included the concession to mint all the coinage in the realm; the collection of various classes of fines, penalties, incomes, and taxes; the right to take possession of estates left without heirs; the right to the income of the royal chancellory; the import and export duties; the income from the iron works and salt marches; and the right to restore the royal property that had been squandered upon the nobility and the Church. The comment of Abraham Neumann that "a more glaring opportunity to amass riches and to reap ill will can hardly be imagined" appears to be justified. The remonstrations of the various *Cortes*, that these tasks should be entrusted to Christians, was met with the reply from the Court that Christian subjects of the king who would serve him equally well could not be found. Since the king, in the interest of a national policy which at the same time was a crusade, could not accede to the complaints that were brought before him, the accumulated bitterness finally exploded in the bloody pogroms of 1391 which broke the pride of Spanish Jewry and sealed their final fate which came a hundred years later. In fear of their lives, numerous of the wealthiest Jews rushed to the baptismal font, but one may add that some of them deserted their faith in order to preserve their status. The administration of the Jewish communities was left in the hands of "tailors and strapmakers" whose greater steadfastness, however, could hardly compensate for their lack of experience and financial potency.

For some two centuries, the king and the nobles had tried to contain the onslaught of the populace who were unable to compete with the Jews and envious as well as contemptuous of the material success which they enjoyed and which contrasted so sharply with their alleged spiritual depravity. The popular rancor was incited by ecclesiastics, both men of the hierarchy and friars of the mendicant orders, and fanned to flames by uninhibited preachers like Ferrant Martinez, whose fiery sermons started the bloody uproar in Seville in 1391. Finally, the Crown, on whose power the Jews relied, was compelled to concede. In 1307, Ferdinand IV could exhort the chapter of the Cathedral of Toledo in threatening language to abstain from exacting from the Jews of Toledo the cancellations of their debts to them because, as he put it, "the Jews and what they have are mine." But when Ferdinand the Catholic in 1481 intended to call the Prior of the Cathedral of Saragossa to account because of his violent actions against the Jews "who are our treasure and our inheritance," the courtiers urgently advised him to abstain from pursuing the matter, so as not to provoke severe public disorder. According to Americo Castro, the decree of expulsion of 1492 was a success of the Church only in as far as the Church was backed by popular sentiment. It is true that the fall of Granada had removed the external threat. It is likewise true that the continued presence of the Jews threatened to put the dubious absorption of the *conversos* or *Marannos*, as the "New Christians" were called, in jeopardy. These were facilitating circumstances; but essentially the expulsion was a victory of the demagogues over the royal policy. The catastrophe of the Jews of Spain shows up with great clarity what price the Jews have to pay for their role as agents of the powers that be: it can happen that they are ground between the upper and the nether millstones.

8

The Jews of Eastern Europe

Every large-scale society is necessarily stratified, and there is a division of labor between the classes of which it is composed. The individuals in these strata must willingly cooperate and their interests must dovetail, if the equilibrium of the total society would not be seriously disturbed. However, a review of history yields numerous situations where a ruling class blatantly disregards the interests of other classes in a society, exploits them, and disregards their human dignity, so that severe disharmony is the result. If nothing is done about it, violent eruptions and even revolutionary upheavals are inevitable. If we look at Jewish history from this vantage point, it is obvious that the Jews nowhere and at no time have been a ruling class or even part of a ruling class throughout the entire history of their dispersion. Yet, frequently, as in Spain, the Jews had to recognize that their interests were necessarily tied with the interests of the ruling class. If this tie had been disregarded, the Jews, being strangers by law and adherents of a strange religion, would not have been granted the right of *domicilium*. Over and over again, the Jews were granted the twin privilege of protected settlement and communal autonomy because they appeared to be useful agents of a single ruler or a powerful ruling class. They constituted an economically active and revenue-producing middle stratum of a population, interposed between the ruling elite and the laboring classes. Viewed from above, they seemed small and insignificant, that is, the rulers regarded them as an object of political manipulation. Viewed from below, they looked large and even dangerous, because they were the visible representatives of exploitative absentee overlords. Frequently, too, there has been present among the lower classes a subconscious awareness that the upper classes, if hard-pressed, might consider "their" Jews expendable, so that one can vex and kick them with impunity while at the same time indulging in the notion that one has confronted a dangerous enemy and performed a heroic deed. Finally, if to a socio-economic and even socio-psychological conflict situation of this kind an ethnic antagonism is added, possibly coupled with religious diversity–in other words: if the ruling class belongs to one nationality and the laboring classes to another–then, one tension is aggravated by another tension and a violent eruption, whereby the wedged-in Jews are likely to be the first victims, is unavoidable. The classic example for such a multiple disaster is the riot of the Ukrainian Cossacks under their *hetman* (leader) Bogdan Chmielnicki against their Polish overlords in the seventeenth century.

The vast plains of the Ukraine were a colonial territory of the old Kingdom of Poland. In these subjected regions, the Polish gentry (*shlakta*) had established huge landed estates on which Ukrainian peasants worked as bonded serfs. But the seigneurial owners were absent most of the time; they lived in grand style in Warsaw, Krakow, or Paris. The people on the spot, the administrators of the estates of the Polish nobles, were Jews. They leased entire villages, collected the tithes, sold the products that the peasants delivered, and satisfied their own needs after they had transmitted the ever-increasing lease payments to the owners. Two sources of income on the estates were felt to be especially oppressive: the fees that had to be paid on the occasion of births, marriages, and deaths, payable to Polish Catholics, were collected in the Greek Orthodox churches of the peasants by Jewish administrators who were entrusted with the keys to the churches. According to Simon Dubnow, it was the intention of the Polish overlords to wean the peasants away from their allegiance to Eastern Orthodoxy. The lease of liquor licenses or the granting of the right of "propination," as it was called, to Jewish lessees meant that innkeeping in rural areas was ostensibly a Jewish business, actually a means of social control on the part of the *seigneurs*. In the village pubs, the peasants would get drunk on credit, with the result that their indebtedness and thereby their enmeshment in servitude became hopelessly irreversible. Consequently, when the free peasants and the Cossacks, who had been settled on the Tatar frontier, revolted, the rural population all over the Ukraine rallied to their side. Most of the noble owners were far removed from the scene of conflagration; but the Jewish agents, administrators, and innkeepers were murdered. Wherever possible, the Jewish population fled to the fortified towns where they could defend themselves against the Cossack bands, side by side with the Polish garrisons; however, in more than one instance the noble commanders attempted–not always successfully–to save their troops and their own skins by abandoning the Jews to their fate as a condition of surrender. Large parts of Poland were laid waste at that time and over seven hundred Jewish communities suffered massacre, pillage, and rape. The number of victims is estimated to have been in the hundred thousands; in some parts of Poland, for instance in Volhynia and Podolia, barely 10 percent of the Jewish population survived. The Jews of Poland recovered from the blow numerically, but never economically.

Numerically speaking, the old Kingdom of Poland, which once extended throughout the entire area between the Black Sea and the Baltic, is the cradle of the Jewish people as we know it today. About ten million of the approximately thirteen million Jews who live in various countries at the present moment, or nearly 80 percent of the total, are descendants of Eastern European, that is, ultimately of Polish Jews. This proportion does not hold true for Israel, where roughly one half of the population stems from Oriental Jewish communities, but it is likely to be higher than 80 percent for the United States and the other English-speaking countries. These facts are well known. What is much less well known is that up to the time of the Hitler catastrophe the German-speaking Jews, in addition to those who spoke Yiddish as their mother tongue, were, to a large extent, of Eastern-European descent. This statement applies particularly to the major metropolitan centers of Berlin and Vienna that by 1930 contained about one half of all German and Austrian Jews. This is due partly to the fact that in the partitions of Poland in the eighteenth century large Jewish populations in Poznan and West Prussia, on the one hand, and in Galicia and Bukovina, on the other, were incorporated into Prussia and Austria, respectively and partly to migratory movements on a large scale that started in 1648, the year of the Chmielnicki pogroms. From that time on, a never-ending stream of refugees from the Polish, later Russian and Austrian, areas of Eastern Europe trudged westward in search of security and an opportunity to gain a livelihood. The Eastern European rabbi and Talmudic student, whose progeny made a name for themselves in the arts and sciences, as well as the Eastern European peddler and beggar

(*Schnorkel*), who was supported and shunned at the same time, became familiar and yet strange figures on the high roads and in the cities and villages of the various German states, of Bohemia, the Netherlands, and Alsace. In the nineteenth and twentieth centuries, the movement swept past Central Europe to the Western Hemisphere, especially to the United States of America, where it created, within the span of a few decades, the largest Jewish community of all time.

From the point of view of Jewish history, this migration has been a blessing in a twofold sense. It has replenished the isolated Jewish communities of the West and imbued them with a new vitality. As far as overseas migration is concerned, it has saved and preserved a large part of the Jewish people, men and women who otherwise would have fallen victim to the Nazi onslaught. But regarding Jewish-Gentile relations, the mass migration of Jews from East to West has reestablished the image of the Jew as a stranger. On a larger scale than ever before, the Jew once again became a man who comes today and stays tomorrow. A newly divisive element was injected into the relations between the Jews and their ambience especially in German speaking areas where the very similarity of the German and the Yiddish languages made the latter appear as a kind of a pidgin-German; the efficacy of this new element is testified to by innumerable cartoons, parodies, and doggerels that were disseminated far and wide throughout the eighteenth, nineteenth, and twentieth centuries. They depicted the Jew as a foreigner in speech and appearance whose special pleading was resented and whose attempt at familiarity were mocked and summarily rejected. The historical fact that the in-migrants were in reality re-migrants was forgotten. The Shapiros, the Landaus the Epsteins, the Ginsburgs–all bearing names derived from German localities–and many others were the great-grandsons and great-granddaughters of those German Jews who in the late Middle Ages had fled to the wide-open spaces of the East; yet, they were looked upon as intruders, not as repatriates. The impression which the Galician street hawkers made upon the agitated mind of the young Hitler belongs to the formative experiences of his stay in Vienna. This impression, of distance, even revulsion, which was widely shared and easily communicable, merged imperceptibly with the latent image of the Jew as the universal stranger, regardless of whether he was a migrant or a native.

These observations by no means exhaust the importance of the social and economic history of the Jews in Poland–and later in Russia–for the history of Jewish-Gentile relations in the contemporary world. Within the Jewish mass settlement in Eastern Europe arose a full-fledged Jewish society, amounting to a third Diaspora. According to estimates based on the report of the Jewish Commission appointed by the Quadrennial Polish Diet shortly before the dissolution of the kingdom of Poland (1788-91), the reduced Polish territory contained a total population of about nine million, of whom at least one million were Jews. In numerous small and medium-sized towns the Jewish population amounted to more than half of the total. Clearly, such a multitude had outgrown the confines of a medieval caste. Among them were urbanites and country dwellers, merchants and artisans, traders and beggars, scholars and laborers, the rich and the poor. Initially, to be sure, the Jews of Poland, not unlike other medieval Jewries, had been a commercial middle class. Small Jewish settlements, amalgamated with Slavic and Tartaric ethnic splinters, such as the fabled Khazars, had traded both with co-religionists in the eastern Mediterranean region and with merchants in Prague, Regensburg, and points west. In the later Middle Ages, starting with the Crusades, numerous German Jews fled to the East, which was then a semi-barbaric outpost of Europe. They were welcomed by the rulers of Poland and Lithuania as an urbanizing element along with Christian German immigrants who came at the same time. Over the course of the centuries, the German burghers were transformed into an indigenous Polish middle class through intermarriage and by means of linguistic assimilation. Polish anti-Semitism was born in the competition between the two middle classes and has remained alive among the Polish middle classes to the very end. Emanuel Ringelblum, one of the chroniclers of the Warsaw Ghetto under the Nazis, reports that the harassed and beleaguered Jews found supporters among the working classes and even among some intellectuals, but that the middle classes continued to be their implacable enemies.

The early Jewish immigrants from Central Europe were moneylenders and wholesale traders because the landed gentry as well as the burgeoning cities needed an infusion of capital and opportunities for export, and because the rulers were in search of revenue. But with the growth of urban centers and the urban middle classes, money lending and commercial activities were restricted, as the guilds grew jealous of competitors. The guilds found support, as they did elsewhere, among the clergy who were afraid of "Judaizing" tendencies among Christians that indeed did crop up on one or another occasion. All the anti-Jewish and anti-heretic riots that occurred in Polish cities, chiefly from the seventeenth century onwards, were executed either by journeymen and apprentices, or by students, but instigated by the merchants and the clergy. Against these opponents the Jews found protectors first in the king, later in the nobility. To the rulers of Poland and Lithuania as well as to the Turkish sultans, who provided a haven for many of the refugees from Spain, the Jews were all the more welcome because there were competitors on the scene. The Turks, having incorporated Byzantium, had become dependent in commerce and the crafts as well as in administration on the ever-present but unreliable Greeks; they used their new Jewish subjects as a politically innocuous counterpoise. The situation in Poland and in Lithuania was not dissimilar. The German burghers who had come east were considered indispensable for purposes of economic development, but at the same time feared as political antagonists. Hence, the grand dukes and the kings fostered Jewish economic activities and protected the Jewish guilds and associations. When the power of the Crown declined and the by then Polonized Christian urban middle classes asserted themselves, the Jews settled in the country-towns and on the estates of the nobility. They engaged in a variety of commercial activities, but foremost among these was the administration of the estates themselves. Jews leased entire estates and the villages that were attached to estates; they collected tolls and imposts and engaged in lumbering, flour milling, and dairying, always as managers for a nobleman to whom they paid fees. They sold marketable agricultural products, especially grains, flax, furs, hides, and timber. They took over the liquor licenses on the estates and the sale of liquor against credit to the peasants. The Jewish innkeeper became ubiquitous all over Poland. At the same time, the nobles encouraged Jewish traders, carters and artisans to settle not only in the villages, but also in the urban localities (streets, districts, private towns) which remained under their control. These observations apply to the whole of Poland, but the Jewish administrators as well as the Jewish artisans in the Ukrainian and Belorussian parts of Poland profited from a doubly and trebly interstitial position. They were interposed between the gentry and the commoners as well as between the Polish overlords and the subjected nationalities. Their function as agents and shock absorbers was honored, but the reverse side of the coin was powerlessness and exposure to violence. The Chmielnicki pogroms are a prime example by which to study these complex relationships.

Additional circumstances furthered the growth of a Jewish artisan class. The swelling numbers of the Jewish population constituted an internal market of considerable magnitude. In this respect, conditions had never been so favorable since the days of the Sassanian empire. Conversely, the outlet that existed in the manual crafts facilitated further population growth. To be sure, some of the Jewish craftsmen, like the lacemakers of Krakow and the furriers of Lvov, along with tailors, leatherworkers, carpenters, glaziers, housepainters, and musicians gained a clientele among the Polish nobility. But their decisive advantage was that the Jewish artisans were compelled to undersell the guild-monopolists and thus could serve a mass clientele of Christians as well as Jews. The Jews were led onto this revolutionary avenue by a variety of circumstances. Fiscal discrimination in the field of commercial activities and the general impoverishment of the Jewish community in the wake of the Chmielnicki pogroms drove the Jewish masses into manual occupations, sometimes in connection with petty trade. These marginal craftsmen had to earn a living by hook or by crook. Having learned their craft by trial and error, sometimes with the help of runaway Christian journeymen, their work was likely to be of shoddy quality and had to be sold at a reduced price. Wherever a craft grew out of the pawnbroking business and the trade in used goods, the refurbishing of worn and damaged merchandise added another incentive in favor of doing business by price cutting. That the Jew at any rate was expected to grant credit added the final touch to the mechanism that had been set in motion. In vain did the guildmasters complain about quality infractions and the allegedly lower standard of living of their Jewish competitors. The modern economic role of the Jews in catering to the needs of a growing mass market, especially in the garment industry, is thus adumbrated in the history of the Jewish artisan class in Eastern Europe.

It is obvious from the foregoing that the picture must not be restricted to a consideration of the entrepreneurial side. To each master and small-scale entrepreneur in the garment, leather, and furniture trades, finally in the tobacco, liquor, and foodstuff industries ought to be added several and occasionally dozens and even hundreds of workers occupied in workshops and homes as well as haulers and clerks and beneath these a reserve army of day laborers and occasional laborers who, over the course of the nineteenth century, grew into an increasingly class-conscious working class. The history of the Bund, the independent Jewish labor movement, as well as the history of the Jewish participation in the general revolutionary movement in tsarist Russia, are well known. In the present context, this development is of importance, because it documents our contention that the Eastern-European Jewish mass settlement constituted a third diaspora, essentially different from the second diaspora in medieval Europe and resembling the first diaspora in the Mediterranean area in that it constituted a newly formed and fully stratified society in which large parts of the lower classes only rarely came in contact with the outside world. In the old kingdom of Poland that task was left to the *shtadlanim*, the wealthy traders and leaseholders, who interceded with the authorities in an emergency, while in the late nineteenth and early twentieth centuries it had to be shared with the ambitious new intelligentsia. Consequently, the Jewish masses never felt the need of acquiring more than a scant knowledge of the Polish, Lithuanian, Ukrainian, or Russian languages. Remaining among themselves, they retained the middle-high German speech of the original immigrants from Central Europe and developed on this basis, merely incorporating scattered Hebrew and Slavic linguistic elements, the Yiddish language as a separate vehicle of popular communication and literary expression. Hebrew was retained for the purpose of sacred learning. There were manifold economic relations between Jews and Gentiles, but hardly any social mingling. Throughout the seventeenth and eighteenth centuries, Jewish lessees managed the gentry's estates, but they were treated contemptuously and often brutally, whenever the noble owner put in a rare appearance. Salomon Maimon's memoirs offer a vivid example of that kind of relationship. Jews sold alcoholic beverages produced by Gentiles–something they had abstained from doing in the Middle Ages–but Jews and Gentiles were rarely seen drinking in each other's company. In the nineteenth century, the Jews were removed from the villages, but they remained important in the trade with agricultural products, especially the lumber trade of the estates. However, the typical Jewish habitat was the small country town, the *shtetl*. In the *shtetl*, the Jews lived their own life. In many instances, they constituted the majority of the town's population. The *shtetl* was surrounded by peasant villages and its inhabitants were aware of the threat of pogroms in periods of depression, but they felt superior to the peasants. While the Jews were not well off economically, they were better off than the peasants, who were dependent on them for selling their products and acquiring other goods in return. Even these commercial relationships did not exist for women and children, the working poor, the beggars, and the elderly. The Jews of the *shtetl* lived in splendid isolation.

Finally, mass settlement coupled with ecological separation and cultural differentiation furthered the growth of organs of self-government. Local Jewish communities, although subject to arbitrary imposition from the outside, were largely autonomous. This was true elsewhere as well as in Poland. What was added in Poland was that the organized Jewish communities (*kehillot*) of Great Poland, Little Poland, Russia, and Volhynia were coordinated into the "Synod of the Four Lands" (*Vaad Arba Arazot*) and that the representatives from these regions met regularly at the time of the Lublin fair; a similar setup existed in Lithuania. The Synod of the Four Lands functioned like a parliament; it issued directives and ordinances, appointed officers, and engaged in arbitration. It was dissolved in 1765, when its usefulness as a tax-collecting agency for the central government ceased and collection from individuals was considered to be likely to yield more revenue. But its abuses notwithstanding–the Synod laid heavy imposts of its own on the Jewish communities in addition to those levied by the government–there is no doubt that it was an instrument of cohesion as long as it lasted. All signs pointed to a situation where the Jews had ceased to be a caste and become a people. Political reformers, therefore, spoke already in the eighteenth century of "two nations" who dwelled together in "one country."

Two further factors were added to the foregoing preconditions in the nineteenth century: the oppressive tsarist policy that created the Pale of Settlement and the contagious example of budding nationalistic movements. The Pale of Settlement restricted the area where the vast majority of the Jewish population was permitted to live to the western and southern regions of European Russia, chiefly those that formerly had constituted the kingdom of Poland and even there only to the cities. The Jewish population was expelled from the villages early in the nineteenth century. Thus the Jewish masses were drawn still closer to one another and separated from the mainstream of society. As the average Jew was immersed in his own world, it mattered little to him that he did not enjoy full civil rights, but it did matter to the Russian-educated intelligentsia. They became aware of despotism, corruption, and exploitation and of socialism as a possible solution to the world's ills. The news of nationalistic movements, especially in Poland, in the Balkans and among the peoples of the neighboring Habsburg monarchy, but also the cruel disappointment in the wake of the pogroms that were instigated after the assassination of Tsar Alexander II (1881) and later at the time of the Russo-Japanese war (1904-05), worked in the same direction. It is therefore not amazing that over the course of the nineteenth and twentieth centuries Eastern Europeans, chiefly Russian, intellectuals, men such as Pinsker, Smolenskin, Birnbaum, Lilienblum, Bialik, Achad Ha'am, Borochov, Eliezer Ben Yehudah, Dubnow and many others formulated the credo of Jewish nationalism and subsequently disseminated it throughout the Jewish world. It matters little whether this general movement took the special form of cultural autonomism and Yiddishism, chiefly in the countries of Jewish mass settlement, or of political Zionism, with its aim of creating an independent Jewish commonwealth in Palestine, or of Labor Zionism, with its combination of political nationalism and socialist idealism, or of a host of related political and cultural expressions. What counts in the present context is that the awakening of collective memories, which was indicated by all these stirrings and strivings, would not have sufficed to bring about the powerful nationalistic movement that captured the Jewish masses without the *vis a tergo* of economic and political harassment, of bitter hostility, and of bloody pogroms. The combination of geographic proximity, even intermingling, and ethnic differentiation in Eastern Europe created sharp conflicts which proved impermeable to efforts at reconciliation. The warring ethnicities could neither merge nor separate in a clear-cut fashion. The third alternative of cultural autonomy, which had provided a working solution in earlier times, was likewise incompatible with the newly arising intolerant nationalism of the majority peoples. The anti-Semitism of the Eastern European peoples, nurtured on centuries of antagonistic symbiosis, erupted orgiastically in the period of the Nazi occupation. The near-total extermination of the Jewish population in many localities throughout Eastern Europe was made possible largely by the hearty cooperation of the Gentile population in these areas with the Nazi machinery of genocide. The lesson that history as yet has not arrived at the point where "two nations in one land" can dwell side by side in peace has not been lost on the survivors.

9

The Ghetto

In the eighteenth century, the institution of the ghetto appears more sharply etched than at any other period in history, but at the same time its walls begin to crumble, physically as well as figuratively, and a new era in Jewish-Gentile relations was initiated. The growth as well as the decline of the ghetto was a long drown-out process, which is frequently misinterpreted. In trying to comprehend what the ghetto meant, it is not helpful to confuse congregation and segregation. Rather, one must distinguish between a settlement in which co-nationals and co-religionists voluntarily congregate, and a segregated settlement imposed by legal or otherwise compelling restrictions, that is, by external force. Historically, in the cities of the Roman and Sassanian empires, people of various ethnic backgrounds lived in separate quarters. Thus, large Jewish communities dwelled in particular parts of town in Alexandria, Antioch, Rome, and the major cities of Babylonia and Persia, where they congregated around their own institutions, as did Greeks, Syrians, and others. St. Paul found numerous separate but not segregated Jewish communities on his apostolic travels. Yet, individual Jews were not hindered from living outside the Jewish quarter, and individual Gentiles were found within, as for instance, in imperial and early papal Rome, but on the whole kinsmen, compatriots, and co-religionists chose to stay close to one another. In the early Middle Ages, groups of Jewish families settled in the cities of Europe under special charters and in specifically designated quarters, as they did later in the Kingdom of Poland, without compulsory concentration or restriction of activities (*Juiverie, Juderia, Judaca, Judiaria, Judengasse, ulica_zydowska*, etc.). The Jewish quarter in medieval cities was likely to be in the center of town, adjacent to the marketplace, which indicates a favored location. Also, the fact that the Jewish quarter frequently was separately walled points to a privilege rather than a restriction. If must be added, however, that both rabbis and churchmen were intent on keeping Jews and Christians socially apart, the rabbis to prevent possible contaminations by idolatry and the churchmen to forestall Judaizing proclivities among the Christian laity. As time went on, the rabbis relented, starting with the disputations about the Talmud in the thirteenth century, insofar as Christians were exempt from the designation of idolaters, but the hedges upon hedges that had been erected about the daily conduct of the Jew, especially concerning eating and drinking, continued to make social intercourse with Gentiles exceedingly difficult, to say the least. Johann Jakob Schudt reports from Frankfurt at the beginning of the eighteenth century that a Jew, when imbibing wine in the company of a Gentile, used to have a big tub of water standing beside him, so that he could rinse the cup after every gulp the Gentile had taken, or else, he would not take a gulp form the same cup again himself. Yet, Schudt added that in the villages, and also in Italy, this rule was frequently disregarded. At the close of the eighteenth century, Goethe relates that he attended circumcisions, weddings, and holiday observances in the Frankfurt ghetto, that he met with exquisite hospitality on those occasions and that he was invited to return. And he does not forget to observe that the Jewish girls seemed pleased with his polite advances.

On the other hand, Goethe's brief but acute comment also refers to the insulting engraving beneath the bridge tower at the entrance to the Frankfurt ghetto where one could see a Jew riding backwards on a huge sow in conversation with a horned devil who is likewise marked as a Jew while two other Jews drink avidly the sow's milk and urine, and a Jewish woman in the background rides a goat that bears close similarity again to the image of the devil. All this is topped by the likeness of the corpse of a martyred Gentile boy, allegedly the victim of a ritual murder. This disgusting picture well epitomizes the fact that the Church had succeeded in quenching possible Judaizing proclivities by exposing the Jews to public contempt. Papal Rome, while subtler in approach than the imperial city of Frankfurt, provides an especially striking example because it is the center of Christendom. There, Pope Paul II instituted in 1468 the infamous Jews' race during the Roman Carnival: amidst race of asses, buffaloes and horses, Jewish delegates had to run in the nude wearing only a loin cloth, exposed to piercing whistles, the rude practical jokes, and the derisive laughter of the populace. In 1688, this degrading obligation was commuted into an annual payment of three hundred scudi. For a much longer time, the Jews of Rome had to pay homage to a newly elected Pope, offering him a scroll of the law which he accepted saying: "We sanction the Law, but your belief and your interpretation we condemn, because he of whom you say he will come has come, our Lord Jesus Christ." These were the words of Innocent VIII in 1484, but other popes used similar words on similar occasions.

The growth of the voluntarily established Jewish quarter into the segregated ghetto was due only in part to the desire of the Church to keep Jews and Christians apart, attitudinally as well as physically. The Church's insistence on segregation found support among the merchant and craft guilds, who were bent upon restricting the scope of Jewish economic activities. In addition, the violent mob attacks on Jewish quarters that started at the time of the First Crusade (1906) made effective control a necessity. The development from the Jewish quarter, first as a privilege, then as a protective device, to the Ghetto as a disability can be best observed in Morocco and Spain. In the wake of an anti-Jewish riot that occurred in the city of Fez in 1280, the Merinide prince Abou-Youssef-Yacoub ordered all Jews to move to a special place outside the commercial town and in the shadow of the Kasbah (the sultan's castle), where they would be protected behind walls and gates. But what was meant to be protective isolation also meant inevitable stigmatization and exposure to a concentrated rather that a mere sporadic mob violence whenever the protector was found napping. The bulk of the Jewish community complied, but some of the wealthiest Jewish merchants chose to accept Islam in order to avoid the dreaded move. However, the near-universal deterioration of living condition in the Jewish quarters in Muslim countries dates from the seventeenth century. The Moroccan institution is called *Mellah*; the name used in Tunisia for ghetto is *Hara*, in Persia *Qua'at al-Jahud*. In Spain the transformation occurred between the thirteenth and fifteenth centuries, when the development was cut short by the expulsion. In 1248, three spacious parishes in Seville, hardly a Ghetto, were appropriated to the Jews and surrounded by a wall and in 1300 the Jews of Majorca even claimed residence in their quarter as a right when its demolition was announced. But in 1412, the ordinances of Valladolid threatened all

Jews and Moors who failed to transfer to separate enclosures with confiscation of property and corporal punishment. Yet, compliance with the ordinance seems to have been largely circumvented or at least postponed. Even the stipulations of the Third and Fourth Lateran Councils (1179 and 1215), prohibiting Christians from lodging among Jews and entering into the service of Jews and imposing upon Jews the wearing of a distinctive yellow badge, were not always rigorously observed until the period of the Counterreformation, when the bull *Cum nimis absurdum* of Pope Paul IV (1555) enjoined the consistent enforcement of the medieval principles of segregation. The ghetto of Rome, to which all Jewish inhabitants of the Eternal City were forcibly transferred, was established in 1556. The name "ghetto," probably derived from an iron foundry located near the Jewish quarter, was first used in Venice in 1516. In that era, an area for Jewish settlement was set aside in a poor neighborhood, shut off from the rest of the city and provided with Christian watchmen. The Venetian ghetto became the model for other ghettos in Italy.

Within the ghetto, the Jews enjoyed a considerable degree of autonomy, under short-term contracts. There was no assurance of continuity. When faced with an offer of expulsion, as happened in Prague as late as 1745, they did not insist on a right to stay where they were born, but realizing that they resided at a place by grace of the sovereign, they resorted to petitions and, if everything else failed, to bribery as a last resort. But as long as the settlement lasted, the Jewish street or quarter formed an officially sanctioned independent corporation with its own religious, judicial, charitable, and recreational institutions. Local pride was not absent and at times even extravagant, but economic activities were restricted to despised or unhealthy occupations, such as pawnbroking, door-to-door peddling, repair trades like mending old clothes and refurbishing used mattresses. The tax burden, both to the protection agent and internally, was oppressive. Physically, the ghetto was a single lane or courtyard, or a series of interconnected lanes and courtyards, even initially barely sufficient for the number of people admitted to it. As population increased and lateral expansion proved impossible, houses tended to be stacked up until they rose to unusual height, with consequent congestion, fire hazards, and the spread of unsanitary conditions. In the ghetto of Frankfurt, a horse-drawn carriage was not able to turn. The low-lying Roman ghetto was annually flooded by the Tiber. To add to the ill repute of the place, prostitutes were at times placed in the ghetto or adjacent to the ghetto. The ghettos were enclosed by walls and gates and kept locked at night and during church festivals, for example during Holy Week. Even so, looting and pogroms were not always prevented. Venturing outside invited harassment at all times.

By the eighteenth century, even if the Church had not relented on principle, some of the most degrading of the earlier restrictions, such as the enforced wearing of the "Jewish hat" and the yellow ring on the outer garment, had fallen into neglect. Also, there were no ghettos in the strict sense in some of the newer settlements, such as Hamburg or Hanover, and in the villages. Nevertheless, Jews remained clearly discernible from the remainder of the population by their distinctive dress, the long gabardine, the fur-lined hat (the Polish "Shtreimel"), by their appearance, such as beards and earlocks, by their bearing, their gestures, and by their speech. The Jewish languages, so-called Judaeo-Spanish (Spaniol), Judaeo-Arabic, Judaeo-German, even splinters like Judaeo-Persian and Judaeo-Piemontese, are a truthful mirror of the interpenetration of acculturation and separation that characterized the Jewish way of life prior to emancipation. The Jewish languages, so-called, preserved antiquated Castilian, Arabic, and middle-high German grammar and vocabularies, interspersed with variously pronounced Hebrew and Hebrew-derived expressions and idioms. Most of these linguistic amalgams later dissolved. However, in Eastern Europe, where the surrounding population spoke strange Slavic tongues and where, in addition, compact Jewish settlement made for some amount of Jewish self-sufficiency, the initial Judaeo-German dialects developed into a separate language, Yiddish, which toward the end of the nineteenth century acquired literacy status, thus contributing to the transformation of an enlarged ghetto into modern peoplehood. We have referred to this process in the preceding chapter and shall return once again to the same theme below.

The ghetto denotes a way of life, in addition to being a habitat. It promotes human warmth and mutual help, but also ostentatiousness, jealousy, and narrowness of outlook. In the ghettos were not only schools and academies, but also bathhouses, dance halls, societies for providing shelter to vagrants, dowries to poor brides, and burial for the dead. Since Jews, as a rule, could not hold real estate, the rabbinic institution of *hazakah*, forbidding a Jew to bid for the rental of a house occupied by another Jew, was used to prevent exploitation by Gentile landlords. If a bride could bring to marriage the right to occupy, say, one eighth of a house as a dowry, she was eagerly courted. But there was also the attempt by the wealthy to outdo competitors in the display of showy dresses and costly jewelry, so that sumptuary regulations had to be issued by the rabbis and community leaders. These were, however, frequently honored in the breach. There was bitter contention for positions of prestige in the community and for special trading privileges that were granted by the sovereign, but carried with them the opportunity to dominate one's fellow Jews. The surreptitious drive for recognition among the well to do found its counterpart in the public hustling, haggling, shoving, and yelling among the poor hawkers and peddlers. This restless competition, which was eagerly interrupted by complete rest on the Sabbath and the religious holidays, was the aspect of ghetto life that aroused the attention of the Gentiles and created the dual impression of greedy striving and lazy idleness from which the image of the Jew came to be composed. Judas Iscariot, who bargains for thirty pieces of silver, became the incarnation of the plotting Jew in the popular Passion plays which proliferated in the sixteenth and seventeenth centuries. The positive aspects of Jewish life, piety, love of learning, family cohesion, were rarely, and, at best, only grudgingly acknowledged. On the Jewish side, the fear of the Gentiles was counterbalanced by an ardent, if often suppressed desire, to participate in the opportunities of the wider world. Otherwise, the phenomenon of the Jewish apostate could not be fully explained. The internal contentiousness and the external harassment that characterized Jewish life in the declining Jewish community of Regensburg prior to the expulsion of 1519, drove one of the most outstanding apostates of the late middle ages, Antonius Margherita, the son of a Regensburg rabbi, into the opposite camp. But once a Jew had ventured outside, he was likely to be rebuffed. To use another example from Regensburg, a Jewish cantor who had been attracted by the contemplative calm of a Dominican monastery, was driven back to the shelter of the ghetto as a result of the rude treatment that was meted out to him by the bishop's servants. The marginality of the modern intellectual Jew, who is lured by opportunity but repelled by prejudice, is thus foreshadowed in the ghetto. Israel Zangwill has given us a poetic description of the tragic aspects of the dilemma in his story "Joseph the Dreamer," which transports us into the Rome of the Renaissance, and the eighteenth century has provided us with one of the prototypes of the marginal Jew, the philosopher Solomon Maimon.

Solomon Maimon's autobiography, which carries the reader from his native Lithuania to Koenigsberg and Berlin and from a primitive religious school to conversations with Moses Mendelssohn, has all the earmarks of a desperate attempt to escape from the superstitious restrictions of the ghetto, but it also indicates the transcendence of the ghetto in the third diaspora of Eastern Europe. A similar impression, although less strikingly demonstrated, may be gained from Israel Cohen's description of Vilna and Majer Balaban's portrait of Jewish life in Lublin. Maimon tells of his growing desire to flee both from the brutality and rapaciousness of Polish nobles and the narrowness and contentiousness of Jewish life to the scientific achievements of a larger European civilization, but the world he comes from was not confined to the dark ghetto lane. His childhood was spent in the open country, where his grandfather was the lessee of an estate, and the small towns where he subsequently lived were largely inhabited by Jews from all walks of life. There was no dearth of open space, ecologically and even less so socially: the Jew moved in an almost total Jewish environment. The Polish case was a case of quantity transmuted into quality. The Jews of Lublin and also those of Krakow and other places in Poland, occupied an entire Jewish town beside a Polish town, where they were granted the right *de non tolerandis Christianis* (i.e., the right to exclude Christians from settlement), in analogy to the corresponding right *de non tolderandis Judaeis* in the Polish town. Moreover, both rights were often disregarded. Christian merchants disputed the privileges of the Jews, and Jewish hawkers, tailors, and furriers offered their wares and looked for work in the Christian towns. The guilds protested against the intrusion, but the municipal council and the nobility—against payment—were on the side of the Jews. The Jews of Vilna were able to defy the attempt of the Christian burghers to confine them to three narrow lanes. To be sure, the charter of 1633 did precisely that; but after a stubborn struggle extending over more that a century, a royal court settlement of 1742 finally decreed that Jews could dwell in and buy houses in all parts of the city, save in two streets. There were just too many of them. This growth in numbers did not prevent the exposure of the Jews to hostility, especially when the guilds instigated their apprentices and unruly seminary students to violence or when contending armies considered the Jews fair game. Nor did numbers erase from the Jewish mind a pervasive sense of insecurity; but numbers of transformed Jewish existence from the isolation of the ghetto to the larger reality of ethnicity.

Still further reaching transformations occurred in Central and Western Europe at the same time. A small but significant economic elite among the Jews broke out of the confinement of the ghetto to mingle with the high and mighty, and an intellectual elite arouse simultaneously. Even more important was the elevation of the Jews as a community to the rights and obligations of citizenship. Unavoidably, the ghetto had to be broken up, to become a lingering remembrance of times past in the minds of Gentiles and Jews, as the Jews were drawn into the whirlpool of social change all around them. A new era was in the making. But in retrospect the question is posed as to what extent the change was fundamental and to what extent the continuity of history had been reasserting itself all along.

10

Court Jews and Bankers

The problem of the significance of the Jewish participation in the development of modern capitalism has been treated differently by different authors. Some, like Werner Sombart, have focused their attention on what Sombart called the "spirit of capitalism," namely, the restless striving after commercial profit. But the profit motive, that is, the calculation of advantage and disadvantage in monetary terms, is nearly universal, not tied to a particular time or place. It is impermissible inside a tribal society, but typical of outsiders to a society, that is, of "strangers." We have seen that the Jews, who in their dispersion were cast in the role of ubiquitous outsiders and who devoted themselves to commercial pursuits, are prototypical strangers. However, modern capitalism arose inside European societies, when the wholesale trader became pitted against the guild merchants and craftsmen, who were interested in securing a "living," not making a profit. When Jacob Fugger of Augsburg, the head of the most potent commercial and banking enterprise of his time, at an age where he could have conveniently retired, said he "wanted to make a profit as long as he could," he expressed what one may call the "spirit" of capitalism. At that time, in the sixteenth century, there was, far and wide, no Jew who could have competed with him. But other authors, such as Karl Marx and Max Weber, define the rise of modern capitalism differently, namely as a phenomenon inherent in the growth of industry. The position of Marx, to be sure, is not clear. On the one hand, in an often-quoted passage Marx considers the profit motive as specifically "Jewish" and capitalism as the "Judaization of the Christian world," but a statement of this kind is hardly to be reconciled with Marx's general position which derives profit from the exploitation of labor, that is from the ever-increasing employment of a propertyless working class in the industrial process. It is precisely the conspicuous absence of Jews from entrepreneurial activities of this kind which led Max Weber to the statement that "hardly a Jew is found among the creators of the modern economic situation," namely the continuing and rationally conducted enterprise. But Max Weber's position, in which politically secured commercial and financial operations, as contrasted to economic activities of an independent "bourgeois" nature, are designated as "pariah capitalism," is not satisfactory either. First, a statement of this nature comes suspiciously near to the proto-Nazi contradistinction between *schaffendes* (creative) and *raffendes* (rapacious) capital, of which one is supposedly "Aryan" and the other "Semitic." Second, the Jewish purveyors and agents of the Baroque age, men who were proud of their achievements and of haughty demeanor, did not conceive of themselves as "pariahs." Finally, the disparaging term "pariah capitalism" fails to do justice to the twin phenomenon of modern entrepreneurial capitalism, namely modern bureaucracy. The emergence of industrial society, as Max Weber himself emphasized is predicated on the establishment of unified law over a sufficiently large territory, that is, on the growth of a central governmental apparatus and of orderly financial procedures to sustain that apparatus on a continuing basis. It was at this point that the Jewish contribution became conspicuous and highly relevant.

The development is different, if one considers England and the Netherlands, on the one hand, and the German states on the other, with France occupying a middle position. In Western Europe, the colonial expansion favored the emergence of a national bourgeoisie and strengthened the central government vis-à-vis the feudal forces. Fugitive Spanish and Portuguese Marannos, whether they returned to Judaism or remained Christians of a sort, almost all of them belonging to a merchant elite, played an auxiliary role in this development in some places, especially in Bordeaux and in Amsterdam, but nothing more. The picture is entirely altered, if we look at the German territories and, as far as France is concerned, at France's newly incorporated eastern provinces, Lorraine and Alsace. There, the religious conflagrations, especially the Thirty Years War, had left a once-flourishing economy in tatters. Vast stretches of the countryside were devastated, thousands of villages disappeared, the population declined–in some areas by more than one half–and the wealth of the cities was a tale of the past, a mere pretension in the present. In the midst of the ruins lived a narrow-minded generation, jealously watching over their privileges, even after the substance was gone. But the medieval conception of the role of money and commerce, which had been shared by Martin Luther and the Lutheran theologians, had lost its virulence. That money was the *nervus rerum* was painfully obvious. Already while the religious wars lasted and later during a sequence of dynastic wars, especially the Wars of the Spanish Succession, the generals were confronted with unprecedented logistic problems. The armies consisted of mercenaries and the hired soldiers that needed to be paid, fed and properly equipped. When the rubble of the war's devastation had been cleared away, enlightened territorial sovereigns felt the need to found manufacturers, to stimulate exports, to draw cash and precious metals into the country, to create an efficient administration and to erect monuments to their exalted paramountcy. In this situation the remnants of the medieval Jewries gained a new lease on life. They had been precariously preserved in the villages of the imperial knights and counts, after their expulsion from the cities and the larger territories. To be sure, the majority of these Jews were as impoverished as the rest of the population. They eked out a miserable existence as peddlers and as *Gelegenheitshaendler* or *Nothaendler*, rendering services here and there as occasions arose and dealing with whatever merchandise they could lay their hands on. These marginal traders had at least the right of residence while Jewish vagrants (*Betteljuden*) either singly or in hordes wandered from place to place, frequently mingling with gangs of dispossessed peasants and unemployed journeymen, accepting occasional employment, but chiefly engaging in thievery, robbery, and extortion. This footloose multitude was vastly increased in the wake of the Chmielnicki pogroms. There may have been more frequent and more intimate contact between Jews and Gentiles in the lower strata of society at that time than at any other period in history. The Yiddishisms in the German *Ganovensprache* (the language of thieves) are a testimony to that. But as far as the settled village Jews were concerned, new opportunities beckoned. In the villages, guilds and guild restrictions meant little and the protection of the territorial sovereigns was more effective. In the villages, the Jews perceived a chance to break out from the narrow confines of pawnbroking and to reenter merchandising by opening up markets for agricultural products, such as cattle, wine, grain, and hides. Jews were also useful as news purveyors, general advisers, and connoisseurs of coins. In addition, they provided credit for the acquisition of parcels of land that the peasants held on lease from the nobles. Loans were further needed by peasants to pay taxes and to tide them over the lean period before harvest time. The peasant could not afford to travel great distances and at prohibitive cost to reach larger markets and the city merchants were not inclined to grant small-scale and often risky loans to unknown debtors or to accept produce in lieu of cash. This gap was filled by the Jewish traders. Peasants as well as Jews knew that they needed each other. To be sure, it occurred that a peasant could not extricate himself from debt, so that his land was sold through the courts or otherwise alienated, but as the peasant could lose his holdings, so could the Jew lose his money. If the Jew worked with borrowed capital himself, the operation might spell disaster for him, even if the sums involved were diminutive. Ordinarily, therefore, not much gain was to be realized from transactions of this kind which were in the nature of a subsistence capitalism. But when the armies needed vast quantities of grain, wine, horses, and meat on the hoof, the Jewish dealers knew where to get what was desired. It was sufficient to commission one Jew who was more aggressive and possibly somewhat more affluent: he would engage ad hoc poorer relatives, in-laws, acquaintances of all kinds as subcontractors, agents, helpers, and go-betweens, and extend credit on delivery. These men were of an individualistic and rationalistic cast of mind, alien to the conventional estate system and therefore the natural allies of the territorial sovereigns. A few of them rose to heights of affluence and influence.

Another opportunity where guild restrictions, at least in part, could be evaded, offered itself in the trade with luxury goods, such as pearls, precious stones, and metals suited for coinage. The latter item was more than a luxury because of the preoccupation of the mercantilistic state with the idea that hard cash, either in coins or in bullion, was to be imported in order to pay soldiers and officials, and to stimulate manufacturers who could be expected to produce for export. The place where all these transactions can best be observed is the city of Metz which was transferred from the sovereignty of the Holy Roman Empire to that of the king of France in 1567 and which subsequently became the operational base for the extension of French influence over Lorraine, Alsace, and to some extent over the entire left bank of the Rhine. The Jews of Metz could draw from this outlying area horses, when hostilities were about to break out, grain, when a famine threatened, and coins, sometimes clipped or of inferior alloy (*billonage*), to satisfy the royal administration in an emergency. In the words of the intendant Turgot (1728), the Jews were something like a neutral nation and therefore most suited to the import and export trade. Their extended correspondence, their wide-ranging travels, the hospitality they enjoyed among themselves, he thought, enabled them to gather the most reliable information about prices and opportunities for procurement. Besides, the Jews had retained their usefulness as a source of revenue. In the beginning of the eighteenth century, the Jews of Metz constituted one-eighteenth of the general population of the city, but paid one-sixth of the capitation tax and more than twice as much for licenses as their Gentile competitors. Moreover, only a very small number of Jewish householders carried that burden. In 1710 were counted twenty Jewish horse dealers, eighteen dealers in old goods, ten haberdashers, twelve moneylenders, and five family heads too young to engage in trade. Since about 400 Jewish families lived in Metz at that time, it follows that about 335 families were without regular income and were, at best, servants, hangers-on, and occasional agents. A document from 1741 gives a more detailed occupational breakdown, but as Robert Anchel correctly observes, these lists are incomplete and too precise at the same time, because most Jewish dealers traded in all kinds of merchandise that came their way, either on their own account or on commission, so that Turgot could say about them that they "*ils se mêlent de tout.*" This principle of taking everything in stride, born of the necessity of being a commercial generalist, is confirmed in the famous memoirs of the Glueckel of Hamelin who relates about her father that "he traded in jewelry and, like a Jew in anything else which could be profitable." A hundred years later, Nathan Meyer Rothschild could list as the reasons for his success in business: "1) What somebody else can do, I can do likewise, and 2) I am a businessman who acts on the spur of the moment ('*aus dem Stegrief*'), that is, I accept what occasion offers and conclude every business on the spot." This acquired habit of versatility and ingenuity has remained a characteristic of Jewish entrepreneurs and intellectuals and as such will claim our attention later on. At the time, it contrasted sharply with the ingrained inflexibility of the guild merchant while at the present moment in history it is generally recognized that it has become a requirement for survival for all of us. Still, even now, it is expected of a Jew that he be a jack of all trades and that he can find a way out of each and every predicament.

The same principle of versatility underlies the steep rise of the court Jew and the subsequent emergence of the state banker. The court Jew, a general financial confidant of a territorial sovereign, was well equipped for his role. As a result of strategically placed marriages, he disposed over family and business connections covering a wide area–Glueckel von Hamelin and her husband corresponded and traveled from Danzig to Amsterdam and Metz and from Copenhagen to Fuerth and Vienna–and these connections enabled the agent-trader to engage in purchases and sales, mostly on credit, which the local merchant would and could not consider. As soon as the agent had acquired a princely charter, he could provide today forage for the horses, tomorrow uniforms for the armed forces, the day after tomorrow jewels for the privy box of the duchess. If the guild-dominated estates declined to grant the prince the necessary taxation, he could advance cash and provide credit against the pledge of state revenue, establish a tobacco or salt monopoly, import raw materials, promote manufacturers of luxury goods, and see to it that the products were sold and the coffers of the duke or the prince-elector, or even the emperor, amply supplied. The wars of Prince Eugen and of the Spanish Succession, the mint experiments of Frederick II of Prussia, the prince-electorate for Ernest August of Hanover, the royal crown of Poland for August the Strong of Saxony were financed by the Oppenheimers and Wertheimers, the Itzigs, and Ephraims, the Lehmanns, Behrends, and others, down to the agent or agents of the smallest imperial knight. At times, there was bitter competition among two aspirants to the coveted position, as between the Models and the Fraenkels of Ansbach, leading to accusation, conviction, confiscation, expulsion, and even execution. The jealousy of courtiers was added to the strife of competitors. Frequently, reckless treatment was encountered on the part of the very treasury of the sovereign, especially, when debts were not acknowledged after the emergency had passed, so that the formerly indispensable financial wizard eventually was driven into bankruptcy and his heirs into virtual pennilessness. This was the fate of the estate of the most ingenious organizing talent among the court Jews, the great

Samuel Oppenheimer. Always surrounded by petty jealousy and court intrigues, Oppenheimer enabled the emperor to carry on during the protracted wars against the Turks and the French, that is, to keep the armies in the field and to sustain a central administration. The achievement was possible because of a Europe-wide, if loose, organization of agents, contact-men, cousins, and in-laws and on the basis of Oppenheimer's seemingly unlimited credit, which was anchored in his reputation for efficiency coupled with integrity. Yet, when success was assured and the House of Habsburg established as the paramount power in Central Europe, the Emperor simply refused to honor the debts he had incurred. Litigation against the imperial chamber was to no avail.

Considering the human side, positive as well as negative entries into the ledger may be made in connection with the court Jews. General respect from man to man after long centuries of mutual distrust and bitter hostility appears for the first time in the relation between Samuel Oppenheimer and the most prominent among the imperial commanders, Marcgrave Louis of Baden. In a forthright way the "Tuerkenlouis" threatened to give up his command and to enter the service of the English, if the Jewish contractor was replaced by an incompetent Gentile competitor. Still more remarkable is what Glueckel von Hamelin reports about the wedding of one of her daughters to the wealthy Elia Cleve, a subject of the elector of Brandenburg-Prussia. Prince Maurice of Nassau and Prince Frederick, later King Frederick I of Prussia, the latter then but thirteen years of age, requested to be invited to the sumptuous celebration. Glueckel relates with a Jewish mother's prideful satisfaction that the princely guest held the hand of her five-year-old son in an admiring and caressing manner throughout the proceedings. This gathering at Cleve was a meeting of almost-equals, and unheard-of event when it occurred, foreshadowing a juridically more formalized equality that was to follow in due time. It was not a gathering of lordly masters and "pariahs." Nor was an Elia Cleve or a Samuel Oppenheimer "raised from the depths," as Lewis Coser assumes. These were independently wealthy men who were attracted by the glamour of the courts and the opportunities that beckoned there. The reverse side of the coin was not so much the callousness of the rulers but the continued hostility of the citizenry. The commissars, agents, servants, and employees who made up the entourage of the court Jews received the privilege of residence in cities from which Jews had hitherto been excluded. Their transactions circumvented the barriers of the guild regulations and intruded upon the turf, as it were, of native business, while the newfangled state monopolies at the same time increased the burden of taxation. Added to the perceived economic threat was a social-psychological ingredient. The sight of the despised Jew-trader of yesteryear who now appeared as a *seigneur*, strutting in the glaring light of his princely connections, was plainly intolerable-as is the sight of ostentatious, yet powerless affluence at all times. The absolute ruler of a country could safely disregard the indignation of his subjects. But the pent-up hostility rose to the surface, when the occasion offered itself where the alliance between the financier and the sovereign could be broken. On such an occasion the Jew was beaten, but the economic policy of the mercantilistic state was meant. The death on the gallows, after trumped-up charges and an outrageously unfair trial, of Joseph Suess Oppenheimer ("*Jud Suess*") the former court-agent of the duke of Würtemberg, was a symbolic act. But the establishment of an effective, centralized governmental administration could not be halted.

What can be said is that Samuel Oppenheimer's bankruptcy and Joseph Oppenheimer's death on the gallows were indicative of the continuing fact that wealthy Jews, even if they were riding high at a particular moment, differed little from their poorer brethren in that they had no irrevocable rights of residence and remained dependent on the will or whim of their sovereign. Their roots were not so much in the locality but in the family; it is fascinating to observe to what extent they succeeded in combining a family-centered religious traditionalism with courtly association. The more precarious the latter was felt to be, the more unswerving was their loyalty. The fickle favors of the sovereign were not only anchorage, but to shift from one employer-protector to another, while facilitated by the mobility of Jewish capital, was a risky step that was more often contemplated than effectuated. However, while individuals rose and fell, a new Jewish elite had been formed whose potency as a class could not be overlooked. Otherwise, the Prince of Prussia would not have wanted to be present at the wedding at Cleve. Jewish writers of the pre-Hitler period and later, in their understandable enthusiasm over the achievement of equal rights, have frequently failed to recognize that the ideas of the Enlightenment, in and by themselves, would not have sufficed to bring about the emancipation of the Jews, if it had not been for the fact that the liberal ideas were at the same time an expression of socio-economic realities. There was to be no taxation without representation. To be sure, the philosophy of the Enlightenment may have prepared the way for the *Toleranzedikt* of Emperor Joseph II (1781), which freed the peasant and "transformed the Jew into a human being," the Great Revolution in France (1789), which established the sovereign nation as the totality of its individual citizens, and the subsequent liberal legislation in Prussia (1812) and elsewhere. These events, especially the French Revolution, are political landmarks of the utmost importance, but the forces that became operative in these events, did not reside exclusively or even primarily in the realm of ideas. As far as the Jews were concerned, the connection is transparently clear in the case of the Alsatian Jewish communal leader, banker, and royal agent Cerfberr. In recognition of his services as contractor for the king's armies he had been presented with a royal letter patent granting him the right to purchase and own real estate in the city of Strasbourg, but the city of Strasbourg, where no Jew was permitted to stay overnight at the time, contested Cerfberr's and his relatives' and employees' (seventy persons in all) right of residence. Litigation started in 1775 and was not yet concluded when the Revolution broke out and disposed of the issue. In the course of the litigation, however, Cerfberr not only warned the king that he might cease to furnish his armies with provisions, but he also turned for support to the Jewish philosopher Moses Mendelssohn in Berlin, who in turn asked a Gentile friend, the Prussian state official Christian Wilhelm Dohm, to write the desired brief. The outcome was Dohm's celebrated book *Ueber die buergerliche Verbesserung der_Juden* (About the Civic Improvement of the Jews) which Cerfberr subsequently had translated into French and which in its German as well as in its French edition influenced both Emperor Joseph II and the protagonist of Jewish emancipation in France, the fiery Comte de Mirabeau. Thus, one of the most influential documents of the Enlightenment owes its very existence to the litigation of a Jewish court-banker. The burden of the argument was that the Jews of Alsace, then in ill-repute because of their practice of usury, could be made into "useful citizens," if the cruel restrictions which for so long a time had hemmed them in, were removed and legal equality established.

Indeed, the pressure for the removal of legal restrictions, where they still existed, and the effect of their total or partial removal increased and became more potent in the decades after 1789, not only because of the contagious example of the Revolution itself, but also because the need for the services of the Jewish court-bankers, who by then had become state-bankers, had grown more urgent. The Napoleonic wars brought about an unprecedented rise in military expenditures as well as the establishment of a permanent civil service. When peace was restored, these bureaucracies were consolidated while independent economic development unfolded at the same time. The new climate of economic liberalism favored the growth of Jewish enterprise because the Jews had been accustomed to fending for themselves for a long time. The Christian merchant insisted on proceeding on sure ground while the Jewish entrepreneur was not averse to innovation and risk taking. State-credit had been risky business since time immemorial: in recent memory, the Fuggers of Augsburg as well as Samuel Oppenheimer of Vienna had foundered on it. But their credits had been in the form of loans by individuals or interlocking conglomerates of individuals. The Jewish state-bankers, especially the Rothschilds, prided themselves on having established a public market for government bonds, thus tapping sources of capitalization on a hitherto unheard-of scale. On this basis of the successful floating of government loans, the Jewish bankers entered into the field of commercial credit, stock exchange speculation, and speculative enterprise in general, as for instance trade in grain futures, real estate operations, and especially the building and operation of railroads. Railroads, the key industry of the nineteenth century, were so risky an undertaking that only the combination of governmental grants and Jewish venture capital could cope with the task. There was not a single major continental railroad prior to the 1870s that was not built and promoted by capital provided by Jewish bankers, such as the Rothschilds, the Foulds, the Pereires, the Bischoffheims, the adventurous B. H. Strousberg, and the most daring of all railroad entrepreneurs, Baron Maurice de Hirsch, whose nickname "Tuerkenhirsch" derives from his establishment in protracted efforts of politico-economic diplomacy of the gigantic network of the Oriental Railways, linking Vienna with Constantinople (Istanbul) and the lesser Balkan capitals. These promotions yielded enormous profits to the promoters and opened up wide areas for private enterprise.

Jewish banking operations started with state credit and stock exchange operations in the interest of state credit, but proceeded inescapably, through the intermediate stage of railroad construction, to the promotion of private enterprise. Among the nine signatories of the first list of the newly established Berlin stock exchange were five Jews. Three Jewish bankers provided 81 percent of the Bavarian state loans in the years 1801-1804. These were the beginnings. But when the Bayerische Hypotheken-und Wechselbank was founded in 1835 to take care of general economic expansion, still 63 percent of the shares were taken over by a consortium of Jewish bankers in Munich and Frankfurt. The joint-stock bank, surely a continuing enterprise and a potent promoter of continuing enterprise throughout the economy, was a Jewish invention, logically following the invention of the capitalization of government loans on the open market. In both cases, the needs of capitalization surpassed the capacities of individual bankers or even groups of bankers. Consequently, in each case the next step had to be taken. There is hardly a French, Belgian, Austrian, or German joint-stock bank which has not been organized by Jews, as for instance, the Crédit de Bruxelles, the Kreditanstalt, the Boden-Kreditanstalt (Vienna), the Deutsche Bank und Diskontogesellschaft, the Darmstaedter Bank, the Dresdner Bank, the Berliner Handelsgesellschaft and so on down to provincial banks, like the Mitteldeutsche Creditbank, the Bayerische Vereinsbank and many others. Without the combined resources of these large banking enterprises and the private banking firms which were their founding fathers, industrial development and the very growth of cities would have been nipped in the bud. Nor is this the whole story. Many hundreds of small and medium-sized Jewish banking firms that came into existence in the second half of the nineteenth century along with the joint-stock banks devoted themselves to providing small and medium-sized industrial and commercial enterprises with the indispensable credit and to making it possible for private bank customers to participate in the profits of larger enterprises. Thus, not only the directors of commercial enterprises, but a broad public among the middle classes availed themselves of the services of a Jewish banker as a trusted friend and advisor, as they availed themselves of the services of Jewish lawyers and medical doctors. Salomon Heine's wide popularity in Hamburg, based on his numerous private and public services and his generous charities, is a good example. For the first time in history, the liberal era thus brought about a genuine cooperation between the Jews and their erstwhile competitors and adversaries in the middle classes. On the other hand, the joint-stock banks underwent a rapid process of de-Judaization. For instance, while in 1906, eighty-seven of 115 private banking firms in Frankfurt and in Munich forty-one of sixty-four firms were Jewish, the picture was entirely different with regard to the joint-stock banks: only six of twenty-one such banks in Frankfurt and only one of sixteen public or joint-stock banks in Munich had Jewish directors or leading employees. The risk had been removed from the banking business, and thereby the need for the services of Jews.

A still more significant and surely more ominous development must be recorded. The shining star in the firmament of European haute finance, around which the lesser stars assembled, undoubtedly was the House of Rothschild. The founder of the firm, Meyer Amschel Rothschild, had started as a court Jew of the prince-elector of Hesse-Kassel, one of the wealthiest men of the dying eighteenth century; the Rothschilds have at no time afterwards abandoned their affinity for prince, state, and government–any government. Apart from Frankfurt-on-the-Main, their starting point, they opened branch enterprises in Vienna, Paris, London, and Naples while they had at least correspondents in Berlin and New York, always in the service of imperial or royal cabinets, never in intimate alliance with the bourgeoisie. Whether they thereby consciously attempted to escape close ties to the growing and increasingly militant bourgeois nationalism, as Hannah Arendt suggests, is dubious, but the upshot of their activities certainly was that they became antagonistic to national-liberal movements. Prince Metternich and Salomon Rothschild were heart and soul in Vienna, while brother James supported Louis Philippe and Napoleon III in Paris; another brother, Nathan Rothschild in London, was on friendly terms with the Duke of Wellington. The London House of Rothschild made it possible as late as 1878 for Lord Beaconsfield (Benjamin Disraeli) to acquire in one swoop the crucial 44 percent of the shares of the Suez Canal Society from the portfolio of the heavily indebted Khedive Ismail of Egypt. All ambitious Jewish bankers of Europe dreamt of business connections with the Rothschilds, who, avoiding mesalliances with lesser stars, preferred to hobnob with princes and counts–another international set.

For the Jewish masses in Eastern Europe, the Rothschilds, along with the fantastic Baron Hirsch, were cast in the image of worldly redeemers, not as entrepreneurs, but in their capacity as grandiose dispensers of philanthropy. But the ominous aspect of the legend of the Rothschilds was their image in the eyes of the Gentiles. As a matter of fact, the Rothschilds were businessmen pure and simple, not concerned with questions of power politics, except where the security of government bonds appeared to be jeopardized. They were loyal to governments, not to a particular government. That this was in effect a conservative position is not to the point. What counts is that the general public interpreted the sentence which is attributed to one of the Rothschilds, that he preferred to be the Jew of the kings rather than the king of the Jews, in the sense that the Jew dominated the kings and that on his decision was guiding the fate of nations. Alphonse de Toussenel's pamphlet (1845) on which we will have to say more later, with the telling title: *Les Juifs, rois de l'époque: Histoire de la féodalité financiére*, was not solely meant to refer to the Rothschilds, but the Rothschilds were the symbol of the supposedly imminent worldwide dominance of money in which the Jews, as it seemed, were destined to play a preeminent role. The Eternal Jew had assumed a novel, but nonetheless legendary shape: the pale-faced Ahasver had been transformed into a self-satisfied tycoon who sat on a sack of gold and disposed of the riches of the world. Power, or so it seemed, was now within the reach of money and the very nature of money was presumed to be Jewish. A panic fear seized the minds of many.

11

Galut and Citizenship

By the middle of the eighteenth century, a new stratum of intellectuals had emerged in Western European society, especially in France, in England, and in the Protestant German states, largely of middle-class origin, but detached from the mass of the burghers as well as from kings and nobles, and held together not by the tenets of a religious credo but by a belief in the universality of reason. Several currents combined in this new development. Natural law established the right of every person to the unhampered enjoyment of life, liberty and the pursuit of happiness; utilitarian ethics identified the good with the useful; the philosophy of the enlightenment postulated the supremacy of human nature in the abstract over the limitations imposed by concrete events and allegedly accidental historical circumstances. It is incontestable that the rise of this new grouping of detached intellectuals is coincidental with the rise of the bourgeoisie that is, the middle classes, but this observation does not dispose of the fact that the free artist and writer soon found himself cast in the role of antagonist to the forces that had nurtured him. The members of the new stratum were not even drawn exclusively from the commonalty; some came from the ranks of the nobility and even the clergy, attracted as they were, by the vision of the emerging unity of mankind. If that vision was to be taken seriously, it is obvious that the Jews had to be included in it—they had to be accepted as equals on philosophical grounds. It follows, moreover, that they were to be accepted as human beings, not as Jews. As the Gentile intellectual had to free himself from encrusted historical prejudices, so was his Jewish counterpart expected to shed his "ancient superstitions," as they were now called, when he wished to be included in the brave new world of pure reason. Among the first detached individuals of this kind was the philosopher Spinoza, who was indeed an antagonist of rabbinic Judaism and consequently ostracized by the Jewish community of Amsterdam. But when the movement came to fruition in the eighteenth century, the focal point was Berlin. Typical is the case of Aron Salomon Gumpertz, a grandson of Glueckel von Hameln, who studied medicine at the University of Frankfurt a.d. Oder, an exceedingly rare occurrence at the time. Gumpertz was accepted into the company of such literary men as Gottsched, Nikolai, Mauperthuis, the Marquis d'Argent and others, and he gave French and English lessons to Moses Mendelssohn. The significance of Mendelssohn's position must be appreciated in this context. Gumpertz was the scion of a wealthy Berlin family and hence was in a position to start at least from the margin of respectability, but that a hunchbacked Jew from the ghetto, like Mendelssohn, should show himself to be a master of elegant prose and philosophical reasoning seemed to border on the miraculous. There were further complications. On the one hand, Mendelssohn's intimacy with Lessing, one of the principle figures of the German enlightenment, stands as the prototypical example of a genuine friendship between Jew and Gentile, not of conventional give-and-take relationship between a princely overlord and his faithful advisor. On the other hand, Mendelssohn was aware of the notion that prevailed among enlightened intellectuals that "natural religion" was incompatible with the ritualistic exclusiveness and the supposedly superannuated usages of the Jews. Consequently, he felt constrained to justify his continued adherence to the faith of his ancestors by the assertion that the principles of reason were inherent in the precepts of Judaism and that no contradiction was therefore implied in being a Jew and a philosopher at the same time. To the question why Jewish identity had to be continued when philosophy offered the same answer on a more inclusive basis, he resorted to what was essentially a historical argument, namely, that the observance of Jewish law was a special obligation of the "House of Jacob." Mendelssohn had the Sinaitic revelation in mind, but from the vantage point of a later generation it is evident that his concern was with the preservation of the Jewish people. Surely, a people should not be offered liberty at the price of suicide. But it is likewise true that the aim of the emancipation of the Jews was the dissolution of Jewish peoplehood. Where the Church had failed, philosophy was to triumph. A new area of conflict opened up, if the Jews insisted on remaining Jews.

The victorious advance of liberal ideas, as we have seen in the preceding chapter, was ensured by the forces of capitalistic development. This broke the fetters of regulations that had outlived their usefulness and they carried a tiny but influential Jewish elite to the pinnacle of economic achievement. As affluent Jews became the financial advisors of the ruling strata in the larger society, they aspired to social recognition and the equal protection of the laws, but not to the rights and obligations of citizenship. The reasoning behind this attitude is not difficult to grasp. All Jews, rich and poor, considered themselves as living in the *Galut* (or *Gola*), that is, in exile or in a condition of captivity, from which they could be released only by means of prayer, repentance, and good deeds that were to bring about the advent of the redeemer. Jewish self-government was instrumental, if not in furthering that end, so at least in making survival in exile a possibility. But the granting of citizenship would have brought about a spiritual dilemma by opposing a secular redeemer to the expected redeemer who was supposed to restore the glory of Zion. There was a likelihood, then, that Jewish observance would be corroded and Jewish allegiance jeopardized, if self-government was replaced by citizenship. Already the absolutistic rulers had looked askance at Jewish self-governing institutions, for the same reasons for which they strove to subdue the barons, to undermine the guilds and to disestablish the estates. They were intent on freeing themselves from feudal obligations and to secure their unencumbered sovereignty. As a subject of the sovereign, everybody was to be like everybody else. In this regard, the philosophers and the politicians were in accord. The ideologues and practitioners of the French Revolution completed what the kings and cabinet ministers had started, namely, the concentration of legitimate power in the central government.

It ought to be understood that the French concept of *la nation* is based on territorial principle which is the heritage of the Roman Empire. To be sure, the term "nation" originally refers to familial bonds and a presumed common ancestry, ultimately to ethnicity. But the French monarchy subjected the various regions of France, such as Provence, Auvergne, Lorraine, Normandy and others as well as *seigneurs*, churches, guilds, and corporations to the same sovereignty, comparable to the process by which the Roman Empire had welded together natives of Italy, Spain, Gaul, Greece, and other provinces in their capacity of Roman citizens. The French Revolution went one step further in denying legitimacy to all corporative forces that are placed between the individual citizen and the centralized state (*forces intermediaries*). The state was identified with the sovereign nation, that is, conceived as the aggregate of its citizens and constituted by their free will. Accordingly, Article 1 of the "Declaration of the Rights of Man and the Citizen" of August 26, 1789 proclaimed that all men are born free and are endowed with equal rights while Article 3 stipulates that the principle of sovereignty resides essentially with the nation. These two statements complement each other. All men were admitted into the *généralité des citoyens*, if they foreswore particularistic loyalties. Conversely, all particular entities, the heritage of the Middle Ages, down to the very names of the ancient regions were abolished: Île de France became Seine-et-Oise, Lorraine became Meurthe-et-Moselle, and so forth.

These ideas and legal principles were bound to have a profound effect on the status of the Jews. Surely, it was assumed that the Jews residing in territories under French sovereignty could and should become citizens and merge with the French nation. But they could do so only as individuals, not as a community. Clermont-Tonnerre provided the classical formula for this position when he declared in the National Assembly that "everything must be denied the Jews as a nation, but everything must be granted them as individuals." It was implied that they may remain members of a Jewish "Church," that is, of a community of worship, although it sought to be added that the Jacobins were more consistent than the moderate Republicans when they demanded during their brief terroristic rule that Jews as well as Christians should abandon their peculiar "superstitions" and unite with all Frenchmen in the worship of the Goddess of Reason. To these "superstitions," as far as the Jews are concerned, belonged, the "inhumane" practice of circumcision, the sanctification of the Sabbath and, indeed, any kind of Jewish worship and instruction. Such was the position of the leftist partisans. But the rightwingers were of like mind. They were represented by those like the Abbé Maury, who maintained that to grant French citizenship to the Jews would amount to the monstrosity of dual allegiance, one conveniently asserted in the actuality of the present and the other maintained *in limbo* until the advent of the expected Redeemer. The Alsatian deputy Reubell went so far as to declare that the Jews of his province, by holding on to their institutions, had clearly excluded themselves from the privileges of citizenship. A few years later, a similar position was formulated by the sociologist de Bonald who said in a newspaper article that might have influenced Napoleon's views on this matter that the Jews seemed more repelled by Christian mores than they are repressed by French laws, and further that their unfortunate status was but a confirmation of the truth represented by the Church. Moreover, both leftists and rightists were equally disturbed by the undeniably widespread money-lending activities of the Jews of Alsace without taking into proper consideration that it had been precisely in that province of France that the Jews had been subjected to the meanest restrictions anywhere in Europe. They were excluded from the cities and the crafts, their residence was confined to a number of rural localities, their occupational activities were narrowly circumscribed by the money trade, the trade in used goods and in agricultural commodities, and they were subject to a vexatious taxation and the petty chicaneries of the local authorities. The consequences of these degrading conditions could hardly be countermanded in the course of a few years.

In spite of disabilities of this kind, it is very true that the leaders and followers of traditionalist Jewry all over Europe were not ready, or at best only reluctantly ready, to assume the rights and obligations of citizenship at the price of what must have appeared to them as the insinuation of apostasy. Such rights and obligations, apart from the impairment of rabbinic jurisdiction that they entailed, included military service, with its implication of the probable violation of the laws of *kashrut* and the sanctification of the Sabbath. As might be expected, the reaction was fiercest in Poland. When Napoleon's constitution for the Duchy of Warsaw (1807) proclaimed equal rights of citizenship for all inhabitants, both Poles and Jews were up in arms. The chassidic and mitnagdic (rabbinic) leaders of Polish Jewry combined in intensive lobbying at court and among the nobles in an effort to have the edict rescinded or at least suspended. A similar protest occurred when Prince Joseph Poniatowski, the defense minister of the Duchy, intended to introduce universal subscription to the armed services. It is said that the Maggid of Kozienice succeeded in changing the minister's mind. In Central and Western Europe the situation was different. The rabbis were hesitant, if not opposed, and the simple Jews incredulous, but the

Jewish merchants could ill afford to turn down the offer of equality of opportunity, and in France in particular the newly proclaimed principle of nationality brooked no exemption, even for conscientious objectors. There was to be no "nation within the nation." Thus, when Napoleon decided to cut the Gordian knot and to put his famous twelve questions before an assembly of Jewish notables from France and the French-administered German and Italian territories and to have their decisions formally ratified by a "Great Sanhedrin," a resounding affirmation of the principal tenets of emancipation on the part of official Jewry was a foregone conclusion.

To be sure, some of the questions posed by Napoleon created a dilemma which, however, had to be resolved, if the great promise of the new era was to be fulfilled. Especially, the reply to the third question, whether a Jew, male or female, was permitted to marry a Christian, could be formulated only after a heated internal argument. The delegates finally agreed that while Jewish law prohibited only unions with idolaters, rabbis could no more consecrate Jewish-Christian marriages than could priests or ministers, but that a Jewish person living in a mixed marriage nevertheless was presumed to have remained a Jew. Questions eleven and twelve, whether Jewish law permits or forbids Jews to practice usury in dealing both with their fellow Jews and with strangers, were likewise of a delicate character, touching, as they did, not only upon the ingrained bitter controversy over interpretation of Deut. XXIII, 19, 20, but also on the acute problem of the ways and means by which many of the Jews of Alsace were accustomed to gain their livelihood. In this regard, the assembly argued that according to biblical and Talmudic prescription charitable loans to Jews should remain interest-free, but that interest may be charged on commercial loans to Jews as well as to non-Jews, if the stipulated interest did not entail an excessive or usurious profit. Otherwise, it was pointed out, Scripture, which elsewhere commands benevolence toward strangers, would be self-contradictory. Moreover, the assembly continued, if in actual practice some Jews are found to charge usurious rates of interest, it would be unfair to impute the vice of individuals to the entire community. As a matter of fact, the theological controversy had long lost its virulence. In addition, in Benjamin Nelson's words, the Revolution contributed mightily to the dissolution of "tribal brotherhood" and the promotion of "universal otherhood," that is, of a society of individuals who were strangers to each other, but who never the less recognized in a general way their common humanity. Contrary to the expectations of fervent revolutionaries, no effective sentiment of fraternity was aroused to replace the communal bonds of old on a higher level. Everybody was on his own, subject only to possible punishment by law. What can be said, however, is that in conditions of liberty the Jewish occupational structure was to undergo a process of rapid transformation, with the result that the precariously living petty trader became a "useful citizen," acquiring wealth in a respectable way and contributing his share to the growth of the Gross National Product.

In the context of our deliberations, the fourth, fifth, and sixth among the questions put before the assembly of Jewish notables were the most incisive. Do the Jews of France consider Frenchmen as their brothers or as strangers? What does Jewish religious law prescribe regarding the relations between Jews and other Frenchmen? Do Jews who are natives of France and French citizens consider France their fatherland? Are they obliged to defend France? Are they obliged to obey the laws of France and to follow the dispositions of the French civil code? These questions went to the heart of the matter. If the Jews of France aspired to equality before the law and to full citizenship, the answers of their representatives had to be unequivocally affirmative in character. Indeed, the delegates expressed themselves most emphatically. "*La France est notre patrie, les Français sont nos frères*." Jewish law prescribes benevolence toward the stranger. Jews live on the same soil with other Frenchmen and are regulated and protected by the same laws. They are obliged to defend France "until death." The impact of these pronouncements, which became the credo of the Jewish bourgeoisie, cannot be overrated. The break with the concept of *Galut*, meaning captivity in exile, could not have been more radical, and the emperor was aware of it. In the opening sentence of the "Notes" to the twelve questions, Napoleon referred to Titus's capture of Jerusalem and he added that the present situation in regard to the relations between Jews and Gentiles was unlike any of the epochs that preceded it. Now, under the new conditions of liberty, equality, and fraternity, he continued, the Jews were not asked to abandon their religion, but merely to rectify those aspects of doctrine and custom which had "crept in" in times of persecution. In anticipation of an affirmative response, Napoleon ended with the assurance that he wanted the Jews "to find in France a new Jerusalem."

This sentence epitomizes the fundamental change that occurred in the liberal era regarding Jewish status, Jewish self-understanding, and Jewish-Gentile relations. It shows clearly that the initiative in the movement for emancipation came from above: the modern nation-state, that is, the state in which sovereignty rested with the generality of its citizens, could not tolerate a competing corporate entity within its borders, certainly not one which both the protagonists and the foes of emancipation considered to be "a nation within a nation." Where formerly the Church had been intent on keeping Jews and Christians apart, matters had now come to the point where the liberal state was intent on integrating them. Christian Wilhelm Dohm's position marks a beginning. Having in mind both conditions in Prussia, where the social integration of a Jewish elite had already vigorously started, and those in Alsace, where the avenues of economic diversification and hence of social advancement remained severely blocked, he predicted that the Jews would register decisive gains in civic virtues, if they were permitted to enter without impediment into agriculture, the crafts, the professions, and a wide variety of commercial pursuits. Under such conditions, he concluded, the free exercise of the Jewish religion would be unobjectionable. The Jacobins, anticipating the communists of a later day, went further and considered all theocratic religions as inimical to the new secular religion of reason and destructive of the loyalty to the state as the embodiment of reason. Napoleon never went as far as that; he merely imposed on French Jewry a consistorial organization which as nearly as possible was adequate to the spirit of the time inasmuch as it sharply separated nation from religion. What this meant was that adherence to the nation was stipulated as an obligation of all citizens, but that an empty shell of religion, entirely cut off from its historical roots, which were designated as "abuses," was benignly, yet reluctantly, tolerated. Jewish peculiarities were explained as the results of "oppression" and expected to evaporate in the light of liberty. France provides the ideal-typical model of that development, which, with alterations, spread to many lands.

In the German states, where emancipation was introduced either arbitrarily under French influence or half-heartedly from narrow interests, by "enlightened" bureaucrats, then taken back under pressure granted again piecemeal and finally achieved in a protracted struggle, in which the Jews were active participants, only in the 1860s, the clarity and deceptive simplicity of the French model was never achieved. But the trend was in the same direction. Under the impact of the gruesome experience of the Hitler period, Jewish as well as Gentile commentators have spoken harshly of the protagonists of emancipation. They made it appear as if the generations that were engaged in the struggle for emancipation had thrown their dignity overboard for a mere mess of pottage, that is, at the very best, a grudging acceptance in the larger society. There is a semblance of truth in that statement as far as integration in a larger social context is concerned, but politically speaking the picture is entirely different. In the political arena, the initiative was not with the Jews, but with the governments. The common citizenry was reluctant to accept the Jews as equals, but the aim of the liberal bureaucracies in the German states, including Austria, was integration to the point of amalgamation of Jews and Gentiles. However, the French idea of the nation-state was blurred and the guiding idea instead was to absorb the Jews into a Germanic version of Christianity. Already in the draft to the Prussian law of 1812 concerning the status of the Jews the view was officially expressed that "the intention to transform the Jews into useful citizens was to be realized only by means of a gradual amalgamation with the Christians." The idea was conversion by kindness rather than by coercion. Liberals, like the linguist and statesman Wilhelm von Humboldt, and conservatives like the philosopher Schelling, were of one mind in this regard. One area where the intention as well as the measures taken for its implementation can be clearly observed is with reference to the family names that were imposed on the Jews in the various German states by administrative fiat. Hebrew names were permitted only in rare instances like in the case of a Rabbi Levi of Gailingen in Baden, who had to put up a fight for its retention. German names, partly derived from localities and occupations, partly from sheer fancy (Goldstein), frequently Germanized Hebrew names (in the case of my own family: Kahnmann for Cohen or Kahane, Schuelein for Jehoshua) had to be substituted for them. But the purpose of the emancipators was achieved only very partially and mainly among the financial and intellectual elite: the children and grandchildren of Moses Mendelssohn, who all became Christians, are a good example. The case of the family Mendelssohn is of particular interest because the descendants were still subject to the racial legislation of the Nazis after 1933 although they had been Christians for several generations. The reason is that they had intermarried chiefly with other baptized Jews! In other cases, however, especially with regard to aristocratic families, who were not averse to replenishing their fortunes by means of the ample dowries of the daughters of Jewish bankers, the amalgamation was complete. But with regard to the bulk of the village and small-town Jews, nothing of the sort took place. Emancipation, particularly where it had been withheld for a long time, was ardently desired, but Jewish affiliation was not abandoned in order to achieve it. Until the middle of the nineteenth century even Hebrew first names were retained; when they were replaced by German, even Germanic first names, it was chiefly to avoid or ward off anti-Semitic slurs, not to forsake Jewish allegiance.

While the programmed physical amalgamation of Jews and Christians was not achieved, another more psychic amalgam, composed of fervent patriotism plus continued allegiance to Judaism was formed in the minds of the Jews in Central and Western Europe. To the average Jewish businessman both may have been either sincere sentiments or protestations for appearance's sake, but the combination, at any rate, was a psychological fact that was taken for granted in the Jewish community and expressed with conviction by the spokesmen of Reform and Orthodoxy alike. A comparison of the positions taken by Abraham Geiger, one of the foremost spokesmen for Reform and of Samson Raphael Hirsch, the protagonist of modern Orthodoxy (*Agudat Yisroel*) illuminates the situation. Hirsch's motto was "*torah-im-derech erez*," meaning the combination of Jewish learning with the ways of the world, both in everyday life and in higher education. Geiger's way of bridge building was his suggestion that Jewish theological faculties be established at state-supported universities, a postulate, by the way, which was never fulfilled. Although both men argued against each other in their time, the positions they took appear to be amazingly convergent in retrospect. To Geiger, Israel was a people endowed with a "genius for religion," while for Hirsch the Jewish people, unlike others, was a "religion-people," that is, a cohesive community only in as far as it adhered to the Torah. For both, Jewish religion and German nationality were distinct, yet complementary realities. A position of this kind may have looked like a halfway house if viewed from the vantage point of either traditionalism or egalitarianism, but it must be admitted that it corresponded to the requirements of the situation as these men saw them. It may have been Hungarian nationality in Hungary, Italian nationality in Italy, in addition to German and French nationality which were the prototypes, but the combination of a sentimentally conceived patriotism and a lofty interpretation of Judaism was the same everywhere. What had been started by Moses Mendelssohn, namely the coalescence of particularity and universality, was completed by the Neo-Kantian philosopher Hermann Cohen, the esteemed head of the Marburg School of Philosophy. I have in mind not so much Cohen's ill-fated pamphlet on "Germanism and Judaism," but the magnum_opus of his old age, *The Religion of Reason according to the Sources of Judaism.* Reason, the universal court of appeal of the philosopher, was shown in this work as not only compatible with Judaism but as the very essence of it. The concept of *galut* was preserved only insofar as the promise of redemption by means of reason remained unfulfilled. But the world was thought of as moving in this direction. It was a grandiose vision in truly messianic style, but hardly in tune with the situation in which it was conceived. Cohen's last work was at the provincial University of Marburg and retreated to the Hochshule fuer die Wissenschaft des Judentums (Academy for the Study of Judaism) in Berlin, on a special assignment to teach the philosophy of Judaism. The situation was one of a homecoming to Jewishness rather than of fraternization with an environment that was about to grow increasingly hostile.

12

From Liberalism to Racism: The Dialectics of Catastrophe

If we want to understand why the liberal era, which started so hopefully, ended in the cruelest catastrophe ever experienced in the history of Jewish-Gentile relations, we must recall once again the close affinity of the Jews and the princes at all times, but especially at the beginning of the modern era. This affinity was reinforced with the emergence of the nation-state because of the enormously increased financial needs of the newly established bureaucracies, the enlarged armies, and the expanding means of transportation. These needs could not and would not be satisfied by the Gentile middle classes, partly because they were lacking the necessary organizational set up, but chiefly because they were traditionally mistrustful of the central authorities. The Jews, on the other hand, although economically beginning to rise to the level of the middle classes and in some cases even beyond that level, remained socially outside the established class structure. Apart from France, their political emancipation, not to mention their social integration, remained incomplete well into the second half of the nineteenth century. Emancipatory efforts were carried forward from above, that is, by the governments, against the inertia and, frequently, the opposition of the citizenry. The masses of Jewish beggars, peddlers, and occasional hunters indeed, remained a problem and were finally disposed of either by education or emigration, but the Jewish moneyed elite had become indispensable. Their inter-European connections enabled them to be of service whenever needed, while their lack of a secure footing in the social structure of a particular country made them loyal supporters of the central state power. Thus, contradictory as it may seem, the international bankers became reliable patriots and pillars of the nation-state. The Jewish middle classes followed the lead of the financiers, with the emphasis on loyalty reinforced by the fact that their commercial activities were more localized. In retrospect, one can say that the liberal honeymoon lasted as long as the nation-state, and the inter-European system of nation-states remained the order of the day. With the replacement of the nation-state in the twentieth century by the twin forces of imperialism and racism, the civic position of the Jews was corroded and ultimately laid open to the destructive onslaught that cost the lives of millions of innocent men, women, and children. It is this fateful development that we must now retrace.

The contradictions of liberal era–freedom and disintegration, exploitation and opportunity–are still awaiting intensive analysis. As far as Jewish-Gentile relations are concerned, a new Jewish reality had come into existence: money power, formerly politically impotent, now appeared combined with effective political participation and hence was destined to become frighteningly paramount. The outcast was seen as the power that pulled strings. However, as much as the opposition to Jewish penetration in the economic and political spheres was aroused by the sight of the big financiers, the Rothschilds, and others, its manifestations went far beyond the point of departure. A great many widely divergent and yet intimately interconnected currents were to flow together until Heinrich von Treitschke's phrase "The Jews are our misfortune!" could be made the catchphrase of an infernal work of annihilation. All we can do here is to point out the main lines of a complex chain of events.

The Conservative Objection to Emancipation

The feudal opposition was the first in the field, but it did not have the last word. The noble gentlemen minded not so much the economic but the social advancement of the Jewish parvenus. The aristocrats and their literary spokesmen, who in Berlin were already loosely organized in the Christlich-deutsche Tischgemeinschaft in about 1810, excluded from membership "Frenchmen, Jews, and Philistines," thus linking the Jews both with the external enemy–the ideas of the French Revolution–and the internal opponents–the rising middle classes. They would have tolerated Jewish wealth, if prestige had not been associated with it. They could not free themselves from the image of the protected Jew, whom one could use and tolerate, even taunt and mistreat, if he were only somehow kept alive and not irrevocably prevented from minding his own business. The highborn gentlemen were joined and soon outdone by literati who shared with the old-style conservatives a dislike of bureaucrats and foreigners, but whose point of departure was different. Rather than being satisfied with preserving the status quo, they stressed freedom of expression for the individual and for the group into which the individual was born. One can say that the cult of personality and of nationality was intimately combined in this romantic version of liberalism. Another definition of nationality, different from the one established by the French Revolution, made its appearance. Nationality was now understood as ethnicity, not as citizenship, as an enlarged kinship group, not as an inclusive territorial principle. Within this frame of reference, the inclusion of the Jew in the nation became a problem. The Jew appeared as the proto-typical "stranger," even if he was transformed into a fellow-citizen, truly as a man "who comes today and stays tomorrow." He was not considered assimilable.

Representative of this mindset was the Heidelberg professor Jacob Friedrich Fries who in a review of a book by his Berlin colleague Friedrich Ruehs, published in 1816 under the title *About the Jewish Threat to the Prosperity and the Character of the Germans,* characterized the Jews as (1) a particular nation; (2) a political association; (3) a religious party; (4) a huckster and peddler caste. To be sure, the first three categories can be combined under the designation of an ethno-religious group; it had been precisely this collective aspect of Jewish existence that emancipation strove to eliminate in favor of the acceptance of the Jews as individual human beings and as citizens. At this point, one can observe a confluence of ideologies. Ruehs and Fries as well as other prominent writers of the time, for instance the Protestant theologian H.E.G. Paulus, were liberals insofar as they were ready to accept Jews as individuals but conservatives insofar as they doubted that the Jews were able and willing to fulfill the obligations of citizenship in a "Christian state," that is, to detach themselves from their Jewishness altogether. Again, the emphasis on the incompatibility of rabbinic law and the traditional expectation of a worldly redeemer with the alleged Christian character of the state was a conservative trait, but the emphasis on the incompatibility of being a Jew in the accustomed sense with the rights and obligations of citizenship was of liberal derivation. Especially forceful, if not to say rude, was the formulation of the radical philosopher Fichte, who held that where not the rights of men, but the rights of citizens were concerned the only solution to the Jewish problem was to decapitate the Jews and then provide them with new heads in which "not a single Jewish idea was kept alive." As this procedure was believed to be impossible to effectuate, the conclusion was that the Jews might be considered as fellow humans, but could not in all sincerity be granted the status of fellow citizens. However, all these liberal and radical ingredients not withstanding, designation by Fries as a contemptible "huckster and peddler caste" was a truly conservative notion. It was doubted that the Jews were capable of ever rising above their caste. As early as 1819, a low-level comedy with the title *Unser Verkehr* (With Whom We Socialize) swept the German state, heaping coarse ridicule upon Jewish upstarts. But even though the Jews might become as educated, law-abiding, and patriotic as they wished, the low-caste stigma remained with them. Bismarck, as a younger man, before he became the first chancellor of the Hohenzollern *Reich,* expressed sentiments of a continued social distance of the kind just mentioned when he declared in an 1847 speech delivered in the Prussian Diet that as a Christian he was sure he would "feel deeply depressed and restrained" if he should be compelled to recognize the authority of the king in the person of a Jewish official. But these arguments by themselves were of no avail. Even Bismarck changed his mind toward the end of his career. The spirit of liberalism, which dominated the thinking of the period, demanded that achieved status was considered equal to or better than ascribed status, which meant that a moneyed as well as an intellectual elite was to be considered on par with inherited rank and ultimately could overshadow it. The foremost example of achieved status was the newly arrived Jew. One can therefore say that the Jew was hit, but liberalism was meant. In the meantime, however, a pervasive discrimination was maintained against professed Jews in public employment throughout the nineteenth century, especially in the Germanic countries. Only commercial activities and the free professions were available as avenues of advancement. The conservative element in these restrictive policies is unmistakable.

The Radical Attack on Wealth

The right-wing conservative opposition to the Jew as the representative of liberalism was matched by the left-wing radical opposition to the very same Jew as the representative of capitalism. Historically speaking, one might say that a populist brand of anti-Semitism is endemic to Europe. The massive, murderous outbreak against the Jews throughout the centuries, from the period of the Crusades to the Chmielnitsky uprising, had been carried forward by impoverished craftsmen, unemployed apprentices, and disinherited peasants; and although their onslaughts were primarily directed against the nobles and the Church, it was the exposed and defenseless Jews who were the foremost victims of the popular furor, whenever it was unleashed. By the nineteenth century, the situation had become more fluid. Free enterprise advanced by leaps and bounds, legal restrictions were lifted, individual Jews appeared prominently on the public stage, and, most importantly, free-floating intellectuals, alienated from society, emerged in the major cities of Europe, lending their pen to the formulation of socialist or semi-socialist theories. They were aiming at a society dominated by an intellectual elite. The history of socialist movements in France is paradigmatic in this regard. Except for the St. Simonists who were friendly to industry and held Jews in their ranks, the major spokesmen of French socialism were sharp antagonists of the Jews. Fourier called the Jews "a nation of swindlers"; Toussenel, a leading Fourierist, considered the terms Jew, usurer, haggler as synonyms and "finance feudalism" the chief opponent, with the Jews as its most gifted representatives. Proudhon saw the peoples of Europe sacrificed to the Rothschilds and other powerful money lenders; Pierre Leroux declared that the Jewish spirit was the spirit of commerce, speculation, profit-making, and selfishness. Edouard Drumont, the author of *La France Juive* (1886) and one of the principal movers in the campaign of vilification against Captain Dreyfus, was an ardent admirer of Toussenel's widely discussed book *Les Juif, rois de l'Époque*, which Drumont thought of as an "incomparable masterpiece." Compared with former centuries, the image of the Jew as the arch-exploiter was reinforced in the writings of these men: with the Jewish religion relegated to the background, the so-called inborn nature of the Jew had become the main culprit. It is well known that Karl Marx, although of Jewish descent, held the same conviction. He saw in capitalism the Judaization of the Christian world.

The official socialist parties, largely Marxian, were not straightforwardly opposed to the propagation of the new image of the Jews as devils. A widespread conviction among socialist leaders was that anti-Semitism was the socialism of "blockheads," meaning that the followers of anti-Semitic parolees were ill-informed; but they were socialists at heart who ultimately would come to see that capitalism as such, not merely "Jewish" capitalism, was the principal evil force in the world. Hence, the French socialist leaders, including Jean Jaurés, at first tried to go along with an anti-Semitic propagandist such as Drumont in the belief that his propaganda might be used to their advantage; they changed tactics only when they realized that agitation against Dreyfus was aimed at the overthrow of the Third Republic. The German social-democratic leaders Bebel and Liebknecht, although convinced that anti-Semitism was a diversionary maneuver of the bourgeoisie, nevertheless persuaded themselves that "the social-democrats would ultimately reap where the anti-Semites had sowed." The official party organ *Vorwärts* consoled its readers after the success of the anti-Semitic parties in the parliamentary elections of 1893 with the thought that "anti-Semitism is the last phase of the moribund capitalistic society." However, apart from the doctrinaire belief in the inevitability of a socialist future, there may also have been present in a position of this kind the recognition that anti-Semitism was widespread among the voters and that it was not opportune to combat it head-on. Besides, the socialists, not unlike the conservatives in this regard, considered the Jews to be an integral part of the new "ruling class." What is certain, though, is that the social-democratic parties were not racist. They never wavered in their defense of the worth of the individual. Many of their leaders, especially in Berlin and Vienna, were men of Jewish descent; some, like Paul Singer, a Berlin garment manufacturer who was known for his selfless service to the cause of labor, were the idols of the electorate. But most of these Jewish socialists thought that anti-Semitism was a passing phenomenon and that corporate Jewish existence would become meaningless in an egalitarian society. In line with leftist ideology, they played down their Jewishness and painstakingly avoided identification with specifically Jewish aspirations. In Austria, where they favored a federation of nationalities and the recognition of each nationality's language and culture, they bitterly opposed the recognition of a Jewish nationality. Whether or not this attitude helped Jewish-Gentile relations remains dubious. The Austrian social democrat Engelbert Pernerstorfer, who was a German nationalist, reports with some annoyance that when he asked a Jewish party comrade,

Robert Danneberg where he belonged, Danneberg replied that he was a "cosmopolitan." Pernerstorfer's comment is revealing: "That is a magnificent answer on the part of a logician, such as Danneberg surely thinks he is. Every human being belongs to a particular people. But Danneberg neither wants to be a German nor does he wish to admit that he is a Jew, an affiliation which could be honorable enough." An example such as this shows that those Jewish socialists who believed they could gain acceptance simply as human beings in actual fact straddled the fence.

The Contending Jewish Elites

Wedged between the contending and not infrequently intermingled forces of conservatives, liberals and more or less socialist radicals, the Jews as well as the churches had to take their stand. The churches were clearly on the conservative side, but, as we will see later, a populist ingredient, supported by leading churchmen, changed the character of the conservative movement to a point that it became unrecognizable. What is certain is that the Catholic Church as well as Protestant spokesmen were disturbed about the spirit of the times and frequently attributed the dissolution of social bonds to the nefarious influence of the Jews. To be sure, the moneyed Jews tried to maintain the best possible relations with the forces of "throne and altar," but the intellectual Jews, the writers, journalists, and political propagandists, disturbed the peace. The close alliance between the Jewish financial elite and the princes and nobles is a continuing theme of Jewish history, but the existence of a contending intellectual elite must not be overlooked. What changed after the emancipation was both the composition and the function of the intellectual elite. Throughout antiquity and the Middle Ages, the leaders of the Jewish community, both within its own community and throughout the world, had been rabbinic scholars. But as peripheral pressures increased and survival was fought for again and again, the predominance of the men of means became more firmly established. The language of finance convinced the rulers and the potentates. It was, of course, possible, to combine the role of financier of the court and political intermediary with a high level of scholarship as exemplified, for instance, by Don Jizhak Abarvanel, the last Jewish grandee of Spain, but such an occurrence must not blind us to the fact that scholars and businessmen were intrinsically opponents. In the old kingdom of Poland, wealthy leaseholders, who enjoyed the favor of the nobles, increasingly dominated the communities, especially after the dissolution of the "Council of the Four Lands" by the middle of the eighteenth century. The classical formulation of the contrast of the two elites prior to the emancipation is found in the regulations of the assembly of German rabbis in Frankfurt am Main in 1603. The rabbis said, "It is known that many uneducated people have become arrogant, trusting in their amassed fortune and their great wealth but if the Lord had not stood by our side, we might have been destroyed and crushed and wrecked and ruined a long time ago." The rabbis threatened to excommunicate all those who evaded their jurisdiction. What had been a severe if essentially already empty threat in the seventeenth century became entirely ineffective in the nineteenth. The predominance of the man of means was now an accomplished fact. To be sure, the chairman of Napoleon's Sanhedrin was Rabbi Sinzheim of Strasbourg, but the fact that he was related by marriage to the state-banker Cerfberr merely enhanced the status of the business community. However, a new elite of independent intellectuals, chiefly literati and journalists, arose at the same time.

The secular intellectuals engaged in pitched battles on all fronts. They barely escaped from the restrictions of the ghetto, were ambivalent about the Jewish heritage as they knew it and indelibly marked by the cruelty and contempt of the general population; yet they eagerly grasped for the promise of a new freedom which, however, evaded their enthusiastic embrace and confronted them instead with the cold fact of discrimination. Nonetheless, they still expressed themselves on all matters for artistic and political impact, letting the chips fall where they may. They turned their sharp wit against their persecutors. They attacked the Church that had stamped the Jews as outcasts, the aristocracy that had held them in thrall, the very notion of a "Christian State" that seemed devised to legitimize their continued exclusion from public employment, and the narrow outlook of the average philistine that deprived them of the appreciation they thought was their due while gleefully applauding every affront to which they were exposed. The aggressiveness the intellectuals exhibited is thoroughly understandable although it was hardly designed to win friends. But the liberal current swept the intellectuals much farther. Taking the credo for the new freedom seriously, they felt themselves to be Jews merely by force of circumstance but citizens of the world by free choice. Whenever cultural particularities were upheld, they suspected that the purpose was to justify their exclusion and, indeed, their return to the ghetto. Consequently, the defense they engaged in which frequently took the form of a counterattack, was a defense of civil rights, not of Jewishness. One hardly exaggerates if one says that Jewish particularities in speech, dress, food taboo, forms of worship, and communal organization seemed even more reactionary to many Jewish intellectuals than other particularities because they were thought to be an obstacle to the integration of the educated Jewish elite into the larger society. The nouveau riche Jews became a favorite object of parodies and caricatures in radical Jewish publications, so as to contrast their lack of sophistication with free-style intellectualism. It was all the more galling that Jewish money gained acceptance where Jewish intellect was rejected. The intellectuals were further antagonized by the fact that the men of means, who had access to the powerful and were steadfast supporters of the status quo, were the recognized representatives of Jewish interests and that they, the intellectuals, were dependent on them. The love-hate relationship between the impecunious poet Heinrich Heine and his wealthy uncle, the banker Salomon Heine, comes to mind even though Heinrich Heine must be considered an ambiguous figure. He simultaneously detested and admired the charitable and domineering financial magnates, such as his friendly relative in Hamburg and the more remote Foulds and Rothschilds in Paris, whom he called "the (entrepreneurial) rabbi of the Right Bank" and "the rabbi of the Left Bank," respectively. The magnates, in turn, tithed the poet with occasional handouts because they were afraid of his biting pen. But then, Heine also wavered between a position that considered Judaism a "collective illness" and a "misfortune" and another that expressed pride in being "a descendent of those martyrs who gave the world a god and a morality and who fought and suffered on all the battlefields of thought."

The position of a renegade Jewish intellectual like Karl Marx is much clearer. In Marx's view, the Jews were a financial clan whose "foremost representatives everywhere were the leaders of the counterrevolution." On another occasion he explained to his readers that "we find every tyrant backed by a Jew, as the pope by a Jesuit." The latter remark is especially significant because in associating the Jewish establishment with the Church, both could be tarred with the brush of clericalism. Anti-clericalism became a surrogate Jewishness for freethinking Jews, marginal Jews and ex-Jews. Indeed, while Jewish literati, from Ludwig Boerne to Kurt Tucholsky, were bitter social critics who convinced republicans and fervent fellow-travelers of revolutionary movements, the Rothschilds were reliable supporters of the Hapsburgs and the Bourbons and maintained close contact with Louis Philippe and Napoleon III; the fabulous Baron Maurice Hirsch was a personal friend of Prince Ferdinand of Saxe-Coburg-Gotha, the later King of Bulgaria, whose mother, Princess Clementine of Orleans, was a daughter of Louise Philippe. As late as 1888, Hirsch contributed 2.5 of the 4 million francs that were in the hands of the royalist committee to the cause of the Orleans family. From the point of view of Jewish-Gentile relations, the outcome was that the two competing Jewish elites maintained contacts with entirely different strata of the larger society. The magnates, Hannah Arendt's parvenus were not always accepted in the highest social circles, but were on excellent terms with the heads of governments, while the intellectuals, Hannah Arendt's *pariahs*, mingled with radicals and revolutionaries, likewise not always accepted among their peers, but always spirited, always in the thick of battle at the same time advancing their own cause in every tilt with universal injustice.

Both elites bifurcated into those that were actively Jewish and those that were escapists. Among the magnates, some were baptized; and some, without taking to the baptismal font themselves, at least succeeded in marrying off their female descendants to the money-hungry scions of the aristocracy. A conspicuous example is the Cologne banker Simon (Baron von) Oppenheim whose daughters and grand-daughters became Countesses Bredow, Arco-Valley, Leyden, Plancy, Pocci and Baroness Kaskel, Franckenberg, Hauerstein-Loxten, Vivier Deslandes, etc. Others, like the Rothschilds and Maurice Hirsch, were leaders in Jewish affairs, both in local communal matters and in international philanthropic efforts. It is remarkable, however, that the Rothschilds kept aloof from other Jews to the extent that they married either their cousins or members of the European aristocracy. Nobody else seemed to be of equal birth. The Rothschilds never failed to support Jewish religious and charitable institutions, generously if they could place one of their satraps in a position of influence, niggardly if such was not the case. They were ready to protect and represent other Jews, but they carefully avoided mingling with them. No Jew, no matter how respectable or educated, was ever invited to a reception of Baron Nathaniel Rothschild in Vienna, to the amazement of a prominent member of the Austrian aristocracy who would have been curious to meet a Jew with whom he could converse. "Is there no Jew in Vienna who is worthy of Baron Rothschild's company," he asked. Yet, when another member of the high aristocracy was assured that he would not encounter Jews at Baron Rothschild's house, he replied: "Baron Rothschild does not socialize with Jews and neither do I." In spite of strenuous efforts at adaptation, the acceptance even of slang Jews was less than perfect.

Among intellectuals, baptisms and other forms of denial also occurred, as in the cases of Heinrich Heine and Moritz Saphir; but these were acts of despair in the face of the unwillingness of governments and universities to admit non-baptized Jews to salaried positions. Heine's bitter witticism that his baptism was merely "the ticket of admission to European civilization" is well known. The term "civilization" is revealing. It stands for an elusive economic security, but it also points to a quasi-religion of universal progress that helped its devotees to keep clear of outright apostasy (or, as in Heine's case, deny that apostasy had actually occurred) because it transcended both Judaism and Christianity. Not unlike the financiers who strove to be accepted into the ranks of the ruling elite, the intellectuals were intent on joining "the larger society." They did not wish to be encumbered by what they thought to be the outmoded beliefs and customs of the average Jew. The "Rights of Man," not the Decalogue of Moses, were their "Ten Commandments." But society resisted a surface treatment of this kind. A conservative observer, the German sociologist Wilhelm Heinrich Riehl, expressed a collective judgment when he stated that the typical Jewish intellectual had "abandoned genuine Jewishness without embracing Christianity, rejected in like manner the Germanic state and Jewish theocracy." The secular state, of course, was not in Riehl's view. He rather concluded that having escaped severe coercion and civic disability, the bulk of the Jewish intellectuals had become incapable of appreciating historical forms of any kind. Clearly, by the middle of the nineteenth century the Jewish writer had become the prototype of marginality.

A clarification of the concept of marginality in relation to the terms "parvenu" and "pariah," as used by Hannah Arendt, would seem to be necessary at this point. The term parvenu as applied to financial upstarts, is self-explanatory; but the use of the term pariah requires explanation. Hannah Arendt's parvenus are upstarts in the eyes of onlookers while her pariahs–not to be confused with Max Weber's pariah in Hannah Arendt's sense is a state of mind. In a similar vein, Eleanore Sterling observes that until the end of the eighteenth century the Jews took it for granted that they were different, but that they became "a problem to themselves" in the liberal era. Like Hannah Arendt, she had in mind not so much the financial magnates and still less the average Jew, but the Jewish intellectuals. The moneyed aristocrats knew how to help themselves, and the average Jew never intended to leave the fold. But the intellectuals who separated themselves from the community of Israel but were not accepted in the larger society as anything else but Jews, presented a problem. Ludwig Boerne (1786 - 1837) explained the emotional state of these men and women perceptively, when he confessed about himself that "some accuse me of being a Jew, others forgive me for being a Jew, still others praise me for it, but all of them reflect on it." Surely, his desire to be considered a human being pure and simple could not be granted. Hence, he and those like him were floating between the camps as true outcasts, that is, as belonging to no caste or class. Theirs was marginality with a vengeance. The comparison with pariahs stems from Michael Beer, scion of an emancipated Berlin Jewish family and brother of the composer Giacomo Meyerbeer, who wrote *The Pariahs,* a thinly disguised dramatic play about the Jewish condition as he saw it. A more accurate designation for the marginal intellectuals would be the one of "frustrated escapists." They were unable to escape, yet unwilling to return.

By the same token, because they had placed themselves precariously at the edge of both Judaism and Christianity, the escapist Jewish intellectuals were incapable of challenging the financial elite for leadership. That task fell to another breed of intellectuals, namely, to men who formulated the credo of secular Jewish nationalism. The nationalist movement, in both its autonomistic and Zion-centered branches, arose in response to the anti-Semitic rejection, even defamation, of Jewish participation in the larger society. The forerunner was Moses Hess, the author of *Rome und Jerusalem* (1862). Hess was a refugee German socialist living in Paris who, to the amazement of his socialist friends, became a fervent Jew. There is little doubt that Heine, had he lived longer, would have rallied to his side. But the main protagonists of the new response were Russian Jewish intellectuals who were disappointed with an enlightenment that was powerless to prevent pogroms. In addition, these men, from Peretz Smolenskin and Moshe Leib Lilienblum to Leon Pinsker and Ahad Ha-am, came from an area of a large-scale Jewish settlement, where "peoplehood" in the sense of a segmented society was a natural phenomenon, not a mere postulate. On the basis of his folk background, Ahad Ha-am (One of the People) could castigate the position of the assimilationist intellectuals as "slavery in freedom," yet remain in the tradition of enlightenment. By far the most significant figure among the nationalist intellectuals, though, was the Viennese writer Theodore Herzl, the convener of the first Zionist congress (1897). Herzl's first strategic idea in laying out the plans for the creation of a Jewish State was, indeed, to bargain for the support of the "rich Jew," especially Baron Maurice Hirsch and the Rothschilds. In a fascinating interview that Herzl, the author of *The Jewish State*, had with Hirsch, the most munificent Jewish philanthropist of all times, Hirsch called Herzl "an intelligent man" but "with such fantastic ideas." Herzl, in reply to the question about where he would get the money for unrealistic enterprise, said defiantly that he intended to "raise a Jewish National Loan Fund," meaning that he would seek to gain a broad financial base that would make him independent of the lords of international finance. Only a week later (June 7, 1895), Herzl sketched in an entry in his diary three stages of the foreseeable development of his movement. The first and second stages were conceived as being dominated by "The Rothschilds" and "the midget millionaires," but the third stage was by "the little people," with Herzl adding that "... if it comes to this stage, the first two will rue the day." Indeed, the intellectuals and popular leaders that had risen from the ranks were to call the tune in the Zionist movement. The millionaires, midgets and others, while still indispensable, were relegated to the role of auxiliaries.

The Dilemma of the Churches

The churches, like the Jews, were caught in the crosscurrents of the times, and Church attitudes toward the Jews were affected accordingly. The earlier objection against the emancipation of the Jews, that they could hardly be expected to abandon their ancient autonomy, came to naught in view of the fact that the Jews had embraced the liberal credo with alacrity. But to the extent that the Jews appeared as the protagonists as well as the beneficiaries of liberalism, the churches necessarily assumed a critical stance toward them, in both the avant-garde and the business community. Surely, if one considers the entire history of Jewish-Christian relations from the earliest time until the heyday of the liberal era, one can hardly blame the Jews, especially the intelligentsia, if they promoted now, when the opportunity arose, the separation of Church and State, a progressive family legislation, freedom of the press, and an educational system free of clerical interference, even if their choice of words at times was unfortunate. Neither can one blame the Jewish merchants for taking advantage of the principle of freedom of trade. But one must likewise understand that the churches meant to defend the traditional positions. Their point of departure was conservative, but in line with the general deterioration of conservative thought and practice; the means employed, more often than not, were demagogic in character. The nature of the case was such that an appeal to popular anti-Semitism was by no means spurned when it seemed to serve the interests of the Church. What in another context would have been considered as damnable revolutionary excesses was hailed as the expression of the "healthy sentiments of the people" when directed against Jews. Certainly, the related images of the commercial Jew as exploitative, the intellectual Jew as corrosive, and all Jews as enemies of Christ were readily available and avidly utilized. What the churches failed to understand was that hostility against Jews had to assume a racist character in an age in which religious bonds were subject to a rapid process of dissolution and that the churches inevitably would be sucked in the whirlpool of destructive nihilism that was to arise in the wake of the renunciation of spiritual values.

In retrospect, this truth was evident only to a few far-sighted minds by the middle of the nineteenth century, one of them being the progressive Viennese rabbi Adolf Jellinek. While most Jewish spokesmen considered the Church the main enemy and anti-Semitism as a mere "remnant of the dark ages," Jellinek predicted that the antithesis Christians versus the Jews was likely to be replaced by the antithesis Aryans versus the Semites. He thought that this new controversy might go a long way towards uniting Christians and Jews against racism as the common enemy. The hope expressed was in line with the liberal optimism of the period, but the observation was more accurate than that of the general run of conventional commentators. Much to the point was the anonymous Gentile author of a pamphlet issued in Vienna in the revolutionary year 1848 who warned against the subversion of Christian values. It read: "Those Christians that have lost faith in Christ will turn out to be the most furious enemies of the Jews. . . . When the Christian people will have no more Christianity and no more money, then, Jews, you will have to fashion skulls of iron for yourselves–with mere skulls of bone you won't survive history." While the Gentile pamphleteer addressed himself to the Jewish intellectuals and their liberal friends, the poet Heinrich Heine, himself a revolutionary in his sympathies, warned the Christians, but in vain. Heine's vision of the ancient Germanic god Thor who, once roused from his slumber, was to wield his gigantic hammer and shatter the Gothic cathedrals, was not heeded until the cities of Europe lay in ruins.

The anti-liberal stance of the churches in the second half of the nineteenth century must be viewed against the background of the Manchester liberalism of the time and of Social Darwinism, which was its ideological expression. The utilitarian thinking prevalent in both was incapable of comprehending collectivities. What was good for the individual was presumed to be good for the community. However, even if it was true that the mechanism of the market would see to it that only the fittest survived, the commonwealth was not served if innumerable small craftsmen and businessmen lost their independence and the living standard of the laboring man was depressed. A variety of solutions was offered. The socialists promised to end the struggle between capital and labor by expropriating the means of production, but the conservative forces, including the churches, availed themselves of the rising Christian-social movement to remedy the excesses of liberalism and to keep the socialists at bay at the same time. Legislative measures were proposed to restore the imperilled equilibrium. The beginnings of social security legislation fall into this time, initiated by Bismarck as a piece of unabashed Tory socialism, but conceived by Albert Schaeffle and other academic socialists (*Kathedersozialisten*) in a larger Christian-social context. Social security legislation, although instigated from above, nevertheless was forward-looking. But a kind of rearguard action in favor of the middle classes was politically more effective.

The demand was for legislation designed to protect the small independent producers by means of licensing procedures and other curtailments of unhampered competition. The stock exchange crashes of the 1870s, especially in Berlin and Vienna, and the ensuing economic depression that lasted from the late 1870s until well into the 1890s, undermined the belief in the efficacy of the philosophy of social harmony, which had been the centerpiece of classical liberalism. The economic reverses generated noisy populist movements that started with a Christian-social ideology advocating cooperative rather than competitive attitudes, but soon adopted anti-Semitic slogans that were in line with the resentment of the disappointed middle classes. Austria is symptomatic in this regard. The Christian-social ideologist Baron Vogelsang, a true conservative who attacked the prevailing materialistic greed of the business society, referred to the Jews merely as protagonists of such a society, not as the root-cause of its ills. But a clerical politician, like Prince Alois Liechtenstein, abandoned the ethical stance for political propaganda when as a speaker at the second general meeting of Austrian Catholics (*Katholikentag*) he attacked liberalism as a force that ". . . entered the stage in the garb of Nathan the Wise (Lessing's generous Jewish philosopher), exuding enlightenment and promoting happiness, but soon assumed his natural role of Shylock, insisting on his bond and demanding his pound of flesh." The ancient image was conjured up and proved to be as virulent as ever. The Christian-social movement was not racist, but it made good use of ingrained popular prejudices. However, there is a grain of truth even in the most prejudicial notions. The Shylock image is a distortion of reality, but it cannot be gainsaid that liberalism was the ideology of achieved status and wealth and that Jews were prominent among its beneficiaries. Accordingly, when property qualifications for voting were removed (1895), it was revealed that liberalism had no mass base in Austria and the Jews of Austria no defender in the political arena. The situation was not essentially different in Germany and France.

Economic Insecurity and Political Frustration

The vulnerable position of the Jews in the social structure was reinforced by the periodic economic crises of the nineteenth century. Every depression has the effect of restricting the market and increasing competition. Nobody objects to the success of a competitor in times of a business upswing, when making ends meet is no problem. But in times of a downturn, one is inclined to overlook one's own miscalculation and to ascribe the decline of one's fortunes to what one believes was the unfair machinations of the very same competitor, especially if he is a Jew. One must further consider that Jews, either as bankers or as commodity merchants, frequently were the creditors of farmers and small entrepreneurs. The prices for the debtor's products decline in a depression, with the effect that his income is curtailed while his debt becomes proportionally more onerous. Hence, anti-Semitic movements of the nineteenth century can be observed to rise and fall with the ups and downs of business cycles. For example, the economic crisis that immediately followed the end of the Napoleonic wars made possible the infamous Hep-Hep riots of 1819, which led to serious property damage and physical attacks on Jews over wide areas in southern Germany and in their wake delayed the full emancipation of the German Jews for decades. Conversely, the business upswing which lasted from the mid-1850s to the early 1870s coincided with the completion of legal emancipation. The depression which extended from the mid-1870s to the mid-1890s, in turn, brought about a racist backlash and the growth of political anti-Semitism. We will return to the story of racism later.

Political frustration and economic insecurity went hand in hand. All the countries of continental Europe where political anti-Semitism became virulent, namely Austria-Hungary, France, Russia, and Germany, had experienced military defeats and shocking infringements on national self-confidence: Austria after the battle of Koeniggraetz (1866) and the definitive exclusion from the newly created German *Reich*; France after the conclusion of the Franco-Prussian war (1871) and the humiliating revelation of official corruption in the Panama scandal; Russia after the diplomatic retreat at the Congress of Berlin (1878) and the assassination of Tsar Alexander II; Germany after the shattering defeat in World War I (1918) and the ensuing inflation that wiped out the savings of the middle classes. In the case of France and Germany, hurt national pride demanded that a "traitor" be found: in the case of Austria and Russia, it was the fear of inexorable fate that diverted the rage toward a convenient target; in Austria, the fear of the German nationalists to be overwhelmed by the Slavic majority; and in Russia the fear of social revolution on the part of the tsarist bureaucracy. The only country that weathered the crisis was France, possibly because it came early, when the antibodies in the social structure were still strong enough to fight off the infection. But when economic dissatisfaction, even despair, was added to political frustration, as was the case in Germany after Versailles and the inflation of the 1920s, the counter-forces that might have forestalled a catastrophe were disastrously paralyzed. In the circumstances, the demagogic anti-Semitism, which subsumed all evils under a single common denominator, grew to a social movement of destructive force and intent. The tensions in the German social structure had developed throughout the nineteenth century, but the point is that the dikes broke when the foundations that had been undermined were manned by a feeble defense.

In periods of economic decline and political frustration the counter-image of the Jewish domination of the economy, never entirely absent from the public mind, looms larger than ever. However, the prominence of the Jews in commercial activities, particularly those that were speculative in nature and politically oriented, like the building of railroads, must not induce us to assume that Jewish businessmen wielded effective political power. The notion of Jewish wealth as a world power, a myth fed by the Rothschild legend and virulent as a fantasy, nevertheless was the result of a mistaken perspective. Save for the Jewish mass settlement in Eastern Europe, in which millions of people eked out a miserable existence, the average Jewish businessman in Central and Western Europe had worked himself up from modest circumstances to a comfortable existence, but not to striking affluence. Some had made quick fortunes in stock exchange and real estate operations, but fortunes of this kind were lost as quickly as they had been gained in the ups and downs of the business cycles. At no time, not even at the zenith of the liberal era, was the Jew steering the national economy. This is obvious for a country with a long established capitalistic structure and a concomitant state of mind, such as England. However, in Germany, and even more so in Austria, a rapid capitalistic development was superimposed on a social structure that had retained strong feudal features, thus creating an unresolved contradiction. New wealth was widespread, but status was not necessarily achieved with the acquisition of wealth; it rested largely with older aristocratic and bureaucratic strata, especially the armed forces. Referring now exclusively to Germany, access to these strata in terms of position within the structure was almost entirely barred to Jews. To be sure, Jewish state bankers occupied conspicuous auxiliary positions well into the last third on the nineteenth century; but by the 1870s, the private bankers began to be superseded by the joint-stock banks, which had few Jewish directors. The process was completed by the turn of the century. Some Jewish banking firms remained instrumental in promoting industrial growth, but such promotion again amounted to hardly more than support services. By the end of the century, the older ruling strata entered into a liaison with the tycoons of iron, steel, and armaments; but apart from Upper Silesia, Jews were conspicuously absent from the management of heavy industry. In the chemical and machinery industries, Jews were also scantily represented. When a Jewish entrepreneur attained prominence in the electric industry, as did Emil Rathenau, or in shipping, as did Albert Ballin, he was considered an exceptional case. Significantly, long before the onset of Nazi rule, the leading directorates in both the electrical and the shipping industries had been taken over by Gentiles. Even when Jews had started an industry, they became supernumerary as soon as speculation, innovation and risk-taking were replaced by routine bureaucratic procedures. Jews were both numerous and prominent chiefly in those branches of business that either retained a speculative character or dealt closely with the consumer. To the former belonged the wholesale trade in metals, textiles, furniture, antiques, agricultural produce, and real estate operations, to the latter the retail trade, primarily in the soft goods, garment, leatherware, liquor, and similar industries and businesses. Department stores, trading in "everything that might be profitable," like Glueckel von Hamelin's father's business owed their growth to Jewish initiative. Some of the largest metropolitan newspapers were in Jewish hands and many of their writers were Jews. However, in the insurance business, another branch of business that is close to the consumer, Jews were not managers but agents. In the professions, Jews rarely penetrated officialdom; instead they clustered in the business-like and consumer-oriented free professions of the lawyer, the doctor, and the journalist. Finally, we must return once more to banking and especially to the stock exchange, both of which were considered the stronghold of Jewish domination. In the early 1870s, when speculative fever was at a high pitch in Berlin and Vienna, the stock exchanges, to be sure, were teeming with brokers, agents, fly-by-night lawyers, adventurous promoters, and financial reporters who were largely Jewish and very conspicuous. But the actual beneficiaries, the managers, directors, and members of the board of the leading institutions in investment, banking and railroad speculation, who were often times scions of renowned aristocratic families, as well as the corrupt government officials who were in the same league with them remained in the background. When problems arose, these beneficiaries would maintain that they had been misled by Jewish promoters. As the famous quotation from Lessing's *Nathan the Wise* states, "the Jew will be burned" when matters go awry. In the latter part of the nineteenth century, when political anti-Semitism had just arisen and had merely set out to make the Jews the scapegoat of everything that was evil in modern society, the "burning" was symbolically performed. But in Auschwitz and Treblinka, as we have since learned, the burning was exceedingly real. The least that one can say in the present context is that the fact that the Jew was burned proves that he was not occupying the seat of power. An additional circumstance was bound to create a mistaken perspective. "The wealthier Jew," as *Nathan the Wise*, further states, was not always "the better Jew," but he was the kind of Jew that represented the Jewish community in its relations with the Gentiles. The social psychologist Kurt Lewin has shown that embattled minorities that are discriminated against tend to be led at least at a certain stage in the development of their political consciousness, by spokesmen whose prime motive is not to serve the interests of their own ethnic group. These leaders are marginal men, "poised in uncertainty between two conflicting worlds"–the ethnic world that shelters them and the larger society in which they aspire to be accepted. Had they not been rebuffed by prejudice they would have preferred high positions in a general social context rather than that of Jewish affairs. Becoming successful Jewish businessmen and professionals who consented to accept the presidency of a Jewish community or the chairmanship of a Jewish institution was not their first choice. The notion that in this capacity they could more effortlessly socialize with high-placed Christians was likely to be in the back of their minds; that they represented Jewish interests was the price they were willing to pay. But the wealthier Jew, even without representing any interests other than his own, had ways and means of affording himself access to high officialdom and to publicity in the papers. He could donate to charities and engage in conspicuous consumption. He was the *shtadlan*, the man of influence, who could throw his weight around and thereby help the community. Men of modest means had more modest aspirations. They satisfied their need for socializing within enlarged kinship groups and around the synagogue. Poor Jews were either working for Jewish employers or taken care of by Jewish charity. We have no records of a Jewish working class employed by non-Jewish entrepreneurs, not even in places with a large Jewish proletariat, such as Alexandria, Salonika, Lodz, Vilna, or Warsaw. The requirements of Jewish holiday observance militated against it. Jewish employers were obliged to respect these requirements, but Christian employers were unwilling to do so. Generally speaking, the Christian world was profoundly disinterested in Jews without money, except in cases where Jewish tramps and beggars made a nuisance of themselves. Even the Judaic scholar was hardly in the public eye. Thus, it is understandable that an eminent social scientist like Albert Schaeffle, who should have known better in his capacity of minister of commerce in the Cabinet Hohenwart and as negotiator for a German-Czech modus vivendi in Bohemia, was not keen on making the acquaintance of the selfless Adolf Fischhof, the foremost expert on nationality problems in Austria, while he attempted to take advantage of the scheming real estate Alex Scharf and the intelligent but unscrupulous railroad speculator Victor von Ofenheim. Is it amazing, then, that Schaeffle concluded that "Jewry essentially and instinctively could only adhere to the party of moneyed interest?"

The Transmutation of Liberalism: The Alliance of Imperialism and Radicalism

Actually, the reason why the Jews adhered longer than others to the ideology of liberalism was not their inclination toward the pursuit of material happiness, as prejudicial judgment assumed, but the plain fact that they owed their freedom to it. But liberalism deserted its own cause. The twin-ideas of individual self-determination and national sovereignty had been liberalism's point of departure but were abandoned for a number of interlocking reasons. In the economic sphere, the self-determination of the individual brought about the rise of the bourgeoisie; and this capitalistic class grew increasingly apprehensive that popular sovereignty, consistently pursued, might ultimately lead to expropriation. Consequently, the right to vote remained tied to property qualifications practically everywhere throughout the nineteenth century. In addition, the prerogatives of the elected representatives were effectively hedged in.But the handwriting was on the wall: the classes had to learn how to manipulate the masses. At the same time, the leadership of the bourgeoisie was transferred from bankers to industrialists. In the single case of England the industrialists remained free-traders at the expense both of domestic farmers and less advanced competitors abroad; but on the continent, two successive steps were required to achieve a comparable result. The continental industrialists allied themselves first with nativistic currents in order to secure the home market by means of protective tariffs. With protection achieved, they proceeded to seek foreign markets for their increased production, precisely as the English industrialists had done before them. In other words, as industrialists began to outrank bankers in financial strength and to supercede them at the seats of power, the foreign relations of all the economically advanced nations of Western Europe turned imperialistic. Externally, the scramble for colonies and spheres of influence became the order of the day; internally, the cartels of the heavy industries, themselves a concomitant of the economic depression, depressed the living standard of the middle classes. Since the small proprietors would not dare to move against the powerful combination of the old feudal strata and the newfangled industrial barons, a mood of frustration began to spread far and wide. Simultaneously, governmental authority had to be exercised to keep the labor movement in check and mass support had to be enlisted at the polls. In England, the laboring as well as the middle classes benefitted from the imperialistic exploitation by means of cheap food imports and more exports of industrial products, with a racist sense of superiority over "the lesser breeds without the law," which was engendered thereby, turned against the colored colonials in the overseas possessions.

On the European continent, that kind of outlet became successively less available as one proceeded from France and the Benelux countries toward the landlocked area in Central and Eastern Europe that had been settled by Germanic and Slavic peoples. Here, popular movements with their attendant racist sentiments largely turned against internal, that is, domestic opponents.

One effective way to do this was to take advantage of the resentment that had arisen among the middle classes and to direct it against Jewish competition in the economic and cultural fields rather than against the ruling elite. To move against "Jewish" capital was a daring operation. One had to see to it that the malcontents were not further alienated by denying them the modest capital accumulation they desired. More importantly, one had to make sure that the attack on Jewish capital was not to be the opening wedge for an attack on capital per se. This statement does not imply that political anti-Semitism is the invention of high-placed people in power. The question of whether political anti-Semitism was instigated from above or whether it welled up from below cannot be answered in an either/or fashion. It is true that the campaign of the Prussian preacher Adolf Stoecker was at first encouraged and ultimately called off by the government; but of greater significance is the demagoguery of a far more independent actor on the political scene, the Reichstag deputy Otto Boeckel, who wrote that "the money-grabbing capitalist, whether Jew or Gentile, strangles our people by depriving them of their employment." The spirit of revolt was not clearly articulated in these words, but it was heard. A better articulated social resolution was indeed what the social-democratic leaders believed they could "calmly watch and wait" for. Vigilance was needed, or else, the anti-Semitic movement and the labor movement might coalesce. Perhaps it would be better to say that social unrest was growing vociferous in the 1880s as well as in the last years of the Weimar Republic, but the powers that be believed that it could be channelled and directed. The precautionary wisdom that says whoever rides a tiger cannot dismount was personified by von Papen, Hugenberg, and Thyssen, who persuaded themselves that they could use Hitler for their purposes, as well as by their predecessors in the late nineteenth century. The idea was to deflect the populist tendencies inherent in the anti-Semitic movement, so that they could be turned against the Jews rather than against greed and exploitation itself. This purpose was supposedly served by the differentiation between "useful" and "harmful" capital; "useful" capital was depicted as capital employed in agriculture, industry and "honest" trade, "harmful" capital as "non-working," that is, speculative and chiefly Jewish capital. The terminology was coined as early as 1893 by another Reichstag deputy, Liebermann von Sonnenberg, who had been elected on an anti-

Semitic platform. It was resurrected three decades later, when semi-socialist Nazi ideologues, such as Dietrich Eckart and Gottfried Feder, refashioned it as "creative" and "rapacious" capital. The terminology is meaningless from the point of view of economic theory, and no attempt was made to translate it into practice either; but it did serve to exonerate those who made use of it. One merely had to count oneself among the "creative" capitalists to be safe from damnation. At the same time, its effectiveness rested on the fact that it invoked the ingrained image of the mythical Jew.

The new mass movement required a new leadership that was available among the detached intellectuals whom Hannah Arendt calls the "mob." These intellectuals had long lost their belief in the Goddess of Reason and had fled into a romantic cult of personality. Conventional rules of conduct had been declared inoperative for the great man who incorporated the Hegelian World-Spirit–an Alexander, a Caesar, a Napolean. A host of would-be great men took their cue from this generous dispensation. The anti-capitalistic inclination of these *epigoni* could be harnessed to the needs of the captains of industry because their elitism kept the misunderstood geniuses from joining the proletarian movement. At the same time, they became rabid anti-Semites as they faced the competition of Jewish intellectuals. A racist philosophy served to keep the Semitic rivals at bay and established blue-blooded superiority in the face of inferior achievement. Racism, as we have seen, likewise appealed to the small fry who had lost out in the marketplace. Here, then, was the amalgam that became explosive: the disintegration of the classes joined the discontent of the masses. The industrialists had not created the situation; they merely availed themselves of what seemed to be a happy opportunity. Not unlike the churches before them, they failed to realize that the nihilistic nature of the racist movement, once released, had the power to destroy but lacked the ability to reconstruct or even stabilize. No aspect of the racist movement reveals its inherent destructiveness more glaringly than pan-Germanism, which was the platform upon which the larger movement grew to prominence.

Racism versus the State: Austria as a Proving Ground

It is a mistake to equate racism with nationalism and a still greater mistake to compare it with patriotism. Racism replaces love of one's country and its people with an allegiance that transcends boundaries. The story of nationalism is more complex. Modern nationalism finds its expression in the territorially circumscribed nation-state; but the very victory of the nation-state spelled its own doom as soon as the concept was applied outside Western Europe where it originated. Nationality, understood as ethnicity, and the territorial state, both hardly coinciding even in France, cleaved widely apart in Central Europe. Many ethnic and linguistic groups lived inextricably intermingled in the "shatter-zone" east of the Rhine and between the Baltic and the Black seas. Every boundary that conceivably could be drawn included potentially disloyal minorities along with a majority that showed every intention of becoming a sovereign nation. Even today, after a period of forced migrations, wholesale expulsions and outright genocide, the quais-independent states of the region are uneasily balanced and their frontiers by no means stabilized. This observation applies to Poles, Czechs, Slovaks, Magyars, Croats, Serbs, and others as well as to Germans, but the German problem has a particular aspect to it. The German Federation, which after 1815 had kept the various German states loosely tied together but was rendered nearly inoperative by the bitter contention for hegemony between Prussia and Austria, finally was forcibly dissolved in 1866. Prussia emerged paramount and Austria excluded. Although Bismarck's "little German" solution was exuberantly hailed by contemporaries as if it meant the achievement of the nation-state, it actually was an acknowledgment of the fact that a unified Germany was a political impossibility. The Germans in Austria, who had been split up to achieve the union of Prussia with the remainder of the German states, felt abandoned and frustrated in a dynastic state that now had a Slavic majority. The seeming advantage that the German language remained the *Staatssprache*, or *lingua franca*, merely deepened the sense of betrayal because it made it difficult to discern friend and foe linguistically. Linguistic Germanization was seen to go hand-in-hand with ethnic de-Germanization. This was one reason to espouse the race ideology. But Oscar Karbach has pointed to another more decisive aspect of the pan-German movement in Austria. The unification of all Germanic groups in Central Europe in a pan-German (*gross-deutsches*) *Reich* of the future now appeared possible only if the Hapsburg monarchy and therefore the entire system of the balance of power in Europe was corroded and utterly destroyed. This was the aim of the Austrian pan-German leader, Georg von Schoenerer.

What had to be done to achieve that end? Supporting the monarchy were the clergy, the aristocracy, the army, the bureaucracy and– the Jews. Accordingly, it was the loyalty, that is, the very patriotism of the Jews that cast them in the role of opponents of the pan-German idea and made them a prime target of attack. However, there was a deeper reason why this was to be the case. The racist definition of a Jew, which the pan-German partisans employed, extended far beyond the boundaries of the religious Jewish community. It included everybody who ever had been a Jew and everybody with an ascertainable Jewish ancestry, even a single Jewish grandparent or great-grandparent. The application of this principle clearly had the force of dynamite in old Austria, a country where, more than anywhere else, numerous baptized Jews and their descendants lived, along with half-Jews, quarter-Jews and so forth. The number of Jews who had escaped and ex-Jews was perhaps as great as the number of professed Jews. They were largely concentrated in the educated classes, including the bureaucracy of the empire and in the aristocracy. The usefulness even of cabinet ministers, like Count Aehrental, who, although Catholic, were of Jewish descent or at least might be suspected to be of Jewish descent, could be seriously impaired. To revile Jews who were easily recognizable as such when one meant to attack a larger target was nothing new; but under the circumstances, the element of race had to be entered into the equation if the purpose, namely to paralyze the entire machinery of government, was to be achieved. In that sense, racism was merely a means to an end. Schoenerer and those who thought like him, among them the young Hitler, realized that "dynastic patriotism" and "racial nationalism" were incompatible.

The emphasis here is on the word "racial." The multi-national state was not to be transformed into a federation of nationalities or a multiplicity of nation-states, for this would have entailed either genuine cultural pluralism or a vast dislocation of populations and the consequent abandonment of outlying German settlements. Rather, all of Central Europe was to be refashioned into the utopia of the racial state, wherein the master race was to dominate the subservient *Bedientenvoelker*. Still, in 1920, when the Hapsburg monarchy had ended and the remaining Republic of Austria had not yet been incorporated into Germany, the very first point of the twenty-five-point program of the National Socialist German Workers Party was "the union of all Germans in a pan-German state." This demand was an unmistakable, yet a continually overlooked confirmation of the derivation of the Nazi Party from the pan-German movement in Austria prior to World War I. Even pan-German fellow-travelers in Germany proper hardly understood that the desired pan-German *Reich* not only was to include the German-speaking rump-Republic of Austria and the rimlands of Czechoslovakia, but all Germans, that is, those in Hungary, Yugoslavia, Rumania, territories further east and even territories overseas, if they contained large or small German settlements or were thought to be suitable for German colonial expansion. Everybody who was suspected to be of even remote Jewish ancestry was branded as a Jew, so that those whose ancestry might have been German or part German could be reclaimed for the Nordic race. The entire scheme, from its initiation in the 1880s to its disastrous culmination at Stalingrad, was an orgy of nihilism. It spelled the destruction of an inter-European system that had been in existence since the Congress of Vienna (1815) and likewise implied the rejection of a democratically constituted United Europe that could have replaced it. In the last analysis, it was not merely the multinational state or the nation-state or even the system of alliances between sovereign states in Europe that was negated, but the state in any shape or form. Hitler was explicit in this regard. He declared in *Mein Kampf* that the state, far from being an end in itself, was merely a "means for the maintenance and advancement of a physically and emotionally homogeneous group of human beings," meaning that governments were established to enhance the race and, conversely, to combat whatever was detrimental to the race. In other words, the state was to be nothing more than the executor of racial policies. As a supreme power, the state was superseded by the Party. Herewith, the very fact that the Jews were fervent patriots now came to count against them. They continued to rely on a protector who turned out to be but a poor image of his former self. The state had ceased to be the arbiter of social forces and the guarantor of internal peace. If the party-state, as a racial agent, was to crush all the challengers of the Nordic master race, the Jews, who were considered the arch-challengers and the very incarnation of the counter-race, were faced with an implacable foe.

13

The Actual Jew and the Mythical Jew

If one wants to answer the question of how the relations between Jews and Gentiles on the person-to-person level developed during the nineteenth and twentieth centuries up to the final catastrophe of the Holocaust, one must be cognizant of the dialectical tension between the actual Jew whom he encounters in day-by-day contacts and the image of the mythical Jew which permeates these contacts. The tension is epitomized in the story that has been told about a Jewish storekeeper in a small town in Germany shortly before Hitler's seizure of power and his Gentile neighbor of many years who one day started wearing the sign of the swastika on his lapel. "We have always been good neighbors," the storekeeper is supposed to have said in amazement, "so why are you now turning against me?" The neighbor assured the storekeeper that he bore not the slightest grudge against him as a person but that he was unalterably opposed to "international Jewry." In other words, what was happening was that the actual Jew was well enough liked, but that he was slain to exorcize the perceived threat of the mythical Jew with whom nobody could come to grips. Moreover, if we confine our observations to Central Europe, where the decisive development took place, we shall see that human relations in the early period of the emancipation were uneasy at best and frequently of a hostile nature while they took on an increasingly more integrative character in the later period, especially after the turn of the century. Yet, the uneasiness was merely neutralized, not removed. The process of integration turned out to be deceptive because the phobic image of the mythical Jew had grown to monstrous proportions at the same time. In subtly transitory stages, the actual Jew attained more and more the coloration of the mythical Jew. In the end, mass psychosis overwhelmed even the best intentions. We must now try to unfold the story in greater detail.

The Acculturation of the Stranger

At the beginning of the nineteenth century, the tsarist government in Russia, which had taken over most of the territory of the old Kingdom of Poland, expelled the Jews from the villages, where they had been occupied as lessees of estates, innkeepers, traders, and agents of various kinds. As a result, most of these people increased the proletariat and sub-proletariat in the Jewish quarters of the country towns as well as the larger cities where, apart from market day, they hardly had a chance to be in contact with the Gentile population. In addition, emancipation in Eastern Europe was delayed until the beginning of the twentieth century and, in many ways, until the revolution of 1917. All these factors combined to preserve the linguistic and thereby the social separateness of the Jews in the Russian pale, if one excludes from consideration a very thin upper layer of assimilated merchants and intellectuals.

The situation was very different in Central Europe. There, emancipation was decreed from above–although in many areas in halting steps–but the personal relations between Jews and Gentiles were only minimally altered for a considerable time to come. The vast majority of Jews lived in a restricted number of villages and small towns, which they left on Sundays, heavily laden with merchandise or simply in search of an opportunity to strike a bargain, to return on Friday noon for the celebration of the Sabbath in the family circle. They were highly visible, ubiquitous, an inseparable part of the landscape, familiar with the ways of the peasantry, but they were strangers. That quality of strangers militated against the entrance of young Jews into the crafts on anything but a small scale, the well-intentioned efforts of the bureaucracy and of some Jewish leaders notwithstanding. The vast majority of Christian masters refused to accept Jewish apprentices, partly because they feared future competition, partly because they would have had to excuse Jewish apprentices from work on Jewish holidays. In turn, Jewish apprentices would not have been able to accept room and board with Christian masters, for reasons of *kashrut*, and Jewish parents would have to look for a nearby Jewish home to accommodate a young man. Such places were hard to find and, if found, might have been beyond the financial ability of a poor tradesman. Apart from economic conditions, then, the difference in worship was most telling, and to worship "other" gods is an essential attribute of the stranger. One can say that the very familiarity with the phenomenon of the Jewish presence, coupled with the religiously sanctioned observation that, as a people, the Jews had no home, deepened the impression of strangeness in which awe was mingled with fear and fear with contempt. The story that Berthold Auerbach, the author of the once-popular *Schwarzwälder Dorfgeschicnten* (Village Tales from the Black Forest), tells of an occurrence in his youth is most illuminating in this regard. On his way home from an errand, young Auerbach was ambushed by three boys who declared that they had no desire to fight with him and that they merely wanted him to kneel down and say: "Christ has risen." On his refusal to comply, the Jewish boy was overpowered and bound in the shape of the crucified Christ. He was doubly a stranger because his attackers came from another village. The redeeming part of the story is that Auerbach's Jewish and Christian friends from his own village took physical revenge on his tormentors afterwards. Even more to the point than the Auerbach story is the rhymed comment on "the Jews in our midst" which an annoyed English poet of the time put in these words:

> A hopeless faith, a homeless race,
> Yet seeking the most holy place
> And owning the true bliss.

Apparently, there was felt to be a contradiction between the strangeness of the Jews–they had no "home"–as well as the seeming hopelessness of their faith–the "Redeemer" for whom they waited had appeared long ago–and their stubborn pretension that they were, and would always remain, the "chosen people." They might have been neighbors, visitors, counselors, even friends of a sort, but they were seen through the veil of mystery.

The situation was only superficially altered when, in the wake of emancipation, the Jews broke out of the magic circle of economic restrictions and constructed their own ladder to pecuniary success and social esteem. The principle of the freedom of trade, even where it was imperfectly realized, enabled them to become retail merchants, wholesalers, manufacturers, professionals, to acquire solid homes in good neighborhoods and to become the benefactors of local charities. But, as we have remarked earlier, the vast majority of the population in town and country found the realization that achieved status was now equal, or even superior, to ascribed status most irritating. While previously the common complaint had been that the Jews were not fit for citizenship because they would not give up their peddling and huckstering, the new objection was that they were taking too great an advantage of their newly won freedom, that they were entering the solid "Christian" occupations such as storekeeping and wholesaling, that they were gaining affluence and acquiring respectability. The common people, on the other hand, sensed at every turn that the security of ancient usage was gone. Consequently, when the liberals in the revolutionary year 1848-49 dreamt of unity in liberty, the irate populace in numerous villages and small towns merely perceived an opportunity to riot against wealth and officialdom and to loot what was the nearest and most accessible object of attack, that is, the houses and businesses of the Jews.

But as time went on, the Jews became leaders in modernity. They created new branches of business and a variety of manufacturing. They entered the professions. They promoted voluntary associations and cultural activities. Utz Jeggle reports about the Jewish villages in Wuerttemberg that local Jews frequently took the initiative in suggesting better means of communication and more advanced schools, that they supported social institutions such as orphanages and hospitals, that their houses were more solidly built, their furniture more representative of the newest taste, their meals more opulent and their wives and daughters better groomed and more fashionable. At least, that is the way they are remembered by their former neighbors. In all these regards, the Jews were admired and imitated, especially by their servants who felt that Jewish families looked after their welfare where others merely exploited them and that they provided a "home-like" atmosphere for them. Many servants remained faithful even in the Hitler years, when neighbors and business acquaintances succumbed to social ostracism. Generally, there is evidence from all over Central Europe that Jews found it easier to establish friendly relations with the ruling strata as well as with the laboring people than with the middle classes. Officials who considered it their business to promote the general welfare or to foster economic development in conservative surroundings found enterprising Jewish businessmen helpful and ever ready for new initiatives in many fields. Workingmen, on the other hand, not only were aware of opportunities in Jewish employment, but also–at least in many instances–of the greater social responsibility of Jewish employers, for instance, when the innovative management of the Tietz department store granted rent and subsistence allowance to its employees in addition to the benefits that necessarily accrued to them as well as to the public-at-large because of the lower prices that were offered. It was the retail merchants who were in an uproar and clamored for protective legislation.

It would be wrong to assume that the latent hostility of the middle classes needed the spur of increased competition. One of the most perceptive observers of the social scene in old Austria, Sigmund Mayer, reports that his parents, upon moving into a house outside the old ghetto of Bratislava, made strenuous efforts to please their new neighbors by buying what they needed in the neighbors' stores, even at a price disadvantage, without being able to penetrate the wall of aloofness or establish some kind of social intercourse. Furthermore, when the Bratislava Jews gained entrance to one of the fashionable coffee houses, they were offered a special meeting room, with the result that the first floor, where they met, in the absence of both orthodox Jews and local Gentiles, became the gathering place for an informal Jewish reform club! Thus the Jews became acculturated, but not accepted and consequently not assimilated. The latter process occurred only in intellectual and artistic circles, but frequently at the price of the abandonment of every semblance of Jewish allegiance and affiliation on the part of the accepted individual. Renunciation of the Jewish heritage was the suicidal advice of such diverse Gentile mentors as Theodore Mommsen, Heinrich von Treitschke, Paul de Lagarde, and Richard Wagner. Obviously, Jewish-Gentile relations lose their substance when, as Wagner put it in his formidable pamphlet, *Das Judentum in der Musik*, the redemption of the Jewish artist "finds its fulfillment only in self-annihilation."

Yet, even Richard Wagner could not do without Hermann Levi, the celebrated Wagnerian conductor who remained a loyal Jew, even if he was a marginal Jew. Whether Wagner was aware of it or not, love, at times, requires distance, so that penetration may be complemented by detachment and devotion by clarity. The problem that is touched upon at this point, perhaps, is too subtle to be analyzed at the heights of intellectual achievement; but if one reduces it to simpler dimensions, the sociological nature of the relationship becomes comprehensible. The best way of putting it is to say that the very quality of the Jew as a stranger renders him a trusted friend. Where the Montagues and the Capulets are locked in internecine strife, only an outsider with no political ax to grind but who nevertheless is intimately familiar with the situation–the man "who comes today and stays tomorrow"–can be an impartial judge. Thus chassidic tales have it that Prince Adam Czartoryski sought the advice of the Maggid of Kozienice at a difficult juncture of Polish history. None of his fellow noblemen could have filled the bill. Still more telling are reports from the life of the common people. Initially, the appreciation of the Jew as an indispensable consultant in situations in which nobody else knows a way out, might have been the reverse side of his reputation for sorcery and witchcraft. This is translucent in the story of the Maggid and the Prince. The Maggid was believed to be capable of working miracles and to be conversant with the ways of Providence. If we go to far-away Yemen or to Muslim Algeria, we find that the illiterate Arab puts his faith in the Jew who, on account of his mastery of the art of writing, is supposed to have acquired the power of healing, the knowledge of debased coinage and the ability that makes him serviceable as intermediary in business transactions. The liberal era has obliterated the magic connotation and humanized the relationship. It must suffice at this point to refer to the creations of two popular writers of the nineteenth century, Fritz Reuter's Uncle Moses and Erckmann-Chatrian's Rabbi Sichel. In Mecklenburg, the jovial Jewish trader is the friend and financial counselor of everybody; and when he dies it is said of him that although his faith was one of a Jew, his deeds were Christian. The appreciation is a bit underhanded–as if a Jew could not be a straight character *qua* Jew–but it was sincerely meant. In Alsace, the small-town rabbi is "le plus grand arrangeur de marriages qu'on ait jamais vu dans ce bas monde." He sees to it that a pretty peasant girl can marry her wealthy suitor and that a Jewish cattle dealer pays on the spot the price for the oxen he has bought from a poor peasant. Sichel's simplistic philosophy is epitomized in the sentence with which the story ends, that to love one's neighbor is to love God and to know his commandments.

The Transformation of the Pattern of Strangeness

It is fascinating to observe how throughout the nineteenth and twentieth centuries old patterns persist, yet are overlaid with new interpretations that are suggested by liberal ideas. For instance, the painter Moritz Oppenheim reports from the beginning of the nineteenth century that Jewish children had no intimate contact with Christian children, except that they had to be on their guard against physical attacks whenever they ventured outside the Ghetto gates in Hanau, a small town near Frankfurt. But the department store executive Georg Tietz reports from the turn of the century that Jewish children in Munich sat in on the Catholic religious instruction in school while Catholic children attended the Sabbath morning service at the synagogue. The mystery remained, but it had lost its frightening aspect. It is still more significant to note how representative Gentile opinion coped with the new phenomenon of Jewish participation in the cultural life of a modern nation. The paradigmatic representative of Jewish penetration was the Jewish journalist because non-baptized Jews rarely gained access to prestigious positrons at the universities prior to the second decade of the twentieth century. Ludwig Boerne and Moritz Saphir, and especially Heinrich Heine are early examples, to be followed by others, with the whole development culminating in the careers of Kurt Tucholsky in Berlin and Karl Kraus in Vienna. These men were biting critics of society, a role to which they were predisposed because of their frustrated academic ambitions and the pinpricks of discrimination. Their criticism was all the more bitter because their Judaism was merely a much bemoaned "background," not a consciously lived reality. Their marginality has been noted by astute, although not overly friendly, observers such as Heinrich Wilhelm Riehl.

The most disparaging literary representation of the Jewish journalist is Gustav Freytag's Schmock, whose confession that he can write "nach jeder Richtung," that is as a partisan of the Left or of the Right, depending on the circumstances, has become proverbial. Here, we encounter once again the versatile Jew who presumably has an answer to each and every turn of events, with the added connotation that his participation in the cultural concerns of the larger society is lacking in conviction. But even the philosopher and sociologist Georg Simmel, whose interpretation of Kant is as deep and sincere as any interpretation of a German culture-hero can possibly be, did not escape the malicious characterization by an academic colleague of "a dyed-in-the-wool Israelite . . . who operates more by wit and pseudo-wit than by solid and systematic thinking." This persistence in seeing the Jew as a scheming intruder who is congenitally incapable of meaning what he says drove sensitive Jewish artists, like the novelist Jakob Wassermann, to the brink of despair.

The story of the ambivalence of feeling and human relations can be pursued still further. Had genuine friendship between Jew and Gentile become a possibility? Lessing's incessantly cited friendship with Moses Mendelssohn stands out as a shining example. Or was it so highly praised because it occurred so rarely? A different picture emerges if we consult Wilhelm Raabe's *Hungerpastor*, a novel that enjoyed considerable popularity among a broad reading public at the end of the nineteenth century. The principal characters, Hans Unwirsch and Moses Freudenstein, become friends, when Hans rescues Moses from a neighborhood gang who mocked and assailed him. Hans is awed, in turn, by Moses's insatiable quest for knowledge and an intellectuality that is unswervingly oriented to the pursuit of worldly success. Moses finally goes to Paris, gets baptized and becomes a professor of Semitic languages at the Sorbonne while Hans, a simple Protestant minister, devotes himself to the service of his fellow man: his imagination, says Raabe, prevails over intellectuality. Unintentionally, the story seems to carry the message that the Aryan and the Semite are psychically incompatible: philistine sentimentality barely conceals the subconscious racism that is at work here. The same can be said about Charles Dickens' Fagin and especially about Gustav Freytag's novel *Soll und Haben* (*Debit and Credit*), with its assortment of more or less greedy and cunning Jewish dealers and business agents. Whatever happens, murder and theft on the one hand and the discovery of a crime that has been committed, on the other, is laid at the door of one or the other Jewish characters. The Jew appears not only as the jack of all trades, he is also believed to be capable of all manner of deeds, fair and foul. All this, even more so than Raabe's account, is beyond the realm of mere "prejudice": The roots are deeper. As Albert Memmi observes, the mythical portrait of the Jew creates a structural and psychological reality that carries its own conviction and offers a rationale for social distance, subtle discrimination and ultimately for genocide–whenever the occasion arises.

However, one encounters in the pertinent literature a distinction between Jewish men and Jewish women that is too striking to be overlooked. In Sir Walter Scott's *Ivanhoe*, Isaac is described as stooped, humble, apprehensive, always trying to curry favor with the powerful Norman knights who treat him with a mixture of pity and contempt. His saving grace, in his words, is that "the hunted fox, the tortured wildcat, loves its young–the despised and persecuted race of Abraham love their children." Isaac's attachment to an intangible value amazes the Norman warrior. But of Isaac's daughter Rebecca it is said that "she bore herself with proud humility . . . while she felt in her mind the consciousness that she was entitled to hold a higher rank from her merit than the arbitrary despotism of religious prejudice permitted her to aspire to." She shows firmness of character, strength of mind, and unflinching fortitude. She is conscious of "the ancient glories of her race," and the knights respect her. The theme of the miserable and money-loving Jewish male and the proud and attractive Jewish female is repeated in other literary sources, with particular forcefulness in two tragic plays by the German and Austrian playwrights Friedrich Hebbel and Franz Grillparzer, namely, *Judith and Holofernes* and *The Jewess of Toledo*. It is Grillparzer who is most conscious of the sexual dimension of the topic. His king, a passionate lover, is portrayed as motivated by physical lust, the king's Jewish mistress as relying exclusively on her bewitching charm. When the attraction of the flesh ceases in death, it is glaringly obvious that the partners in the game of love have remained strangers to each other in their minds and hearts. A step beyond an emotional imprisonment of this kind is taken in George Eliot's *Daniel Deronda*. True, even there it is said that "there is no race like them for cunning in the men and beauty in the women"; but the heroes who show the way out of the prejudicial impasse are now men: Mordecai, the prophet of a new Jewish pride and young Daniel Deronda who painfully rediscovers his hitherto buried Jewish awareness. The fact that this consciousness of being a Jew had remained hidden from himself and stifled for a long time and that his Gentile friends, even after the discovery of his true self, persist in assuring him that it doesn't matter to them whether he is Jewish or not, is the liberal ingredient in the story. Deronda strives to overcome the cover of "benign neglect" by aiming at the reestablishment of a political Jewish nationality and the dignity that is to go with such a renewed openness and visibility. What Deronda has in mind is a conquest of mutual fears and apprehensions: he desires "separateness with communication."

Christian Zionists, like George Eliot, added a new note to the orchestration of Jewish-Gentile relations, one that might have demythified and normalized them, if it had become the dominant theme. It remains a moot question whether it is at all possible, and if possible, desirable, to transform the Jews into a people "like all the nations." But it is certain that the overwhelming reality of the nineteenth and twentieth centuries, from the first signs of the decomposition of liberalism to the demise of Hitler, was the rise of the mythical image of the Jew to dimensions that had never before been imagined. There were portents that ought to be noted. Especially, one must once again refer to the Rothschild legend which by the middle of the nineteenth century had partly merged with the Shylock image and partly superseded it. In a Frankfurt cartoon of Anselm Mayer Rothschild of 1845, one sees an enormously large Jew standing on an equally large moneybag, triumphantly showing off his wealth, with small-scale potentates and marching soldiers subserviently grouped around him. What we have before us is the old theme of Jewish money power, which had grown to potency ever since the high Middle Ages, combined with the new notion, born of the liberal era, that money had now been elevated to being the decisive factor in the game of politics. The same point is underscored in another cartoon that compares the condition of the common man before 1789 with his fate after the Revolution. There, one sees first a ploughing peasant who carries an aristocrat on his shoulders and then the same peasant, now more deeply stooped, carrying along three bankers, all of them with unmistakably Semitic features. There are many facets to the imagery which these cartoons convey. They appealed likewise to those who bemoaned the passing of the "good old times" and to socialist critics of society, to malcontent artisans and to radical intellectuals.

At a deeper layer of consciousness, this manner of viewing the Jew, which we call mythological, appealed to the Manichean tendencies in European thought. By Manichaeism, we mean a cast of mind that not only contrasts light and darkness, good and evil, but disregards their intimate interpenetration in actual life situations and emphasizes instead their inexorable conflict in the realm of thought. The clash of principles knows only victory or defeat and divides the world forever into friend and foe. The philosopher Alfred North Whitehead has called the confusion of concept and reality "the fallacy of misplaced concreteness." In the present context, one is inclined to say that it entails a tragic worldview, which turns its back on a philosophy of live-and-let-live, on a redeeming sense of humor, and on compassion with human weakness. The catastrophe of Jewish-Gentile relations, which occurred within the memory of living generations, is a logical and psychological consequence of the secularization of the Manichaean obsession.

Racism Comes to the Fore

In a Christian worldview, the sharpness of the Manichaean contrasts had been overcome by the idea of the unity of mankind and the hope of redemption. This hope, which had been kept alive in the Kantian concept of the infinite perfectability of man, was transmuted by Kant's heretical pupil, the philosopher Johann Gottlieb Fichte, into the notion of infinite becoming, without a recognizable goal. The unity of mankind was dissolved into a bewildering array of particularities, ultimately into a romantic cult of personality. In his Berlin lectures of 1811, Fichte said that the world truly exists for the sake of a few heroes and that their value outweighs by far the value of millions of common men because the hero expresses the very meaning of existence. This unabashedly existentialist justification of the self-contained personality of artists and rulers was extended to the personality of a nation, especially to the Germans whose original nature was said to have been preserved in their language while the other nations of Western Europe, especially the French, had succumbed to the leveling influence of Latinization. The Germans had remained nearer to the roots of human existence. Whoever would not accept this statement as demonstrable "scientific" truth, Fichte continued, is either an idiot or the devil's advocate. The Manichaean ring of an *obiter dictum* of this kind is penetrating, although its racist character was initially obscured by the linguistic formulation of superiority. But the notion of race as a physical manifestation of spiritual essence necessarily permeated the idea of particularity and of one's allegedly superior ethnic particularity as the ultimate value. Gustav Klemm, an early anthropologist, distinguished between "active" and "passive" races, with Christ, Dante, the conquerors of China and of Central America all listed as light-pigmented Nordics or "white Gods." In such fashion, biology was substituted for theology. Count Gobineau added a note of cultural pessimism, which is contrary to the Spencerian and Darwinian theories of the "survival of the fittest," but follows from the splitting of mankind into warring particularities and the recognition that one's own particularity–which by definition is the best–in stark actuality does not seem to emerge victorious from the "war of all against all" that has become the hallmark of a disenchanted world. A mood of elitist despair, as one might call it, became prevalent in Europe, especially in France and Germany. It did not remain entirely foreign to the Anglo-Saxon countries either, although in classic evolutionary thought the idea of perfectability of man had been retained as the "natural" goal of human progress. But by the turn of the century, social Darwinists among American scholars, for instance William Graham Sumner, had adopted the notion of the societal world as consisting of a variety of eternally competing forces. Brooks Adams gave that notion a pessimistic turn in his "law of civilization and decay," which interpreted the prevalence of moneyed interests as destructive of cultural achievement. Madison Grant, the author of *The Passing of the Great Race*, falls more clearly in line with Gobineau, even expanding the French aristocrat's continental European outlook into a vision of global disaster. Yet, it was on the narrower European scene that the friend-foe obsession reached pathological dimensions. It was there that the fury of fear was directed first and foremost against the Jews as the prototype of the "counter-race."

How did this come about? The nineteenth century transmuted the faith of Christianity into the religion of science. The serious scholar knows that what he works out in his study or in the laboratory is but a steppingstone in an ongoing process. But the "terrible simplifiers," as Jacob Burckhardt called them, embraced a scientific discovery as a permanent and incontestable truth, replacing the truth of religion. Moreover, in the brave new world of science, all that mattered was matter. The spiritual certainties men had lived by were dead. The redemption through Christ, as against the sinfulness of the flesh, was "scientifically" negated in the concept of race; and that concept, in turn, was reified in the actual division of mankind into a redeeming race of Nordic heroes and a darkly plotting counter-race. The Manichaean contrast was thus secularized. The counter-race was represented not so much by the Negro, as one might assume from a present vantage point, but by the Jew. A brief deliberation will serve to make that point clear. Racial prejudice against the Negro, to be sure, is deeply ingrained. The Negro, as James Hunt emphasized in his pro-slavery presidential address to the Anthropological Society of London (1863), was supposed to have his "place in nature" somewhere between the ape and the European. He was believed to be dominated by emotions and of a potentially dangerous disposition, but he could be "humanized and civilized," if only under European guidance. The Negro was thought of as being ahistorical, that is, without a documented collective memory, even more so than the Slavic peoples of Eastern Europe from whom the very name of "slave" is derived; even more than the Slavic peoples were the dark peoples of African origin presumed to be incapable of political organization. Antagonism against the Jew is of a different kind. The Jews are the classic people of history, antedating Christianity, and they are known to be conscious of their election and destiny. For centuries, they were thought of as competitors for dominion because their particularity contained a universal claim that contested the universal claim of Christianity. Now, with its universality submerged in particularity, both Judaism and Christianity appeared in the eyes of a left-Hegelian author, such as Bruno Bauer, as "chimerical" communities–Judaism because it disparages historically concrete manifestations of ethnicity in favor of the "suspended" ethnicity of the "chosen people" and Christianity because it eliminates all ethnicity in favor of the redemption in Christ. Fichte considered the Jewish community not so much as a religion but as a "state within a state," in anticipation, as Bruno Bauer added, of the future domination by the Jews of the peoples of the world, once their captivity was redeemed. Fichte's realms of God and the Devil, as they are called in archaic language, are not necessarily identical with Germanism and Judaism, but they are made manifest in them. In Fichte's view, the Jews constitute an aristocracy of blood-arrogance because, according to the established "scientific" truth of his philosophy, the salvation of mankind depends on the unfolding of the genius of the Germanic peoples. Later in the century and in a different perspective but with the same effect, the French linguist Ernest Renan contrasted Semites and Aryans as the great divisions of mankind. Renan conceded to the Jews a genius for religion, but considered them as a "*race inférieure*" because they were incapable of philosophical, scientific, artistic, and political achievement. Even their religion was branded as "intolerant" monotheism, in line with the general "negativity" of the Semitic mind. When the word "counter-race" finally appears–in Alfred Rosenberg's appropriately titled *The Myth of the Twentieth Century*, which is a major literary document of Nazism, we are already in the entourage of Hitler and close to the deadly *Einsatzgruppen* of the SS.

The liberal ingredient in the new dispensation must not be overlooked, nor must the corrosion of liberalism by racism. To consider the Jewish community as a "state within the state" that must be dissolved was an inheritance from the Enlightenment, even from Jacobinism. To accept the individual Jew, but only on condition that he foreswore loyalty to Judaism, was part of the general animosity of liberalism against "*les forces intermédiaires*." Jean-Paul Sartre's "authentic Jew" is a dubious construction, but he observes correctly that the "abstract liberal," in posing as a friend of the "minorities," demands rights for Jews, Chinese, Negroes as generalized human beings, not as concrete and individual products of history. While racism assumes the immutability of the psychic make-up of the Jew in line with the fixed characteristics of his presumably depraved physical nature, liberalism fails to defend the Jewish quality of the victim that is attacked and thus forsakes him. Moreover, when liberalism merged with nationalism, which happened both in Jacobinism and in the romantic counter-movement to Jacobinism, a further ingredient was added. The Jew was no more asked to transform himself into a generalized "human being" or merely into a "citizen," but instead into a German, Frenchman, or Hungarian in whom no appreciable trace of Jewishness was left. This was essentially the position taken by such a prototypical national-liberal as Heinrich von Treitschke in his famous articles in the *Preussische Jahrbuecher*. Treitschke stirred up a bitter controversy, which became known as the *Berliner Antisemitismus streit* when he demanded of his Jewish "fellow-citizens" that they should desist from being an overbearing and disruptive element in German life and simply become unpretentious Germans. He was an inconsistent liberal, though, inasmuch as he considered those Jews who participated in national affairs as a "misfortune" to the country, exhorting them instead to adhere to their "old and sacred memories." Liberal consistency was more at home with Treitschke's illustrious antagonist, the historian Theodor Mommsen, who expected the Jews to abandon their communal cohesion, so as to confirm their unalloyed patriotism beyond any shadow of doubt. He compared Jews not to Christians, but to Saxonians, Pomeranians, and Holsteiners when he admonished them to sacrifice their particularistic ethnicity on the altar of the unified nation. Cultural pluralism was not envisaged in the heyday of nationalism. In the circumstances, the formula of Paul de Lagarde–not a participant in the Berlin controversy but a forceful proponent of the new nationalism–was most incisive. In Lagarde's view, the Jews who "nestled" within Christian and Germanic culture were not a "misfortune" but a "cancer." He conceded that "friendship with individual Jews was possible but only on condition that they ceased to be Jews: the Jews as a people must disappear." Similarly, as has been pointed out above, Richard Wagner, an ex-revolutionary whose strident blood-and-gold motif enthused vast audiences, could see "the redemption of Ahasver" only in self-annihilation. At this point, the last trace of liberalism had been obliterated and racism had emerged triumphant. For it the "self" in the gruesome combination failed to work, annihilation *sans phrase* was indicated.

From Humanity to Bestiality

Theodor Mommsen was so right when he observed that Treitschke's flippant use of anti-Semitic slogans made the demagoguery of the streets "respectable" in the eyes of the educated public because his reputation as a scholar had bestowed upon their rantings the sanction of science. But historiography was not enough. On the road "from humanity through nationality to bestiality," to use the words of the Austrian playwright Franz Grillparzer, Treitschke's position marked merely a halfway point. The quotation from Grillparzer must be understood literally, for if one wants to destroy an adversary in good conscience, one must deprive him of his humanity and make him into a beast. Racism accomplished this purpose to perfection. In his sharply but obscenely reasoned books about "The Jewish problem as a racial, moral and cultural problem,"

"The Jewish Question as a question of racial character and its detrimental effects on the existence and culture of the people" and others, the embittered anarchist Eugen Duehring argued that the fact that the newer generations had grown indifferent in matters of religion did not mean that the ancient cleavage between the Jews and the Christian peoples had disappeared and that the Jews had become "just like us." Indeed, if the Jews were to abandon their religion entirely, the problem would be posed all the more sharply because their identity would then be camouflaged. The Jews must be recognized for what they are, namely, a "race," separated from other peoples and races by an unbridgeable abyss. Their physical nature is immutably fixed and since behavioral characteristics are declared to be racially determined, so is their morality. Further, as the racial characteristics of the Jews, and hence their moral character, are depraved so that they are "naturally" attracted by conditions of corruption and decay, contact with them is poisonous to the generous nature of the Aryan peoples. The slightest admixture of Jewish blood is likely to be corrosive and even deadly to the unsuspecting host. Only isolation and ultimately annihilation can solve the Jewish problem. Hitler's "final solution" is clearly outlined in Duehring's unrestrained rantings.

Paul de Lagarde, contrary to Duehring in a secure academic position as a professor of Semitic languages at Goettingen, starts more innocuously by saying that the quality of being German rests with the mind rather than with the blood; and he proceeds more inconsistently by conceding that an independent Semitic culture might be tolerable, but his conclusions are no less appalling than those of Duehring. In Fichtean manner, Lagarde asserts that history is not the road to perfection and that individuality is the task to be mastered. But Jewish individuality is destructive of Germanic individuality. The Jews are exhorting the Germans to "learn" from them when, instead, they should free themselves from their "repulsive" Jewish traits. In a famous passage he says that one must hate those who are "too cowardly to crush the usurious insects." And he continues: "One does not negotiate with *trichinae* and *bacilli*, neither can "*trichinae* and *bacilli* be educated: one must destroy them as quickly and thoroughly as possible." One can see what becomes of the mythical Jew when he is defined zoologically. Nor is the kind of "bestiality" promoted by Lagarde an isolated phenomenon. Lagarde was a revered authority by many generations of German professionals, especially by educators who disseminated his pan-German and anti-Semitic ideas among their pupils. Thus, the naturalist Arno Holz compared the Jews to "bedbugs" in the social structure, the immensely popular writer Heinrich Langbehn considered them as carriers of "pestilence and cholera"; and in a perfect echo, the Nazi Gauleiter Wilhelm Kube, thought that "the Jews mean for the morality of white people what pestilence, consumption, and syphilis mean to mankind's state of health." Analogies from epidemiology and bacteriology were applied to what otherwise might have been regarded as human relations, when it came to the topic of Jews.

This trend, long in the making, reached a climax during the Nazi regime. In Hitler's official pronouncements as well as in his private utterances, images of disease, infection, and pestilence occur frequently. "The discovery of the Jewish virus," he said to Himmler in 1942, "is one of the greatest revolutions that have taken place in the world." In the book *Deutschland Ordnet Europa Neu*, published by the representative of the Fuehrer for the supervision of the entire spiritual and doctrinal education in the NSDAP (1941/42), it is emphasized that "conventional methods of historiography" are not sufficient to promote the understanding of racial controversies and that "perspectives taken from the natural sciences" must be added. It is said that "the contrast between the creative and parasitic principles"–light and darkness–is applicable to the life of a people as well as to natural phenomena. The cellular structure of the human body is compared to "a highly organized state" that is invaded by bacteria that are incapable of forming a "state" themselves and that will destroy the invaded organism, or else must be destroyed themselves. The conclusion is that "humanitarian principles" do not apply. Obviously, then, the dehumanization had proceeded to the point where Lagarde's analogy became a reality. Indeed, an official publication of the SS assumes the existence of subhuman beings who are described as "terrifying creatures, facially resembling humans, but spiritually and emotionally on a level lower than animals." One must have such utterances in mind if one attempts to understand what is meant when a member of the Hitler Youth organization, upon initiation, had to pronounce the following formula: "I shall keep no friendship with a Jew. I shall not say a word to a Jew. I shall forget and despise all Jews. I won't any longer see in a Jew a fellow human being." This much neither Lagarde nor any of the proto-Nazi authors had envisaged when they had set the deadly forces in motion.

Nor were epigonic authors, among whom the Americans T. S. Eliot and Ezra Pound may be counted, any clearer about what they were doing. To quote one of many, the pathologically sensitive French author Louis-Ferdinand Céline thought that "the Jews are pestilential in their mass, though there may be a few harmless ones among them, like the microbes Pasteur discovered that had to be sterilized. Pasteur could not stop to differentiate between good, bad and indifferent microbes; therefore, get rid of them all, and the same goes for the Jews." In an afterthought, Céline added that he was horrified by the extermination chambers, but he should have known better. Even prior to the outbreak of World War II and the Wannsee Conference where the "final solution" was decided, the pornographic Nazi newspaper *Der Stuermer* could write of the Jews: "Bacteria, vermin and pests cannot be tolerated. For reasons of cleanliness and hygiene we must make them harmless by killing them off." When the actual killing occurred and the smoke rose from the ruins of the Warsaw Ghetto, a Polish bystander was overheard expressing his satisfaction that "the bedbugs are burning." Murder, the abetting of murder, and approval of murder were the inevitable outcome of a sustained educational process. In view of the mass executions, the death marches, the gas chambers, the sadistic pseudo-medical experiments and the innocent Jewish infants dashed against the walls, goodhearted people have asked themselves how it was possible that human beings could have done all this to other human beings. The answer to this tortured question is clear: the victims had to be denied their human character first. They had to be represented as noxious vermin and as bacteria, so that their extermination could be defined as a sanitary act. Then, and only then, could the bestiality in the aggressors be conjured up.

The Protocols of the Elders of Zion

The story must be carried one step further, to the point of the nihilism that was emphasized in the last chapter with regard to the political aims of the Nazi movement. What is to be added is the delusionary vision of the mythical Jew as a motivating force. This vision was carried to its fulfillment by the famous forgery of *The Protocols of the Elders of Zion*. The *Protocols* have a complex prehistory that can be traced through the writings of many, chiefly French, authors who were stirred up by the social dislocations of the nineteenth century. All these antecedents as well as the *Protocols* themselves are a perfect manifestation of the Manichaean paranoia in that they ascribe the ills of the world not to faults in the social structure but to the conspiracy of evil men, ultimately to the legendary Elders of Zion. Norman Cohn, to whom we owe the most penetrating analysis of the *Protocols* thus far, has observed that the "fear of modernity" is at the core of all the gruesome accounts of plots and counterplots that are envisaged as endangering the security of human existence. But the term "modernity" stands in need of definition. The French Revolution, which is the point of departure for the literature that led up to the *Protocols*, marks not so much the demise of the absolute monarchy but the replacement of ascribed status by achieved status and the measurement of achievement in terms of money. The rise of the House of Rothschild became the symbol of the new development, so much so that the Jew was imagined by many as the master of the epoch. Capitalism was considered akin to revolution; and it was the fear of the unleashed forces of capitalism that alienated from political liberalism the strata that felt imperiled by it, chiefly artisans, small businessmen, some lesser officials and insecure intellectuals. These same strata had a long tradition of antagonism to the Jews, which was now reinforced by the spectacular advance the Jews had made. In this situation, racism became the refuge of wounded self-esteem and conspiracy theories served the purpose of explaining why the "inferior race" was rewarded with superior achievement. It is further significant that the *Protocols* were actually concocted in Russia, under the guidance of the tsarist secret police, from a medley of antecedent literary sources, some of whom had mentioned the Jews in a variety of contexts while others had not mentioned them at all. The absolute regime of the tsar, in mortal fear of revolution, tried to avert the danger of directing the rising discontent toward the Jews. Officially instigated pogroms were one answer, the exposure of an alleged conspiracy by an international Jewish crime syndicate was another. The fear seemed subsequently justified by the success of the Bolshevik Revolution and by the fact that many of the Bolshevik leaders at that time (as well as of the Mensheviks) were Jewish intellectuals, even if they were estranged from the Jewish community. Indeed, the *Protocols* were not widely disseminated prior to 1917. But how could it be that the Jews were made to represent the forces of capitalism and socialism at the same time? The *Protocols* of the Elders of Zion gave a perfect answer to that query. The monsters in human shape who assembled at midnight at the ancient Jewish cemetery in Prague to plot the domination of the world were the personified spirit of negation. They were Satan in the flesh. Comparable to the anti-Christ, the horrifying nightmare of the Middle Ages that was to precede the second coming of Christ, were the fabled Elders of Zion, the anti-Aryan, bent upon the destruction of the established society by means fair and foul, be it the accumulation of capital, the expropriation of Aryan proprietors, the overthrow of governments, the promotion of corruption or the undermining of sexual morality. They were of sub-human nature but of super-human intelligence. As the symbol of symbols of everything that is hateful, they answered the innermost needs of Hitler's evil genius.

Indeed, Hitler took the *Protocols* seriously. They became a mainstay of Nazi propaganda. Even more so, they were the projection of the nihilism inherent in the Nazi movement. The world domination that was the goal of the Nazi movement was attributed to the Jews. In this regard, Hitler expressed himself frankly to his friend Dietrich Eckart: "One can understand the Jew," he said, "only if one knows what he is ultimately driving at. Beyond the domination of the world, he drives at the destruction of the world. . . . While he pretends to elevate mankind, he tortures them to the point of despair, driving them to madness and extinction." What is implied is that the Jews are less than human: they are the "counter-race." But they can be beaten at their presumed game of being the one super-nation that bends the particular nations to its will. Their global conspiracy can be foiled by the counter-conspiracy of the super-race. Hitler all but admitted that the delusionary Jewish plot was a projection when he spoke to Hermann Rauschning, who later deserted the Nazi movement, about the prevailing economic system as a Jewish "super-state, planted by them above all the states of the world," adding that the Nazi movement has now "challenged them with the system of permanent revolution . . ." And he continued: "I have read *The Protocols of the Elders of Zion* and it simply appalled me. The stealthiness of the enemy, and his ubiquity! I saw at once that we must copy it–in our own way, of course . . . It is in truth the critical battle for the fate of the world." The battle, ended with utter defeat for Hitler, but the major German cities lay in smoldering ruins and nearly six million Jews had been wantonly murdered.

The image of the mythical Jew, the dark adversary of the centuries, had reached its culmination with *The Protocols of the Elders of Zion*, but those slain were not frightful monsters with hooked noses and spider feet–half devilishly cunning, half greedy animal but actual Jewish men, women, and children, playmates and schoolmates, neighbors and friends, business acquaintances and fellow employees of their Gentile counterparts, not to speak of those who were medical healers, legal advisors, scientific pioneers, and stars in the arts and literature. At no time were simple human relations between Jews and Gentiles both more numerous and more genuine than in the twentieth century. What then has happened to explain the disquieting discrepancy between promise and performance? In trying to answer that question, we will be led to the core problem of Jewish-Gentile relations.

The Corruption of Human Relations

The account will remain focused on Germany, not because it is assumed that actual or potential enmity toward Jews is alien to other peoples and countries or because it is held that Germans are a morally inferior species of humankind. To adhere to the former belief would be unrealistic, to adhere to the latter would be racist. But Germany is the prototypical example of what is possible in the human condition, if circumstance permit. What were the circumstances? In Germany, an unbalanced social structure, partly feudal and partly modern, and an unsettled political situation, partly unified and partly dismembered, had led to a pervasive sense of emotional insecurity and intellectual restlessness. The vainglory of the Wilhelminian empire, which served the purpose of compensating for these shortcomings, was shattered by the humiliating military defeat in World War I and subsequently by inflation, unemployment, and mismanagement at high places. No other large nation in Europe had a recent history that was similarly unstable. During World War II, again, there was a profound difference between Germany and the rest of Europe. Elsewhere, the Germans were invaders and brutal conquerors, so that protecting Jews became part of a national resistance movement; while in Germany properly opposing one's own government would have amounted to high treason, especially in view of the German propensity of equating patriotism and obedience to German propensity of equating patriotism and obedience to authority. However, it must be added that there was a wide divergence between reactions in Western and Eastern Europe. Polish, Lithuanian, and Ukrainian populations frequently assisted in the extermination of their Jewish fellow citizens; and the support that was forthcoming from them is largely responsible for the thoroughness with which the Nazi policy of genocide could be pursued in Eastern Europe. We shall therefore add some corroborating observations from Poland to the German account.

Hitler was a master demagogue who was aware of the first principle of propaganda, namely, that in a political campaign one must never defend one's own record or divulge one's own plans; one must always attack the opponent's record and vilify his plans. This Hitler did very thoroughly. In Norman Cohn's words, "he attacked the victorious allies, especially the French, for enslaving the German people; and the German republican regime for its failure to cope with the crisis; and the parties of the Left, for dividing the nation; and the parties of the Right for their ineffectiveness; and the plutocrats and monopolists for exploiting everyone else." But his most ferocious attacks were directed against the Jews. Moreover, while everybody else could redeem himself, a Jew, even a half- or a quarter-Jew, was racially fixed and could not escape: once a Jew, always a Jew. These and other features of Hitler's relentless campaign notwithstanding, the most the National Socialist party ever obtained in a free election was 37.3 percent of the total vote (election of July 1932). To be sure, some adherents of other parties, in the first place those of the German-National Party, were not free of conventional anti-Semitism; but exterminatory anti-Semitism of the kind that led to Auschwitz was promoted exclusively by the Nazi Party. However, the fact that Hitler's aim was extermination (genocide) does not imply that the word ever appeared in the official propaganda of the Party prior to 1938 and that those that sympathized with the Nazi movement were clearly aware of it; although to sensitive observers, the murderous aim should have been unmistakable from the start. For instance, one anti-Semitic spokesman, Count Ernst Reventlow, advocated publicly "complete separation and extinction" as early as 1930. Actually, not two, but three stages may be discerned: first, separation of the Jewish group from the bulk of the population; then atomization within the group; finally, after moral resistance had broken down, physical destruction. The first stage extended from the late 1920s when Nazi propaganda mounted to major proportions, until the issuance of the "Nuremberg Laws" in 1935; the second stage from 1935 until the invasion of Poland. With the outbreak of the war, the last stage, physical extinction, was imminent.

Jewish reaction was determined by the nature of the attack and therefore first directed toward the maintenance of contacts between Jews and Gentiles, second toward the maintenance of a community spirit. In the first stage the *Centralverein*, the leading Jewish civic defense organization, advised its members to hold onto their positions in cultural, social, and political organizations within the larger community. This policy succeeded in maintaining most of the embattled positions, but it is also true that the success was questionable because many of these positions could only be maintained in an indirect way: more and more Gentiles would urge their Jewish friends to be content with a silent partnership. This first line of defense broke down in 1933. By 1935 the last traces of human contacts had disappeared: Gentiles could no longer marry Jews, could not enter domestic service with Jews, were ostracized even when seen with Jews. Jewish children, especially in smaller and medium-sized communities, were isolated and humiliated without any opportunity of retaliation. However, in larger communities, Jewish schools, youth organizations and cultural associations for adults made for cohesion and the maintenance of morale. After the "Kristallnacht" of 1938, when synagogues all over Germany went up in flames, even these last supports were removed. With contact severed, livelihoods destroyed, fortunes confiscated and community bonds shattered, Jewish individuals found themselves in total isolation and helplessly exposed to the last blow. When they were herded into the cattle trains, they were only shadows of their former selves.

Concerning the reaction of the Gentiles, one must discern between fanatical partisans, especially members of the SS, and the vast majority of the common people, including even many of the rank and file of the Nazi Party and its civilian affiliates. The mentality of the fanatical partisans has been characterized above. As to the bulk of the rank and file, we have the testimony of six hundred members of the Party whose autobiographies were analyzed by Theodore Abel. It emerges that 60 percent of them did not mention Jews in their accounts; apparently, they were not motivated, and certainly not primarily or significantly motivated, by considerations of an anti-Semitic nature. Among working-class respondents, anti-Semitic replies were in the minority and some respondents even expressly dissociated themselves from the Jew-baiting aspects of the Nazi propaganda. The Nazi movement appeared as a patriotic movement, a social protest movement, a truly and thoroughly populist movement. This impression of a populist groundswell is reinforced by Rudolf Heberle's demographic study of shifting voting patterns in Schleswig-

Holstein 1918-1932, which shows that the majority of the Nazi voters came from the disoriented rural and urban middle classes ("*Kleinbuerger und Kleinbauern*"), with the Jewish issue decidedly in the background. Contrary to appearances, however, it was precisely that "background" which tipped the scales.

For the Nazi fanatics, the "stormtroopers" of the movement–according to Mueller-Claudius, hardly more than 5 percent of the population–anti-Semitism was an expression of the battle between light and darkness where no quarter was given. For the majority of the citizenry, anti-Semitism was so much talk, a propaganda device of passing significance. In addition, plainly opportunistic motives must never be underrated. According to Milton Mayer, "men joined the Party to get a job or to hold a job or to get a better job or to save themselves from getting a worse job, or to get a contract or to hold a contract, a customer, a client, a patient," or, as one might add, to gain a customer, a client, a patient from a Jewish competitor. In that regard, it was implied that "a little bit of anti-Semitism" might do no harm. From a position of this kind, it takes only a small step to condoning even the forcible removal of a Jewish competitor, creditor, business partner, or professional colleague, or of a neighbor who has left pieces of property in trust with a Gentile acquaintance. Emanuel Ringelblum reports considerations of this nature also from German-occupied Warsaw, the dislike on the part of the Poles of the German occupation notwithstanding. Yet, Ringelblum in his marvelously detached wartime diary refutes the assertion that all Christian Poles had gloated over the destruction of the Jews; and he reports a number of instances where individual Gentiles, mostly from the working classes, were helpful to individual Jews, displaying steadfastness and ingenuity and frequently exposing themselves to great danger. Similar cases are reported from Germany. It must be emphasized, however, that all these were individual cases, no matter how meritorious, and that concerted action to save Jews was conspicuous by its absence. Even in Western Europe, concerted action, such as the public protest of the workers in Amsterdam or the daring rescue operation in Copenhagen, was the exception rather than the rule. In Warsaw, when gangs of Polish rowdies, under the eyes of the occupying force, attacked Jewish peddlers or forcibly ejected Jewish passengers from streetcars, some onlookers enjoyed the performance, some others expressed their abhorrence of the "excesses," but nobody dared to rush to the support of the victims. In Wuerttemberg villages, when Jews were harassed, offended, maltreated, and spat upon, their property demolished and their houses of worship desecrated, many of their fellow-villagers were disgusted but nobody did anything about it. If individual help was offered, it was done clandestinely.

It is futile to accuse a whole people of having committed monstrous crimes, such as those that were committed in the name of the German people by the Nazi regime. Crimes on a mass scale are always committed by minorities. The perpetrators are fanatical and footloose people, whether in the uprisings during the Crusades and in the period of the Black Death or in our time. The difference between the high Middle Ages and the recent past is that the atrocities then were furious and spontaneous, with the authorities merely unable to stem the tide, while under Hitler a criminal gang had usurped the reins of government, so that the authorities themselves were the instigators of unmitigated terror. The burning of the synagogues in the "Kristallnacht"was an official action, not the expression of popular resentment. What is comparable, however, is the reaction of the majority of a local population to acts of terror. These acts are almost always carried out by hirelings brought in from the outside, with an assist from townspeople who have nothing to lose. The majority are induced to let their guard down when they are made to believe that the action of the aggressors agrees with their own desires as economically aggrieved or patriotically concerned citizens. This was the case in Germany prior to 1933 and even in the first few weeks and months of the Nazi regime. At this stage, excesses are excused as the over-zealous pursuit of a good cause and explained as the regrettable but passing accompaniment of a revolutionary transformation. In the second stage, the true nature of the terror regime is widely recognized, but the atomization of the social structure has progressed so far that hardly any nuclei of collective resistance are left. By this time, the Nazis had either dissolved previously existing associations that seemed suspicious to them or had replaced the former leadership with compliant stooges or, as in the case of the armed forces and the churches, had emasculated the will to independent action by meaningless concessions and the sowing of internal mistrust. As a result, dissenters were isolated and had to live in fear of being betrayed by false friends. Some that came out into the open were deprived of their livelihood, others were executed as traitors. But many more were cowed into submission.

These general observations must be complemented in the case of Jewish-Gentile relations. In a situation of incipient terror and even more so when a terror regime is firmly established, a process of intimidation is pursued which threatens anyone with "guilt by association" if he consorts with, or assists even to the slightest degree, those that have been declared enemies of the people and public outcasts. What occurs is the "abandonment" of a whole group of people. Those that are abandoned were only yesterday trusted friends and neighbors, part of an ongoing network of human relations. Now, they are cast off because they have been branded as evildoers by their very nature, so that contact with them becomes contaminating and must be shunned like the plague. Whoever associates or merely sympathizes with these stigmatized outcasts is considered as if he had sold his soul: he is excommunicated, he has become a heretic. When the Nazis pilloried persons of this kind as "*Judenknechte*," that is, hirelings of the Jews, they discouraged the maintenance and continuation of bonds of friendship and the expression of simple human decency. Active cooperation first, then kindly assistance, and finally even the impotent display of sympathy were thus stifled. Ultimately, where public sympathy is ostracized, private sympathy withers along with it for lack of exercise. In these circumstances, one must do justice to those men and women who preserved at least a feeble gesture of friendliness, like a barely perceptible nod or a faint smile when encountering a Jewish acquaintance on the street. But this is not all. The reason why the Jews more readily than any other group of human beings are singled out for special treatment, branded as evil-doers and abandoned to their fate is that they have been cast in this mold for a long time. Their resumed role has been imprinted in collective memory. The "enemies of Christ" of times gone by were redefined as a "counter-race" in our time and while this designation was only haltingly accepted by the majority of the population, nevertheless the revived opprobrium attached to association with Jews was effective deterrent to resistance. Somehow, in these circumstances, it is tacitly assumed that the Jews deserve what is coming to them and that some cutting down can do them no harm after they have climbed so high so fast. That the pruning can end in killing is hardly imagined. Thus, despite the fact that popular feeling against the Jews was comparatively weak in Germany and may be similarly weak in other countries, it came to pass that "the red embers of an anti-Jewish tradition which had been slowly dying were brought to a heat which lit the fires of Auschwitz." The fear that like consequences may be unchained, if like circumstances permit, has remained the encumbrance of Jewish-Gentile relations after Auschwitz. For there is no answer to the question whether the experience of Auschwitz was traumatic enough to foreclose the re-enactment of genocide.

14

A Comment about the Soviet Union

Hitler almost succeeded in eliminating the Jews from the continent of Europe, but in the meantime new realities of Jewish existence have arisen in America and Israel, and the question is posed whether the pattern of Jewish-Gentile relations that had been established over many centuries of European history has been essentially altered by the shift of locale. But before we answer that question, it is necessary to take a quick look at the Soviet Union and the Russian satellite states of Eastern Europe where, even after the enormous bloodletting of the Nazi era, over 3,000,000 Jews continue to make their home. After all, it has been the argument of communist theoreticians, even of Marx himself, that the abolition of the private appropriation of the means of production and the establishment of a socialist society will do away with the role of the Jew as a capitalist "exploiter" and therefore with the very raison d'être for the continued existence of the Jews as a separate ethnic entity. It was deduced, that inasmuch as the Jewish people were no more than an economic caste, the enmity against them would lose its point with the disappearance of that caste. The argument overlooks the simple fact that a bureaucratic economy must fulfill the same functions as a private economy. This was clearly recognized by the German sociologist Albert Schaeffle a hundred years ago. Indeed, Jewish employees are presently numerous in the management of the economic institutions of the Soviet Union, especially on the intermediate level. Consumer dissatisfaction can therefore be directed against them. Jewish managers and experts may find themselves in the unenviable position of being blamed for failures in planning–not unlike the position in which the Jewish agent finds himself in a private economy. To be sure, in the first decade of Bolshevik rule numerous Jewish traders, merchants, agents, and artisans were forced into the ranks of industrial labor or remained unemployed; but very soon the rapid expansion of the governmental services placed a premium on managerial, operative, and supervisory qualifications so that it is hardly amazing that young Jews were attracted to the new opportunities. Consequently, the economic pursuits of Soviet Jewry soon became, as in more or less capitalistic countries, concentrated in the administrative, technical, professional, and cultural fields. The data are sketchy, but the general drift is clear. While, according to the last available Soviet census (1959), 1.09 percent of the total population and 2.16 percent of the urban population were persons registered as "Jewish nationality," Jews were 3.22 percent of all high school students, 4.9 percent of those with secondary higher education (doctors, officials, engineers, bookkeepers, etc.) And between 9 and 10 percent of all "scientific workers." Astute analysts of these and related statistical data have concluded not only that Soviet Jews are largely in positions in the economy that are both visible and devoid of political power, but that there is also an observable tendency on the part of the authorities to squeeze them out of positions in which they have attained some prominence or have them simply wither on the vine as soon as Ukranian, Byelorussian, and other "native" young people aspire to administrative and scientific careers. Consequently, there are more older Jewish scientists and administrators than there are younger ones to replace them. These trends may have far-reaching consequences that cannot be pursued at this point.

If the occupational structure of Soviet Jewry and Jewish populations in other Eastern European communist countries such as Poland, Czechoslovakia, Hungary, and Romania is not appreciably different from the occupational structure of Jewish populations elsewhere, it stands to reason that the stereotypical image of the Jew is not much changed either. As a matter of fact, the persistence of patterns is uncanny. Stalin's trumped-up "doctors' plot," that is, the infamous trial in which nine medical doctors, six of them Jewish, were accused of a medically engineered attempt on the life of the Soviet dictator, is reminiscent of the accusations against Jewish doctors in the Middle Ages who were said to attempt to poison their unsuspecting Christian patients whenever the opportunity arose. Khrushchev's regime, in turn, specialized in the prosecution of "economical crimes," such as speculation in gold, jewels, currency, embezzling, counterfeiting, and the like, again with an emphasis on Jews as perpetrators. Khrushchev indicated that the high percentage of Jews involved in these trials was not so much due to "national" prejudice but to the fact that many Jews occupied prominent positions in Soviet institutions of production and consumption; but this can hardly justify the exorbitantly high proportion of indictments of, and severe verdicts against, Jews: 60 percent of the total in the entire Soviet Union and as much as between 86-90 percent in the Ukrainian and Moldavian republics. Nor can it justify the official propaganda line that was indulged in during the 1960s, where synagogues were singled out as dens of economic iniquity, synagogue officials tainted with moral depravity, and love of gain pilloried as a Jewish trait. All of this is not to say that genuine friendship and human generosity are absent from the Soviet scene–Yevtushenko's famous poem "Babi Yar," wherein he identifies himself with the forgotten Jewish victims of the horrendous mass extermination by the Nazis at the outskirts of Kiev–is a case in point. What is important to note is that popular anti-Semitism apparently has not disappeared from the communist countries of Eastern Europe. The combination of age-old notions and the present position of the Jews in the social structure of these countries makes it easy to depict the Jew as a conspirator against commonly held values, be they Christian values or values held sacred in a socialist society. He is seen as economically selfish and politically suspect, even if the accusation is demonstrably fabricated. Many of the economic crime trials of the 1960s were conducted on the questionable strength of officially managed or otherwise distorted testimony. Another example is the terrifying Slansky trial in Czechoslovakia. Eleven of the fourteen Czech officials who were in the docket in this Stalin-inspired witch-hunt trial were Jewish. Although most of them had clear records as anti-Nazi resistance fighters, they were accused of collaborating with the Gestapo, spying for the United States, and being "Zionists"–all three of these things–and condemned after prolonged physical and psychological torture based not on demonstrable evidence but entirely on the strength of the foregone conclusions. Equally telling is the expulsion of the Jewish functionaries of the Polish Communist Party from their positions and, indeed, from the country after the Six Day War of 1967. The purge encompassed men and women in elevated positions and leading intellectuals as well as those in the lower levels of administration, actually as a means of overthrowing one faction of the party in favor of another, but ostensibly because of the alleged political unreliability of the Jews as Jews. The appeal to anti-Jewish sentiments was conveniently employed as a means to furthering political objectives. The nomenclature may have changed in this regard from Stalin to Gomulka, but the procedure remained the same and the outcome was identical. Stalin dubbed his intra party Jewish adversaries "cosmopolitans"; Gomulka denounced them as "Zionists." Either designation places Jewish communist outside the official pale. But the argument is carried further. In Gomulka's latter-day newspeak, "Zionism and anti-Semitism are two sides of the same nationalistic coin"– which is a tortuous way of using a quasi-Hegelian contradiction to say that both are tools in the hands of class–enemies and "fascists." Thus, by a slight-of-hand, anti-Semitism can be denounced as reactionary and consequently declared non-existent *ex definitione* in a communist country while Jews can be maligned, discriminated against, criminally prosecuted and expelled from their country of birth at the very same time. All of these things can be done with perfectly good conscience. Measured against the testimony of the centuries, there is nothing in the policies of the Soviet Union and its satellites that could be considered as turning a new leaf in Jewish-Gentile relations.

15

Is America Different?

Is America different? Has the pattern of the centuries been altered to a considerable degree as the Founding Fathers and the conviction of countless immigrants expected it to be? The question is hard to answer because American history, and certainly the history of the Jews in America, does not cover a large enough span of time to permit a final judgment. Patterns do not emerge in less than two centuries. The Jewish community in America is still in the process of becoming, and so are the relations of various kinds of Americans to each other. Besides, American and European data are not always comparable and the American data are redundant in one regard, deficient in another. For instance, prejudice has been studied over and over again, but the occupational composition of the Jewish population, that is, the structural prerequisite of human relations in a large society, is known only in broad outlines. We must nevertheless try to broach the complexity of the problem.

Much can be said in favor of the contention that America is different. In the view of Israel Zangwill, which was widely shared for a long time, America was "God's crucible" in which the Hebrew, Greek, Anglo-Saxon, Celt, and Slav (blacks were never mentioned!) were to be fused into a new species of man. Indeed, many ingredients of the European situation seemed either absent from the American scene or were profoundly changed. The status of the Jew as a citizen was never contested and no protracted struggle for "emancipation" was necessary. The medieval attitude regarding and charging interest played no historical role; to the contrary, the national symbol of Uncle Sam refers to a straightforward, no-nonsense businessman who knows his advantages, even if he adheres to the principle that "honesty is the best policy." The maxim of Thomas Aquinas that the businessman can "hardly be a Christian" was foreign to Puritan piety. To the contrary, radical Calvinistic doctrine, although it denied that man could buy his way into a state of grace by means of good works, nevertheless considered the incidence of worldly success a mark of divine election. When that religious root had withered, economic man pure and simple appeared on the scene and the end of "success," irrespective of the means, was relentlessly pursued. It seemed that a Jew who had "made it" could be accepted, with no questions asked. Moreover, the Puritan notion of the patriarchs and prophets of the Old Testament as messengers of the Kingdom of God on earth remained engraved on the consciousness of America. Thomas Jefferson, a deist, suggested for the reverse side of the Great Seal of the United States a likeness of the triumph of the Children of Israel, with the tyrant Pharaoh amidst the waters of the Red Sea. At that time, the idea of religious tolerance had begun to replace Puritan zeal. Here was another element favorable to the integration of the Jews. To be sure, the motto *E Pluribus Unum*, which was finally adopted for the Great Seal, was intended to symbolize political union, but religious tolerance was implied. America had become a country of competing denominations whose members had to learn to coexist. The principle of the separation of church and state, which was intended to protect freedom of worship, was guaranteed in the Constitution. There was to be no established church, such as the Church of England, with divergent creeds, including Judaism, at best grudgingly tolerated. But it should also be noted that the Supreme Court of the United States over the decades has tightened the original meaning of the non-establishment of religion, so that it has come to mean that no religious group as such is supposed to be guaranteed or supported in any way. Only the individual's freedom of choice to adhere to one group or another is guaranteed.

The impact of the principle of freedom of worship on Jewish-Gentile relations is not unambiguous. The supreme value realized in the French and American Revolutions is nationality or citizenship; and inasmuch as this zealous God does not tolerate other gods before him, religion is recognized not as an independent entity but merely as an expression of the freedom of association. In other words, religion tends to become a matter of individual willingness instead of being what it originally was, namely, a mold into which one is born and to which one belongs by means of ancestral ties. Religion is conceived in the image of a sect, and in the suburbs the individuation may go so far that a young couple can say they are "shopping around for a church." However, America, to a much greater degree than laicistic France, is not only a multi-denominational but a multi-ethnic society; and ethnicity is a matter of ancestral ties. It follows that the proclaimed principle of uniformity in America clashes with the stubborn fact of diversity. What has happened in these circumstances is that religion has become the protecting canopy of ethnicity. This is true for Protestant denominations, such as the Missouri Synod, which is predominantly German, as against the United Lutheran Church, which is largely Scandinavian in the composition of its membership. The same is true of the Roman Catholic Church, which had to grant recognition to separate Polish, Italian, and Hispanic parishes, with ethnic priests officiating, in addition to its traditional strictly geographical parish organization; even so, the American Catholic Church as a whole has not been able to shed it predominantly Irish character. But Judaism clearly is the classic case of ethnicity and religion interpenetration to such a degree that they form an inseparable whole. The Reform movement in American Judaism has stressed the religious aspect, but the creation of the State of Israel has brought ethnicity to the fore once again of Jewish consciousness; and the impact of the Negro revolt has had the same effect far beyond the confines of the Jewish community. Ethnicity can no longer be wished away or declared a transient phenomenon, bound to disappear with the passing of the immigrant generation. It remains to be seen what this is going to mean for Jewish-Gentile relations.

A glance at the economy offers another perspective. Until recently, the Jewish problem has been relegated to the background because the dissolution of any and all ethnicities, Jewishness included, was confidently expected, but also because it was not so much the Jews as a group that seemed to be involved, but a multitude of individual Jews that struggled for a livelihood. What each of them wanted for himself was a chance to escape from a ghetto that in America was not legally imposed and socially sanctioned, as in old Europe, but merely marked by economic restrictiveness. These economic limitations were overcome not by legal enactment, but by individual effort. Persistent prejudice and discrimination against Jews could be surmounted because the dynamism of economic development in America offered ever new and widening chances for advancement. Petty jealousies were held in check when practically everybody could pursue his particular happiness in the competitive race, when situations of potential conflict, as in housing, were superseded by beckoning opportunities elsewhere, and when the hopes of even those who were running hindmost were kept alive by the popular belief that with luck and perseverance –somehow, sometime–"a fellow was going to get a break." There were hurtful setbacks during periods of depression, but they were soon overcome in a new spurt of growth. Consequently, the traditional anti-Semitism of the lower middle classes was aborted. Finally, the role of the Jews in the economy and the significance of Jewish economic behavior were enhanced by replacing an "inner-directed" by an "outer-directed" mentality, which is the accompaniment of the replacement of a production-oriented economy by a consumption-oriented economy. It must be recalled that the bulk of Jewish economic activities customarily had been directed toward the ultimate consumer. It follows that the role that the Jews play in economic life is emphasized and more highly appreciated when the consumptive capacity of a broad strata of the population rises with a rise in productivity. With brief interruptions, this has been the case in America ever since the founding of the republic and in accelerated fashion since the end of World War II.

America is indeed different, but that does not mean that the position of the Jews in the social structure of America differs correspondingly from what it has always been. Economically, the first major intrusion of Jews occurred in the 1830s, when the Jewish peddler began to replace the Yankee peddler in the expanding American West. Jews were numerous in the small trading towns of California in the 1850s, but even an eastern Jewish community, such as that in Easton, Pennsylvania, consisted chiefly of peddlers until about the time of the Civil War. General Grant, in his famous directive during the Civil War said "Jew" when he meant "peddler." The Jewish peddler served about the same function in America that he had served in Europe, the difference being that the area covered was immensely more extensive here than there and the service rendered to the lonely farmer that much more significant. But the transition "from pack to store" was rapid. By 1890, according to the report by John S. Billings, almost half of the 10,000 heads of Jewish households were wholesale and retail merchants and another fifth were accountants, bookkeepers, clerks, collectors, and agents. The mass immigration from Eastern Europe that set in about 1880 and continued until the victory of the Immigration Restriction League in 1921 and 1924 changed the occupational picture temporarily, but the interlude was of short duration. In 1900, three out of every five Jews who had come from tsarist Russia were industrial workers and more than one half of these were engaged in the garment trades while only one out of five was a storekeeper, a peddler, or an agent. In 1935, only one short decade after mass immigration had been reduced to a trickle. the move into white-collar occupations and business was in full swing. In Detroit, more than one-fourth of the gainfully employed of the Jewish faith were proprietors, managers, and officials and two out of five were clerks and kindred workers. In New York, 60 percent of gainfully employed Jewish youths was engaged in "clerical and kindred" work while almost one half of their fathers were manual workers. Jewish youth constituted 31 percent of the youth of the city, but amounted to 43 percent of those engaged in clerical and sales work, 37 percent of those in the professions and 56 percent of proprietors and managers. These were the proportions in a Jewish mass settlement where the percentage of manual workers among the Jewish population was relatively large.

In a small town, like Stamford, Connecticut, where the Jewish community in 1938 comprised only 3,279 individuals, that is, no more than 5 percent of the total population, the intermediary character of the Jewish occupational structure was even more thoroughly established. Well over half of those gainfully employed among the Jews of Stamford were either in business for themselves or otherwise connected with a commercial enterprise, chiefly in the retail trade. The concentration was most pronounced in the dry goods, cosmetics, liquor, and jewelry business, where practically all the retail outlets were Jewish owned, but the participation of Jews in other branches of business, such as furniture and shoe stores, food markets, and wholesale drug firms was likewise considerable. In industry, Jews were prominent only in two branches, namely, building and the manufacture of women's clothes while in the professions Jews in considerable numbers were found only in the practice of law: forty-eight of the 110 lawyers domiciled in Stamford were Jews in 1938. This contrasts with but thirty-six of 152 medical and dental practitioners and thirty-three of 419 public school teachers. Most significant in this remarkably detailed report is the fact that the Jewish lawyers in town were limited chiefly to the relatively minor aspect of legal work, such as real estate, bankruptcy, collection, and negligence cases rather than having a share in the more lucrative cases, involving probate and estate work, corporation law, and the like. In small compass, this shows clearly that the Jewish advance was into positions in the middle of the socio-economic scale that are consumption oriented and visible, not into the power structure. We will return to this aspect of our story, which is of decisive importance, later in our deliberations. Only one comment might be in order at this point, namely, that the Stamford picture does not seem very different from that of a comparable town in Central Europe.

World War II marks a watershed in the occupational distribution of American Jews, as it does in other regards. The increasingly homogeneous middle-class character of the occupational structure of Jewish communities outside New York, transparent already in the Stamford study, was entirely beyond dispute by 1954, when Nathan Glazer observed that in fourteen local Jewish community surveys conducted between 1948 and 1953, the proportion of Jews in the non-manual occupations had grown to between 75 and 96 percent. In what is perhaps an extreme case, in New Orleans in 1953, more than 80 percent of all Jews in the labor force were self-employed and almost 70 percent were concentrated in two fields–wholesale-retail trade and the professions, chiefly medical and legal services, and semi-professionals. The corresponding observation that the proportion of the total population engaged in non-manual occupations had risen from 20 percent in 1910 to 38 percent in 1950 (if farm owners and tenants are included, to 48 percent) permits a twofold conclusion: first, it indicates that America as a whole had become more middle class and the American economy more "post-industrial" in character, and second, that the Jewish advance had outpaced the general trend. This, again, has a twofold effect on Jewish-Gentile relations. On the one hand, the tendency toward a larger absolute as well as proportional growth in the tertiary sector of the economy as against other sectors is likely to diminish the divergence of the Jewish occupational structure from the general structure. On the other hand, however, it ought to be noted that the rapid transformation among the Jewish population has resulted not so much in the diminution of a one-sided distribution but in a new concentration at the opposite end of the social scale and hence has perpetrated the divergence. If the image of the Jew as a garment maker, pushcart peddler, or junk dealer is replaced by the image of the Jew as a lawyer, doctor, or scientist, *the* Jew is still cast in the intermediary role of an agent and an expert, although on a different level. If anything, the intermediary role has become more pronounced.

The trend can be read from a comparison of the fourteen communities surveyed between 1948 and 1953 with ten communities surveyed during 1935-1945; in the 1950s, the share of professionals had risen on the average from 11-15 percent while the share of clerks and salesmen had declined from 36.5 to 27 percent. Another comparison, namely the one among religious groups, which is possible only for 1957, shows that Jews were then second only to Episcopalians with regard to educational status (four or more years of college); share of professionals among gainfully employed heads of family within a group (Jews occupied first place regarding the share of owners, managers and officials); and total family income (share of those in the two topmost categories of $7,500 - $ 14,999 and $15,000 or more). In addition, it must be assumed that the trend has continued. In seventeen community studies that were conducted between 1955 and 1969, including in such important cities as Boston, Detroit, and San Francisco, statistics show it emerged that proprietors comprised 24-57 percent, professionals 14-36 percent, but clerical and sales personnel only 7-27 percent, and manual workers only 5-20 percent. With almost 90 percent of Jewish youth presently attending college, it can be predicted that the professionalization of the Jewish occupational structure will be completed with a decade. This fact alone will make the position of the Jew within the social structure as precarious as it has always been.

Specifics about the occupational distribution of Jews in the labor force in the period after World War II would be highly desirable, but unfortunately only bits and pieces are available. Most community studies, including the Providence study, do not go beyond the categories of the U.S. Census. In 1935, when the editors of *Fortune* published their rather superficial journalistic reportage about the Jews of America, they were preoccupied with the problem of the imaginary, yet apparently economically based notion of the "power" of the Jews which was conjured up by the *Protocols of the Elders of Zion* on this side of the ocean as well as in Europe. If one were to believe public opinion polls, the strength of that preoccupation has been waning in the meantime. In nationwide polls, the percentage of the total sample who thought "Jews have too much power in the United States" rose from 41 percent in 1938 to 58 percent in 1945, only to fall to 17 percent in 1962. But the questions were formulated differently at different times and were much too vague in any case to give the assurance that the respondents understood them uniformly and unequivocally. In their own impressionistic way, the editors of *Fortune* came to the conclusion that Jews wielded little influence in the key areas of commercial and industrial power, such as banking, insurance, utilities, transportation, and in the steel, coal, rubber, automobile, oil, and chemical industries. They also stated that Jewish doctors were barely represented on hospital boards and in medical associations and that Jewish lawyers played a considerable role in trial work but none in corporation law. They conceded a Jewish preponderance in the entertainment field and in light industries, such as garments, liquor, tobacco, plastics, and the like, but even there more at the distributing end than in manufacturing proper. These are areas of economic activity that are highly competitive, innovative, and close to the consumer–that is, they are areas in which the Jews have excelled at all times and at many places. Perhaps the most significant contributions of Jews to the American economy, the mail order house and the department store, with their diversified offerings, are certainly not peculiar to Jewish commercial activities in America. Already Glueckel von Hameln, in her memoirs, refers to the Jewish predilection for diversification. In the post-World War II period, many struggling small Jewish businessmen, such as owners of candy and stationery stores, tailor and millinery shops, house painters and newspaper vendors have all but disappeared. Their children have made a place for themselves not only in the professions, including teaching, but also in retail chains, the real estate business, book publishing, accounting, advertising, market research and in the host of investigatory, advisory and consulting functions that are the mark of a developing tertiary economy. Even in the absence of specifics, the intermediate character of Jewish economic activities cannot be overlooked.

The data from the 1960s are fascinating. In the year 1967, a Jew moved to the executive desk of the First Pennsylvania Banking and Trust Company; another Jew was named vice president and chief scientist of IBM Corporation; and Edward Hirsch Levi, the grandson of a well-known reform rabbi, became president of the University of Chicago. All these appointments were firsts: prior to that year, Jews were very sparsely represented in the executive suites of America. A few illustrations must suffice. According to a study, likewise undertaken in 1967, only 1.3 percent of the top officers of fifty commercial banks in the country and no more than 0.9 percent of their middle management executives were Jewish. In New York, where about 25 percent of the city's residents are Jews, the nine banks with headquarters in New York had only one Jew among 173 senior officers and nine Jews among 927 middle management executives. In the insurance business, in shipping, railroading, public utilities, and in the aircraft, automobile, oil, steel, paper, and food processing industries less than 1 percent of top management was Jewish. Among five large insurance companies with headquarters in New York, Jews amounted to 4 percent in administrative offices, but to 10 percent in the sales offices. In the same vein, 3.5 percent of the board members of fifty commercial banks were Jews, compared to only 1.3 percent of the top officers. Further, wherever Jews were found in middle management, they were staff experts, such as actuaries, accountants, attorneys, mathematicians, and researchers rather than line officers who might advance to top management positions in the course of time. Apparently, Jews were allowed to provide expertise on the inside or connections on the outside, but not to have a marked impact on decision making. As one ex-officer of a major automobile company said Jews are ". . . not accepted as the kind of individuals the industry looks to for leadership."

What, by and large, is true for the captains of industry, remains also true for the captains of erudition. In 1966, only six of 775 institutions of higher learning were headed by Jews and only forty-five of 1,720 deans were Jewish. But here, the breakthrough was more conspicuous than in the commercial area. In 1967, ten institutions, among them the University of Chicago and the State University of New York in Buffalo, named Jews as presidents and an additional number of Jewish educators were appointed vice presidents, deans, and provosts. As to the professions, the tight quotas that had limited the entry of Jewish students into medical schools in the 1930s have largely disappeared. There is a shortage of medical personnel all over the country and sharp competition from the newer scientific fields. In law, the change occurred in the employment situation rather than in the schools. According to Erwin O. Smigel, the leading corporate law firms in New York ("Wall Street Lawyers"), who hardly made a Jew a partner or associate prior until the last decade, have broadened their search for talent. The old division of labor, with Jewish lawyers appearing in court in civil as well as in criminal cases while the WASP lawyers advised potent industrial clients in wood-paneled offices has not been obliterated altogether, but there have been so many exceptions that the pattern has become blurred. However, the "personal preferences" of the senior partners are still telling and will remain so for a considerable time to come. The most dramatic breakthrough is noticeable at college and university campuses and at research institutions of varied kinds. The Jewish professor is now as ubiquitous as was the Jewish junk dealer formerly was. More than 10 percent of faculty members at institutions of higher learning are Jewish, up to 20 percent at Harvard, Columbia, Pennsylvania, Princeton, and the University of California. In the field of sociology, where only a handful of Jews had attained professorial rank by the early 1940s, Jewish scholars are now in prestigious positions in the Ivy League colleges that actively used to exclude them not so long ago; several of them have been elected presidents of the American Sociological Association. The same is true in other social sciences and in literature. In sociology as well as in literary history and literary criticism, the trend has been so pronounced that Jews are now explaining Anglo-Saxon cultural achievements and the nature of American society to an American reading public. This phenomenon has two sides, in terms of Jewish-Gentile relations. On the one hand, it testifies to the fact that Jews are thoroughly integrated into American life because sociological analysis and the teaching of English literature are sensitive topics that are not usually entrusted to strangers. On the other hand, one cannot help but remember that the prominence of Jewish authors, scholars, theatrical entrepreneurs, and literary critics in German cultural endeavors during the Weimar Republic was greatly admired and at the same time bitterly resented. Whether America will forever remain immune to cultural jealously is a moot question.

The image of the Jew in America has been ambivalent from way back. The Jew as identified with the ancient Hebrew by the Puritans, the Founding Fathers, the Negroes on the plantation: he was the prototype of a liberated slave himself, besides being a lawgiver, a prophet, and a seeker after the Kingdom of God. But the modern

Jew interfered with the image of the ages. For Boston Brahmins at the turn of the nineteenth and twentieth centuries, the noble Hebrew of yore came to be overshadowed by his latter-day descendants. For James Russell Lowell and Henry Adams, the Jew was either the "wretched street-vendor" or the "evil spirit of the age"; in either case he was the epitome of a materialistic civilization. The actual or imagined combination of intellectual ability and financial potency in those Jews with whom these men came into contact–not so much in Boston but in Europe–aroused in them the haunting fear that society might soon be controlled by an emerging moneyed nobility with the Jews as the protagonists of the new Moloch. They could not rid themselves of the notion that the Jews constituted a formidable challenge to their role in economic affairs and in politics and to the values they held dear. The supercilious anti-Semitism of the literary Anglo-elitists such as T. S. Eliot and Ezra Pound echoes this kind of encounter. For Eliot, the Jews were likened to rats "underneath the piles / The jew is underneath the lot" in aristocratic Venice; for Ezra Pound, "gold and work" were contrasted as if they were implacable adversaries in a Wagner-Hitler like fancy. The Rothschild legend was as alive with these men as with any European pamphleteer. One might object that expatriates should not be counted too heavily in the balance, but the Rothschild story was widely popular among average Americans as well as among elitists, both on the eastern seaboard, where August Belmont represented the Rothschild interests, and on the western plains where the remote Rothschild image, fused with a Shylock motive, assumed a quasi-proverbial coloration. The designation of the cash register as a "Jewish piano" may have been in the way of good-natured kidding, but the *Chicago Tribune* was in dead earnest, when in 1863 it contrasted rumors of "a dishonorable peace in order to enrich Belmont, the Rothschilds and the whole tribe of Jews" with an "honorable peace won by Grant and Sherman at the cannon's mouth." One must add, however, that the frontiersmen had no share in the decadent fear complex of the Brahmins. They knew that there were "three Jews in a Yankee" and that the Jews in their midst could help them cope with the eastern seaboard elite. They were proud of the frugality, the enterprising spirit, the solid achievements and the civic-mindedness of their Jewish compatriots. The Jew had become part of the American success story.

The image of the Jew as the prototype of "economic man" may be "traditional," as Charles H. Stember admits, that is, an inheritance from a bygone age; but in a post-medieval setting it is endowed with ambivalence. Thus in recent public opinion surveys, Jews may be considered "greedy," "dishonest," "aggressive" on the one hand, or "able," "persistent," "independent" on the other, although caution is called for in the interpretation of these epithets because the stylized replies have been elicited in response to loaded questions about "objectionable" and "admirable" traits. Stember is on the right track when he fashions the discreet images into a composite portrait, but less so when he concludes from a comparison of later surveys (1957, 1962) with earlier ones (1938, 1940) that unfavorable stereotypes are now held by a shrinking number of hostile persons and that supposedly admirable qualities in Jews contain less hidden hostility than was previously the case. Actually, people don't change attitudes abruptly. They waiver between conflicting attitudes at all times, perhaps with one attitude prevailing at one time and the compensatory attitude at another. The conflicting or compensatory attitude has not disappeared; it is temporarily pushed beneath the level of consciousness. The diminished acceptance or, at least, the attenuated reformulation of hostile stereotypes of the Jew in the 1950s and 1960s appears then as a passing phenomenon, hardly worthy of note in historical analysis. What is likely to have happened is that the impact of Hitler's genocide on public opinion in the 1950s was so overwhelming that anti-Semitic attitudes lost respectability and thus became unacceptable to many people–their own anti-Semitic attitudes included. It had become quite obvious that prejudice can be murderous. But as the impact of Auschwitz and Treblinka wore thin, chiefly as a result of Israel's unexpected victory in the Six Day War, the supposedly vanquished ghost of anti-Semitism has surfaced once again, this time in the guise of anti-Zionism. It seems that the ambivalence is here to stay.

The black-and-white responses that are derived from surveys are likely to be deceptive because they tend to split the human mind into isolated traits; they hardly ever come to grips with the dialectic quality of the total picture. To a degree, all of us are both anti-Semitics and philo-Semitics, liberals and conservatives, depending on the situation. In addition, the brief span of time covered by American history and the even shorter period within which we are able to observe the unfolding of the relations between Jews and Gentiles in America make it difficult to unravel the varied skeins of a texture that is still far from complete. As a result, we are unsure whether the confused pattern that we discern is because of the lack of distance from the object of observation or whether it is a genuine reflection of the situation. John Higham provides a measure of guidance when he refers to three groups in late nineteenth-century America that harbored anti-Jewish feelings that went beyond mere social discrimination: a number of patrician intellectuals in the East, some of the agrarian radicals caught up in the Populist movement, and members of the poorest classes in urban centers. The common denominator in the resentment of these three groups, according to Higham, was their aversion to the prevailing business culture; this sentiment made them susceptible to simplistic racist interpretations of contemporary history. The Jew served as the scapegoat for the sins of the business society. There were shades and grades in the derivation of the aversion: in a patrician Easterner, like Madison Grant, it was the fear of the self-styled elite of being "outbred" by inferior races; in a radical Westerner, like Edward A. Ross, it was the apprehension that "the fiber of the pioneering breed" might be weakened by the influx of immigrants that made him and his friends generally suspicious of newcomers and of Jews merely as their protagonists; among the struggling Irish, German, Greek, Russian, and other immigrants, the Jew was singled out as an antagonist in a subconscious attempt to curry favor with the Anglo-Saxon master-race. However, when the Immigration Restriction League, after decades of unsuccessful attempts, finally attained its goal of cutting off large-scale immigration with the passage of the legislation in 1921 and 1924, the immigrant crackpots were clearly not members of the victorious coalition: the patricians were the leaders while the western and southern populists, the Ku Klux Klaners, the fundamentalists, and last, but not least, the American Federation of Labor–the latter intent on excluding potential competitors from the labor market–provided the main support. Very likely, then, it was not so much anti-capitalism but nativism that united the disparate forces of restriction. But whether the anti-capitalistic or the nativistic animus prevailed, the Jew, nonetheless, was the most convenient target of resentment. Sentiments of this kind, by their nature, are not always explicit, but they are indicative. In the 1890s, when William Jennings Bryan, heading a nationwide populist campaign, cried out that mankind must not be "crucified on a cross of gold," he rallied his followers against Wall Street and the "Eastern establishment" with a battle cry that carried the implication that America was truly a Christian country. In the 1930s, intriguingly, the idea was appropriated by the editors of *Fortune* as the spokesmen for the business community, that is, the national enlargement of what used to be the "Eastern establishment" in Bryan's time. Patronizingly, they explained to their readers that while "all other immigrant peoples accept the culture of the country into which they come," the Jews refuse to do so. Since, as is generally known, the Jews, above all other immigrants to the United States, are in the forefront of those who speak English, support the arts and sciences, and assume the duties of citizenship, what the authors intended to say can only be that the vast majority of Jews have not become Christians. In view of the Jesus movements of the early 1970s, it is dubious whether sentiments of this kind, which cast the Jew in the role of an outsiders, have been muted in the meantime. To the extent to which they are alive, America is not as different as it may seem at first glance.

16

Varieties of Pluralism in America

To speak of "the American way of life" has become commonplace, but closer investigation reveals that the concept of what makes America American has undergone many metamorphoses in the two centuries that have passed since the founding of the Republic. By and large, two ideologies vie for acceptance: one idea that America is a "melting pot" of peoples and races and the other that America is a society marked by "cultural pluralism." It bespeaks of the fascination that the American experience has exerted over the Jewish mind and the earnest desire of Jewish intellectuals to be integrated into America that both terms have been coined by Jews. Israel Zangwill, who was quoted in the preceding chapter, looked upon America as "God's crucible" wherein people from many nations and cultures were fused into a new entity. Horace Kallen, on the other hand, spoke about America as an orchestration of many instruments that had to be attuned to each other. Merger or symbiosis–that is the question. I believe it has become fairly obvious that the melting pot does not melt–certainly not regarding the American Indian, the Negro, the Hispanic-American–but also not regarding a variety of ethnicities that are derived from Europe. But that does not mean that cultural pluralism is a living reality. In my own Brownsville studies, I drew attention to the fact that among the Jewish types that were found in that Brooklyn neighborhood in the 1940s, the most numerous and all-pervasive one was a type that I characterized as "culturally American, socially in the Ghetto." What I meant to say was that the consciousness of the majority of the young Jews who were then living in Brownsville and similar areas and who are now dispersed into suburbia were devoid of Jewish cultural content, except for an attachment to mama's cooking–that their tastes, predilections and pastimes were thoroughly American, but their social life was carried out in an ethnic context. They were aware of their Gentile neighbors and of the larger society across the East River, but they associated with Jews. Similarly, American Jews that are members of a B'nai B'rith lodge do precisely what other Americans are doing in the Knights of Columbus, the Rotarians, Kiwanians, the BPO Elks and other fraternal organizations. They do not differ in behavioral patterns, rituals, professed ideals, social and charitable activities of various kinds, except for one very significant thing–they prefer to associate among themselves. So do other Americans in other organizations–it is the American thing to do. In other words, America is a pluralistic society, but the pluralism is not necessarily cultural in nature. Americans are culturally united, but structurally divided. That is the reason why Milton Gordon, in a felicitous phrase, speaks of "structural pluralism." It remains to be seen that both the cultural unity and the structural divisiveness have been imposed by the dominant White Anglo-Saxon Protestant elite (WASP) and that the recognition of this fact provides the key to understanding Jewish-Gentile relations in contemporary America.

Immigrants were always welcome in America as long as they were willing to do the kind of work that older residents no longer wanted to do. They were expected to be satisfied with a lower level of remuneration and lower social prestige. The immigrant, one might say, was "all right in his place." The Irish were working on the railroads, the Chinese were laundry men, Poles and Slovaks were descending into the coal pits, Italians were truckers and longshoremen. The majority of immigrants were uneducated village folk when they came and hardly able to rise to higher positions. The Jews, likewise, started at the bottom of the socioeconomic scale, yet from a higher level of literacy, and hence moved ahead more rapidly; it was their very success that aroused antagonism. Thus, the German-Jewish immigrant of the nineteenth century was accepted as long as he peddled his wares among the farmers or conducted a modestly prosperous retail business. But the social barriers went up when he attempted to enter the "Yankee" domain of big business and finance. The refusal, in the summer of 1877, of the management of the Grand Union Hotel in Saratoga Springs to admit among its guests the New York banker Joseph Seligman is generally considered to have been the start of "social anti-Semitism" in this country. The action was condemned in the press and from the pulpit, but the pattern took hold. The Jews retaliated by buying several of the leading hotels; the Gentiles departed and soon throughout the Catskills and the New York and New Jersey shores a division developed between resorts with an exclusively Jewish clientele and those that accepted only Christians. Interfaith rhetoric and supporting legislation notwithstanding, it has remained so until the present day.

The Saratoga incident, which didn't start the trend but brought it into focus, is important to the ongoing discussion of whether anti-Semitism in America began at the top and filtered downward, as Carey McWilliams assumed, or whether it was an aspect of popular, even populist, movements. The matter is much more complex than related phenomena in Europe where the attachment of the Jew to the political sovereign provided a safe anchorage until, with the advent of Hitler, the formerly trusted protector became an implacable foe. There is no political sovereign in America comparable to a "foreign power, prince, or potentate" that can serve a protective function. The political scene in the United States is crowded with interest groups that jostle each other, bargain with each other in a variety of combinations, form coalitions and reach accommodations for limited purposes and limited periods of time. It is therefore by no means certain who is "at the top" of the social pyramid at any given moment. At the time of the immigration restriction legislation, it was the Eastern establishment, in alliance with the southern Democrats and the American Federation of Labor. At the time of the Saratoga incident, there is much to be said for John Higham's contention that the anti-Jewish animus did not directly originate with apprehensive patricians who objected to the company of "parvenus" but with upstarts in the world of business who craved respectability and dreaded to be hampered in their "pursuit of happiness," if they were seen associating with Jews. Yet, in a larger sense, the controversy between McWilliams and Higham is insubstantial because in the rough and tumble of the "gilded age" the upstarts were soon to merge with the patricians into a new moneyed upper crust of white Protestant complexion from which Irish and Jewish contenders–there were no others in evidence at the time–were excluded.

The mass immigration of Jews from Eastern Europe strengthened the exclusionary tendencies that had been already well on their way in the 1880s. Again, the Russian influx, although viewed with apprehension in various quarters, failed to produce a serious anti-Semitic reaction as long as Jewish tailors toiled in the sweatshops of New York's garment district or Jewish junk dealers conducted their business in unseemly backyards. But the children of the Russian immigrants were rebuffed when they abandoned beards and earlocks and strove to be admitted to Ivy League colleges and prestigious medical schools. President Lowell of Harvard College was frank enough to recommend a quota restricting the admission of Jewish students in 1922 when Jewish enrollment had reached twenty percent; but other leading institutions, like Columbia University and Cornell Medical College, used a variety of subterfuges, such as geographical requirements, psychological and "character" tests, to cut Jewish registration to the desired size, and numerous smaller colleges followed suit. The commanding heights of the economy and the lucrative professions had to be protected. Compared to the formidable barriers to advancement in academia, populist anti-Jewish resentment, voiced either by rural demagogues like Tom Watson or evangelistic hate-preachers like Gerald L. K. Smith, was in the nature of a minor irritant.

The decades between the conclusion of the Civil War and the onset of the Great Depression of the 1930s were a period of heightened mobility in which customary positions were challenged not once, but perpetually, so that the process of adjustment had to be repeated over and over again. Consequently, in the scramble for what one deemed to be his proper place in a musical chairs game of successively changing arrangements, the outward trappings of achieved status–conspicuous consumption of various kinds and membership in prestigious organizations were highly prized. Paradoxically, however, such membership can be conducive to a new birth of ascribed status if one can hold on to it for a long enough time and fortify the stronghold against newcomers. Thus, it came to pass that for competition's sake, the rules of the game had to be suspended at a crucial point. A prestigious monopoly had to be secured. Accordingly, respectable Jewish merchants who applied for membership in social clubs were blackballed; rejection was extended even to sons of Jewish members in good standing. Jesse Seligman, one of the founders of the Union League Club in New York, resigned in 1893, when his son was so treated. The Philadelphia Club, over which a Jewish Philadelphian, Joseph Gratz, had presided during the Civil War, had no Jewish members after the 1890s. The University Club in Cincinnati broke up in 1896, over the admission of a prominent member of the Jewish community. As E. Digby Baltzell puts it, "the functionless genteel, supported by the newly rich, were seeking social security for their children in a patrician Protestant exclusiveness." But more than that was involved. The clubs monopolized business opportunities. A writer in *Fortune*, observed that "at the Metropolitan or the Union League or the University . . . you might do a $10,000 deal, but you'd use the Knickerbocker or the Union or the Racquet for $100,000, and then for a million, you'd have to move to the brook or the links." Obviously, it was good business to exclude Jews by some sort of "gentlemen's agreement." It is hardly amazing, then, that the Jews responded by creating city and country clubs as well as resort hotels under Jewish sponsorship. Ellis Gimbel, of department store fame, founded the first Jewish country club when he was blackballed by the Union League Club in Philadelphia in 1906. The exclusion came first, the separate Jewish institution followed. Later, in response, Gentiles acquired the habit of excusing exclusionist policies by pointing out that the Jews "have their own lovely club."

In the course of time, the pattern has been loosened here and there, but it remains essentially unchanged. Vance Packard reports that the downtown businessmen's club in a northeast city, in which a large number of merchants are Jewish has restricted Jewish membership to the percentage of Jews in the total population of the city, that is, to a token minority. Benjamin F. Ringer, in investigating the entire range of Jewish-Gentile relations in a midwestern suburban area, has painted a larger canvas. He differentiates between "instrumental" or "social influence" organizations, such as the PTAs, the League of Women Voters, a library committee and the like as against "expressive" groups, whose main purpose is "being" together rather than "acting" together. Ringer makes it very clear that "the edge of friendliness" is reached when "intimacy" rather than "purpose" is at stake. Surely, "expressive" groups want to restrict, "instrumental" groups want to expand. But that is not the whole story. The crux of the matter has been admirably stated by John P. Dean in his investigation of Jewish participation in American community-life, which is based on data from 248 middle-sized American cities. He found hardly any Jewish participation in what he calls "society" organizations, especially the Junior League and the leading city and country clubs and somewhat more in the service clubs, although the majority of the Rotary and Kiwanis clubs, while not excluding Jews outright, usually limited participation to a few select members. But precisely those communities that scored low on social acceptability of Jews, scored high on Jewish participation in community affairs, for instance on the board of Community Chests, non-sectarian casework agencies, and similar institutions. One Jewish community leader stated the matter succinctly: "They'll call on me to lead their Community Chest campaign or help on the Red Cross. But when it comes to the country club, I'm not good enough for them."

The reason why Jews are welcome in the Community Chest, but not in the country club is that–"intimacy" aside–the Country Club serves a variety of "purposes," such as marrying off one's daughter to the "right" partner and huddling together over a couple of drinks in order to decide about the new highway project or the forthcoming election of officers in an "instrumental" organization. Available statistics bear out that contention. According to a nationwide study of 1,152 social clubs with approximately 1,200,000 members, which was undertaken in the early 1960s, about 60 percent of the city clubs (Jewish clubs disregarded) and over 70 percent of the country clubs practiced religious discrimination, with the question left unanswered as to how many of the ostensibly non-discriminatory clubs have only token Jewish participation. Moreover, the topic can be approached from another direction. When Jews do participate in "purpose-oriented" organizations, even when they are the majority of the active membership, the elected president is more likely than not to be an Anglo-Saxon Protestant or possibly a person of Irish extraction, but the office of the treasurer is entrusted to a Jew. (The national anthem at the annual membership dinner is sung by a black woman.) It would seem that the Jew is as welcome in America as he has been at other times and places to provide the *nervus rerum* for public purposes. It might be going too far to say that a Jew is accepted on the condition that he serve that purpose, but he is, at any rate, expected to be most useful as a financial expert. In addition, to be sure, Jews are esteemed as peacemakers and are frequently called upon to fill positions in the judiciary. A Jew has never been elected mayor of the City of New York and only once a governor of the State of New York; but for the last thirty-two years a Jewish jurist has been entrusted by the designers of the party ticket as well as by the electorate with the office of attorney general. Shall we assume that the outcome is due to a game of chance or shall we say that a "stranger," who is neither a Montague nor a Capulet, is believed to hold out the promise of being an impartial judge?

Do Jews prefer intimate contacts with other Jews because they are rejected elsewhere, that is are they forced into segregation by outside pressures, or do they congregate of their own volition? In the early Middle Ages the congregational aspect was clear, but in the newer centuries the matter has grown increasingly more complex. In the context of a modern society, the question cannot be answered conclusively because both segregation and congregation are extremely limiting within the contradictory reality of human relations. Regardless of the motivation on either side, the "five o'clock shadow" is a fact. It may be a "six o'clock shadow," according to a rabbi in Atlanta, Georgia, who commented that "a Jew is accepted anywhere in the city, with any group, up to six o'clock." Participation in civic affairs is one thing, intimate socializing another. In the suburbs, the dividing line runs between "neighbor" and "friendship." "My daytime friends are Gentile, my after-dark friends are Jewish"–that is the summation of a Jewish housewife in Park Forest, a suburb of Chicago. The notion that intimate matters are to be shared with one's own kind is natural: Gentiles and Jews are completely *d'accord* on this question. It is customary to accuse Jews of "clannishness," but what sociologists call "consciousness of kind" is a universal phenomenon. There are exceptions, as we will see, but they prove the rule. As Dean reports, there is Jewish participation in Gentile cliques and Gentile participation in Jewish cliques, but Jews in Gentile cliques are likely to be persons on the periphery of the Jewish community while Gentiles in Jewish cliques frequently are spouses of a Jewish partner or relative of the Gentile spouse. More mixing of this kind is likely to occur as intermarriage rates rise, but all these fluctuations do is to change the composition of one or another ethno-religious group in one or another locality; they hardly ever jeopardize the group's continued existence. As far as the children go, free association across ethnic lines is permitted for pre-adolescents. But as adolescence sets in, lip-service about "romantic love" and the abhorrence of "discrimination" is readily offered by old and young alike, but subtle pressures see to it that not much changes when the dust settles. There are exceptions to the rule of ethnic or semi-ethnic separateness, but they are frequently more apparent than real. For instance, in metropolitan centers the Unitarian Church, the Ethical Culture Society and related humanistic associations provide a haven for those who wish to escape from the confines of ethnicity. The same can be said about artist colonies, large academic campuses and some circles of the "counterculture." However, as many of the participants in these institutional set-ups come from Jewish backgrounds, they tend to congregate, if ever so informally, with their own kind, not withstanding their expressed desire not to do so. They constitute, as it were, an "antitribal tribe." Thereby, some ostensibly "secular" or "non-sectarian" circles and institutions are rendered substantially Jewish in composition – and the rule of structural separateness is confirmed.

Time will tell in what way and to what extent ethnicity will continue to be a major determining societal factor in America. It is possible that Irish and Italian identities—not to speak of the identities of older groups, such as Germans and Norwegians—will become blurred, even structurally. It is possible that these ethnicities will be subsumed under larger, religiously defined headings. In this sense Ruby J.R. Kennedy, in identifying a "triple melting pot" in her New Haven studies, has built a halfway house between the contending nations of the undifferentiated "melting pot" and of "cultural pluralism." In her scheme, the melting pot melts, but in a pluralistic way. But the denominational "Protestant-Catholic-Jew" trichotomy which Will Herberg has construed on top of the "triple melting pot" scheme and related pieces of research, is already being superseded; and if the scheme is going to be enlarged into something like Protestant-Catholic-Jew Eastern Orthodox-Negro-Hispanic-American-American Indian- Asiatic groups, to mention only the major segments that have come into view in the 1960s and 1970s, the entire ethnic aspect of the American scene, including Jewish-Gentile relations, will be profoundly affected. All these groups and groupings are not disappearing, they are emerging. As there were no Italian Americans, only isolated villagers, at the height of the immigration from Italy to the United States, so there were no American Indians, only Navajos, Senecas, Winnebagos, until recently. Culturally distinctive features, such as the knowledge of Chinese language and history among the American Chinese may be receding, but heir structural distinctiveness, that is, their tendency to congregate in search of an identity, is increasing. The foremost example is provided by the American Negro. The black man was deculturated rather than acculturated under slavery, but he was not accepted on the basis of individual merit at any time and was cruelly discriminated against on all levels of human activity. As a result, in the century that has passed since Abe Lincoln's Emancipation Proclamation, a militant black consciousness has arisen that bids well to establish a new ethnicity on American soil. A separate organizational structure – general, fraternal, religious, professional– has been emerging that is gradually extending into a variety of cultural manifestations, such as African hairdos, soul food, jazz and blues music, black theater groups and the like. There is integration to some extent at work and in school, but with blacks and whites seated at different corners in the factory or school cafeteria.

These developments must necessarily influence the American Jew, whose cultural consciousness is the oldest in the western world but has been overlaid with layers of indifference in the course of the Americanization process to which the immigrants and their children have been subjected. Yet, the awareness of being Jewish can hardly be erased as long as Jews have not become Christians, because being non-Christian in a Christian country is as differentiating as being a non-white in a white country. The awareness has remained on the structural level thus far. For instance, it has been observed in Chicago and elsewhere that Jews, in migrating from localities of first and second settlements to the suburbs, have tended to congregate in the high status areas where social respectability can be combined with Jewish affiliation without expending too much of an effort on the cultural involvement of a Jewish character. For many Jewish parents, a modicum of Jewish education, promoting no more than an awareness of being Jewish, seems to suffice. It remains to be seen whether in the years to come Jewish youth will be satisfied with these scant offerings or whether they will find themselves increasingly in the same boat with other "minorities" in that they have a sense of distinctiveness but not of identity. If the latter should be the case, they are likely to discover that they must depend upon themselves, without cultural guidance from the older generation.

A serious question remains, namely, whether the Jews of America indeed are an American minority, comparable to other minorities in America, or whether they are an adjunct to the WASP majority, no matter how discernible. Jewish nationalists, be they outright Zionists, cultural autonomists or advocates of Jewish "peoplehood" within an enfolding general civilization, will tend to opt for the former designation while liberals and assimilationists are likely t be subsumed under the later category. It is not clear where this leaves those radical Jews who follow the "Third World" banner. They might find themselves between the camps, as did their spiritual ancestors in the nineteenth century in Europe. Even without considering them, there are many contradictions hidden in the seemingly clear-cut alternatives that have been posed. The older Jewish settlers, especially those residing in the South and West, apart from vestigial German affiliations (German literary societies, etc.), intended to be Americans pure and simple. They defined themselves as a religious denomination and restricted Jewishness to the universalist Judaism of the Reform Temple, with its quasi-Protestant mode of worship. The children of the Eastern-European immigrants, especially their intellectual spokesman, were by far more radical. They discarded religion altogether, as soon as they arrived on the university campuses, if not earlier. Not unlike young Amsterdam in Myron Kaufmann's novel *Remember Me to God*, these ambitious young people attempted to remold themselves into Anglo-Saxon gentlemen; ethnicity was an obstacle to be overcome. In the next generation, men of the stature of Leon Edel, Lionel Trilling, and Leslie Fiedler established themselves as the foremost interpreters of Anglo-Saxon cultural traditions. Many lesser interpreters have followed their wake. Even on the level of academic administration, the Jewish presence can no longer be overlooked. To offer but one example: among eighty trustees, honorary trustees and life trustees of the University of Chicago, a survey reveals twelve Jewish names, along with fifty-seven English, Scotch, and Irish names (one of these a black scholar) and eleven Scandinavian, German, and Dutch names, but not a single Italian, Slavic, Greek, or Hispanic name. As a result of such observations, especially on campuses and in foundation offices, the impression that Jews are adjunct "whites," not members of a "minority" has not been lost on ethnic representatives.

Indeed, Jews have differed from other ethnics, chiefly because of their rapid economic advance. As a result, relations between Jews and members of other minority groups, especially the Irish (now replaced by the blacks!), have been strained. In the areas of first and second settlements in New York, Chicago, Boston, and other large cities, Jewish street peddlers and schoolboys on their way home lived in fear of violent attacks by Irish street gangs, while the Irish minded that the Jews encroached on their neighborhoods. In *Studs Lonigan*, James T. Farrell describes vividly the resentment of the Irish homeowners and the clashes between Irish and Jewish youngsters on Chicago's south side. A climatic incident occurred on New York's Lower East Side in 1902, when the solemn funeral procession of Rabbi Jacob Joseph was physically assaulted by Irish workingmen who threw iron nuts and bolts and streams of hot water on the marching mourners from the windows of a factory building, shouting "Christ-killers"; on top of it all, the Irish police aided the attackers as soon as the Jews attempted to defend themselves. The relations between Jews and Italians, although less violent, were likewise marked by a mutual feeling of estrangement. Neither the Jewish nor the Italian family had any desire to become closely acquainted, much less to be related to by marriage. Yet, there was symbiosis mingled with conflict from the beginning, as the immigrant Jewish traders and storekeepers and their customary clientele from the old countries, the descendants of German, Polish, Lithuanian, and Slovak peasants, settled near each other after they arrived in the New World. In addition, Irish, Italian, and Jewish businessmen entered into business ventures together. In the course of time, especially in the wake of Franklin D. Roosevelt's New Deal, these contacts extended to the clubhouses and union halls and deepened the alliances that were formed between Irish and Jewish politicians and Jewish and Italian leaders in the garment trades. One recent example is offered by the late Jewish Borough President of Brooklyn, Abe Stark, who started the present Democratic County leader of Brooklyn, Meade Esposito, on his career while Meade Esposito, in turn, supported a Jew as mayoral candidate and selected a Jewish women as a co-leader in his Canarsie club. The difference between these contacts and the contacts of Jews and WASP is that Jewish-ethnic contacts are in the nature of alliances while Jewish-WASP contacts are in the form of attachments. Jewish ethnicity is acknowledged in the former, blurred and, if at all possible, overlooked in the latter. It is not amazing, therefore, that the Hassidic Jews of Williamsburg, in two recent primary fights, preferred an Irish old-timer, Representative John Rooney, to his liberal Jewish challenger, Allard Loewenstein.

Loewenstein's support came from liberal Jews and Protestants in Brooklyn Heights and from blacks. It is likely that the Jewish community will continue to be split down the middle, as far as their relations to Gentiles are concerned, with the Jewish elite associating with the Anglo-Saxon elite and the Jewish middle classes relating to the "ethnic" middle classes in America.

17

Jews and Blacks

America is different because of the presence of the Negro. What is class antagonism in Europe is race antagonism in America, but race and class intertwine in a variety of ways. Similarly, as we know, religio-ethnicity and the position of the Jew in the social structure have coexisted and influenced each other over time. Yet, the formal similarity hides a substantial difference. Blacks not only have been set apart by physical appearance, they have been cast in the role of a menial laborer, so that one is hard put to discern cause and effect. Race has depressed social status; and low social status, in turn, has reinforced color prejudice. The Jew, on the other hand, standing outside Christianity, has appeared to others in the image of a trader; on both counts, he has been a stranger but not a slave. The history of blacks in America is a history of exploitation and the struggle to overcome it; Jewish history in Europe is a history of persecution and the attempt to undo it. These divergent patterns have left their mark.

Various layers and phases of contact can be discerned. As long as blacks lived in the shadow of the plantation, they encountered Jews only occasionally in the flesh, more often in the fancy garb of the ancient Hebrew. Little David played his harp and Moses pleaded with Pharaoh, "down in Egypt's land," to let his people go. Later, Jewish merchants solicited the freed men's clientele; and the black man knew that the store owner would call him "mister," and not "boy," as was the custom at his place of work. But it was only with the translocation of millions of American blacks from the cotton fields and country towns to metropolitan areas and from the southeast to the north and west that black-Jewish relations became a burning actuality. Once again, World War II is the watershed. By that time, the Jewish sweatshop worker and pushcart peddler had worked himself up to the position of a middle-class businessman and his children began to enter the professions on a broad front. The black migrant, on the other hand, escaped exploitation only to a limited extent. He remained "all right in his place" at the bottom of the social ladder in industrial plants and, in domestic service, barely on rung above the position he had occupied as a field hand in the rural south. Little progress had been made in moving from Uncle Tom's Cabin to Bigger Thomas's slum. In comparison, the American Jew, on the average, was well off economically. But it is erroneous to conclude that relative economic affluence erases the precariousness of the Jewish situation when, to the contrary, it exposes Jews to envy and possible violence. From the recognition of this fact flow a number of important consequences for the understanding of black-Jewish relations, extending from the economic to the cultural sphere.

On the first level, the Jews were, and still are, commercial and domestic employers of black employees and service workers; or else the Jews were merchants, landlords, housing and insurance agents and the blacks, customers, tenants, and clients. Escaping from the tyranny of custom, black men and women became subject to the laws of the marketplace; and the executor of these laws, more often than not, was a Jew. Irresponsible conduct on the part of Jewish businessmen, landlords, and housewives may have added fuel to the fire, but even the most exemplary conduct could not have erased the lines of conflict. On the second level, ecological and occupational succession is encountered. Ecologically, when the successive waves of blacks arrived in metropolitan areas, they found it easier to move into Jewish rather than Irish, Sicilian, or Polish neighborhoods because the Jews were ready to integrate to abandon their central city apartments for more desirable neighborhoods. This has changed in the meantime because Jews are not willing to forsake their homes and religious institutions a second or third time; and if such is the case, the clash of interest is as immediate in Jewish as in other ethnic neighborhoods. But initially, areas like New York's Harlem and Chicago's Lawndale district lost their Jewish character and were settled by incoming blacks. Some Jewish landlords and merchants retained their property or place of business in the old neighborhood; and in these instances a quasi-colonial situation ensued, either in actual fact or in the mind of the black onlooker. On the one hand, the Jewish entrepreneur became a stranger to the area where he conducted his business. On the other hand, the Jewish middleman, as the representative of downtown business and large corporations, was interposed between white America and the black masses. In other words, the corporation was remote, but the Jewish merchant or agent was visible. "Goldberg," as it were, was standing in for "whitey." Significantly, when the black ghettoes exploded after the assassination of Martin Luther King, it was chiefly small-scale Jewish property in the ghetto that was burned and looted. Occupationally, a clash of interests is indicated inasmuch as blacks aspire to civil service positions that are held by Jews, especially in the teaching and social work professions. Jews owe these positions to the merit system, which has largely replaced extraneous considerations that had formerly worked in their disfavor. But blacks demand "affirmative action," that is special consideration in view of their disadvantaged start. Again, the Jew appears to blacks as the representative of white privilege while Jews are afraid that the WASP establishment is about to abandon them, in hopes of appeasing the rebellious urban multitude. In other words, the Jews are finding themselves, as they so often did in their history, in a dangerous position between the upper and the nether millstones.

There is a third, namely a cultural, level to the black-Jewish encounter. The Jewish organizational, philanthropic, and scholarly effort on behalf of the human dignity and civil rights of blacks is outstanding. For example, a Jewish social worker, Henry Moskowitz, was among the founders of the NAACP; a Jewish lawyer, Arthur Spingarn was for more than a quarter of a century the unpaid chairman of the legal defense department of the NAACP; and his brother, Joel E. Spingarn was chairman of the board of directors. Other Jews were prominently active in the Urban League and the Congress of Racial Equality (CORE) as well as in the NASACP. Julius Rosenwald's expenditure of a considerable part of his large fortune in the stony vineyard of Negro education, the *amicus curiae* intervention of the American Jewish Congress in civil rights matters and the disproportionally strong participation of Jews in the civil rights movement of the 1960s are likewise worthy of note. Jewish scholars in the social sciences have furthered the cause of the blacks through their research, for instance, the psychologist Otto Klineberg and the anthropologist Melville C. Herskovits. Klineberg has shown that Negro intelligence ratings improve with better schooling; Herskovits has emphasized the strength of surviving Africanisms in the culture of American blacks. Both arguments had in common that they tended to remove the mark of inferiority with which the black man had been stamped for a long time. But other Jewish intellectuals seemed not so much interested in the Negro *qua* Negro as in a crusade for humanity in general. Some of them may indeed have been inclined, as Horace C. Cayton has suspected, to "fight their own battles in terms of the Negro cause." What many liberal as well as radical Jewish spokesmen attempted was to impose their worldview, which entailed a frantic escape from ethnicity, on those who desperately strove to establish their own ethnicity, that is, to actualize the desire to "do their own thing." That kind of imposition could only result in an embittered declaration of independence on the part of the black intellectuals. No people permits members of another ethnic group to tell them what their proper self-image should be.

Some eminent Negro authors have argued with Kenneth B. Clark, that the term "dirty" Jew in a Negro's mouth essentially means "dirty white." That refers to the rantings of black intellectuals, like Harold Cruse, as well as to the emotions of black teenagers. A black educator, Horace Mann Bond, asserted as early as 1964 that a brutal attack of Negro hoodlums on children in a Lubavitch yeshiva in Brooklyn was directed against them as whites, and not as Jews. But why is it, one may ask, do they attack a yeshiva, and not a YMCA? Richard Wright, in describing his childhood in Jackson, Mississippi, provides the answer, when he relates that he and his peers "hated Jews, not because they exploited us, but because we had been taught at home and in Sunday School that Jews were 'Christ-killers'. . . . To hold an attitude of antagonism or distrust toward Jews was bred in us from childhood; it was not merely racial prejudice, it was part of our cultural heritage." Dr. Bond, in reminiscing on his childhood, refers to the same "Christ-killer" syndrome. Indeed, in channeling the aggression against Jews as Jews, and not as "whites," the black man gains the psychological advantage of being part of the dominant majority, if only vicariously. His rage, caged and manacled in so many ways, finds an outlet. However, James Baldwin, in synthesizing Clark's and Wright's analysis, hold that the Jew is caught in the American crossfire. In appearance, he is a white man, but in actuality he is not. "The Negro, facing a Jew," Baldwin maintains, "hates at bottom not his Jewishness but the color of his skin. It is not the Jewish tradition by which he has been betrayed, but the tradition of his native land. But just as a society must have a scapegoat, so hatred must have a symbol. Georgia has the Negro and Harlem has the Jew." Here, the Christ-killer and killer of the American dream are fused into one. One cannot help recalling Hitler's use of the Jew as a symbol of all that is hateful and marked for destruction.

At this point, we return to the question of whether Jews are considered another American minority or whether they are identified with the white majority. As already noted, Jewish opinion, not only the opinion of black and white Gentiles, is divided in this regard. While some Jews are uncomfortable with ethnicity and wish nothing more than that ethnic problems would evaporate into the air of universal reasonableness, other Jews show as clearly ethnocentric cast of mind, to the extent that they are unable to conceive of any other category of human beings but Jews and anti-Semites. One group retreats into self-denial and even self-hatred, the other perceives a genocidal ghost in which there is merely a conflict of interests. These attitudes correspond to a changing American reality. The liberalistic attitude is older, the ethnically accented attitude is more recent; it is possible that the generally mounting emphasis on ethnicity, in which the Jews participate, is an unanticipated consequence of the Negro revolt. If the blacks, who started out with hardly more in common than their dark pigmentation, can acquire a most assertive ethnicity, how can the same recognition be denied the Jews who are the bearers of the most ancient ethno-religious consciousness in the Western world! It remains dubious how many ethnicities will be able to maintain themselves in America, but it is certain that neither blacks nor Jews will disappear from the American scene in the foreseeable future. In that case, what will be the nature of their relations? If they no longer can be based on a presumed identity of interests, will an attempt then me made for Jews and Negroes to participate and coexist as equals in the larger affairs of the nation? The answer to that question may well be the test of a pluralistic society.

18

The State of Israel

The creation of the State of Israel has had its impact on Jewish-Gentile relations. It was a revolutionary event. Throughout the centuries, the Jewish people have never given up their claim to the ancient homeland, and there has never been a time when Jews have not lived in what was then called Palestine; but the restoration of sovereignty has eluded them time and time again. Their prayers for the coming of the redeemer were a mockery to the Gentiles. The claim of the Jews to be the "favorites of God" did not seem to meet with divine acceptance. The contrast between the affluence and even influence of individual Jews, on the one hand, and the powerlessness of the Jewish people "as a *corpo*," on the other, was so glaring as to provoke derision. Even the most influential Jew had to seek the protection of alien sovereigns. The Jewish community could not protect him; to the contrary, Jews who were esteemed and in the seat of power, time and again, have to use their elevated position to intercede for the community. The Jewish people appeared as a ghost people in the image of Ahasver, the wandering Jew, present everywhere but at home nowhere: a mere shadow of their former glory, dead in the eyes of the world, yet refusing to die. Henry Wadsworth Longfellow has expressed this feeling in romantic fashion in his poem about the Jewish cemetery in Newport:

> And thus forever with reverted look
> The mystic volume of the world they read,
> Spelling it backward like a Hebrew book,
> Till life became the legend of the dead.
> But, ah! What once has been shall be no more!
> The growing earth, in travail and pain
> Brings forth its races, but does not restore,
> And the dead nations, never rise again.

For Longfellow, the Jews were a relic of the past. For the historian Toynbee, even now, they are a "fossil," a withered remnant of what he calls the "Syriac" civilization. However, for Emma Lazarus, a Jewish author, Longfellow's sentiment were but a point of departure. In her poem "The New Ezekiel," she asked:

> What, can these dead bones live, whose sap is dried
> By twenty scorching centuries of wrong?

And she answered her own query:

> Yea, prophecy, the Lord has said. Again
> Say to the wind, come forth and breathe afresh,
> Even that they may live upon these slain,
> And bone to bone shall leap, and flesh to flesh.
> The spirit is not dead, proclaim the word,
> Where lay dead bones, a host of armed men stand!
> I open your graves, my people, saith the Lord,
> And I shall place you living in your land.

Emma Lazarus' vision of "armed men" was prophetic, especially if one considers that she wrote under the impact of the Russian pogroms of 1881. A Russian Jew, Leon S. Pinsker, wrote his pamphlet *Auto-Emancipation* under the same impact, with the one significant difference, however, that he, living as he did in Odessa, was close to the events. Agitated mobs encouraged and often incited by the tsarist police had turned upon the Jews in many places, and the Russian intelligentsia remained silent. The dream of emancipation and human brotherhood was shattered; and auto-emancipation, that is, the revival of the Jewish people in their own land, became the new battle cry. The relations between Jews and Gentiles, Pinsker argued, were vitiated by the ghostlike quality of the Jewish people which aroused fear and apprehension. The remedy, as he saw it, was an independent national existence that would make the Jews visible and comprehensible as a people among peoples. Another Jewish writer, Nathan Birnbaum, under the impact of the same events became a co-founder of the first national Jewish student association, Kadimah, in Vienna and the creator of the Maccabaean festival. He and his friends transformed the ancient celebration of Hanukkah from the pious remembrance of a miraculous event of the past into a fiery declaration of independence. His intention was to instill pride and self-respect into

Jewish youth and to create a new symbol that might overshadow the symbols of the past. Theodore Herzl, the founder of political Zionism, merged Pinsker's historical argument and Birnbaum's educational enthusiasm into his famous blueprint of a Jewish state as the "solution" to the Jewish question. Herzl believed with all his heart and mind that the recapture of sovereignty, the creation of "a national home for the Jewish people in Palestine," would go a long way towards removing the causes of enmity against the Jews among the peoples of the earth. Herzl was deeply impressed by the anti-Semitic image of the Jew. He grew up in the midst of the rude German and Austrian anti-Semitism of the 1880s and heard the Parisian mob yell: "Death to the Jews!" during the first stages of *L'Affaire Dreyfus*, which he covered for a leading Viennese paper. He not only recognized the futility of the hope that the rising anti-Semitic movement would leave the Jews in peace, but he also rejected the notion that the motivations of the anti-Semites were beyond comprehension and hence incapable of therapeutic treatment. The *causa remota* of anti-Semitism, he asserted, may be the antagonisms of the Middle Ages, but the *causa proxima* was the overabundance of middle-class and middle-range intellectuals among Jews who necessarily are sharp competitors of the commercial and intellectual middle classes among the Gentiles; the tension could be diminished, in his opinion, if some of these competitors could be removed from Europe. The Zionist argument further maintained that is was deplorable that too many Jews were placed in intermediary occupations and were largely alienated from key industries, from the manual crafts and agriculture. This lopsidedness, it was said, could only be remedied in a Jewish state. It was expected that the anti-Semitic prejudice would disappear "if miserable Jew-boys became proud young Jews," that is, if Jews were to go behind the plough (or drive tractors as we would say now) and if they learned to use rifles and machine guns. The creation of a Jewish state was expected to signify the replacement of one image of Jewish existence by another and the emancipation of an entire people who would thus become an equal among equals in the community of nations.

Have the expectations been justified by events? Dire predictions were not lacking at Herzl's time. One of his contemporaries, the Austrian minister of the treasury von Bilinski, who was a baptized Jew, thought that the Jewish state was likely to be a gigantic trap in which the Jewish people would be caught. Another contemporary, likewise an alienated Jew, the sociologist Gumplowicz, found the notion that sovereignty was a ridiculous solution because it failed to face the problem of how a powerless people could acquire power: nobody would hand power to the Jews on a silver platter. However, by the same token, Gumplowicz would have approved of the events of 1948, 1956, and 1967, if he had lived to see them. Indeed, the emergence of the State of Israel, which was not expected by the political experts and which arose from the desperate resolution of a people that had been dragged to the brink of the abyss, has changed the image of the Jew in the eyes of the young Jewish generation as well as those of the world. The Christian Middle Ages may have receded into the remote past long ago; the Jewish Middle Ages were buried only in 1948. The legendary images of the Jew, a defeated Synagogue, a Judas Iscariot, an Ahasver, a Shylock, a Rothschild, have been dislodged by the images of the Jewish worker and soldier. The Maccabeans are no longer a dream. But closer investigation reveals that this is only one side of a complex picture.

The Jewish masses greeted Herzl's scheme with enthusiasm, but the Viennese Jewish intelligentsia, anticipating Gentile sneers, indulged in witticisms about the "King of the Jews." Indeed, Herzl's majestic appearance recalled Biblical kings. Jews as well as Gentiles were carried away with it. But Herzl's personal impact–a German poet called him "the Moses of our time"–had no immediate effect on the conventional image of the Jew. Rather, the reaction of many, as throughout the centuries, was to contrast the grandiose pretension with the incongruous reality. The alleged Jewish propensity to engage in commercial speculation and to shun productive labor as well as their presumed inability to defend themselves in combat were the recurrent themes prior to Herzl, during Herzl's meteoric career, and after Herzl was gone–until the facts began to speak for themselves. A few examples will have to suffice. The author Hilaire Belloc agrees with early nineteenth-century English travelers in Palestine as well as with the men of the British mandated administration after World War I that only a Jewish army could secure the Zionist experiment, but that the despised race would never face the test of war. Hilaire Belloc conceded that the Jews may have "great power of endurance," but he denied that they could have the "courage of the British kind." His compatriot G.K. Chesterton likened them to locusts who "feed on the community." In France, Anatole Leroy-Beaulieu, assumed that even if the territory of Israel were returned to the Jews, "it would be necessary, in order to attract them to Jerusalem, to construct on Mount Zion a stock exchange, banks, chambers of commerce, and everything needful for those business operations of which they are always trying to secure a monopoly." The height of malicious defamation is reached in the eighth canto of the Austrian writer Robert Hamerling's *Homun Kulus* in which he describes with relish the fancied entry into Jerusalem of the "haggler Jews," the "stock exchange Jews," the "finance barons," the "newspaper Jews," the "art Semites," the "literature Hebrews," and of throngs of "footloose Jew-boys," "buxom Jew-girls," and "Jewish huckster-women," all disparagingly characterized. The gist of the story is that mere speculative ingenuity and critical acumen cannot establish a functioning society in the Holy Land while the world-at-large sorely misses these ingredients. The conclusion is that the Jews renounce the repayment of the loans that the Christians owe them, against the permission to return to Europe. One may say that what is advocated here is a condescending symbiosis of unequals, but the main theme is the confirmation of the hoary contention that the Jews are incapable of engaging in honest labor and devoid of creativity. The Zionist leader Menachem Ussischkin ran into the same attitude *in vivo* in Palestine itself in the early 1920s, when he queried a Christian settler in Galilee about the quality of the swampy soils of the *Emek Jesreel*, which he intended to acquire for the Jewish National Fund. He was told that the suitability of the soils in question notwithstanding, Jewish activities in agriculture were bound to flounder on the inability of the Jews "to make sacrifices." The idea was that the Jews preferred that others did the hard work; only then would they "come and buy it all up." The flourishing Jewish settlements in the *Emek* have long given a lie to that statement. In a similar vein, one may quote what a leading Egyptian intellectual had to say about the negative military virtues of the Jews on the very eve of the Six Day War. Bint al Shâti, a distinguished woman novelist and professor of Arabic literature at Ayn-Shams University in Cairo, wrote on June 2, 1967, in the literary supplement of *Al-Ahrâm* that "the Jews have never entered into an armed conflict by their own choice. Rather, in every period and every generation they used to shy away from a military clash. . . . Cowardice became deep-rooted among them . . .

throughout the ages their weapons were evil and viciousness instead of swords and lances . . ."; and in view of the movement of Egyptian army units into Sinai on May 14 and the closure of the straits of Tiran on May 23, she concluded: "I am certain that Israel will be capable of suffering a measure of degradation, fear and humiliation that no human being could endure and still they would not enter into direct armed clash with. . . ." What happened a few days later is a very different story.

There can be no doubt that the creation of the State of Israel amidst an armed clash with the invading Arab armies, the Sinai campaign of 1956 and finally the Six Day War have made a profound impression on public opinion in many countries. When the British troops withdrew from Palestine in the spring of 1948, nearly everybody–not only the politicians in London, Cairo, and Amman–expected the Jews of Palestine to fold up and frantically apply for help from abroad. Speaking for many, a patient of a New York psychoanalyst confessed that he first thought that the Jews would again be pushed around. He surmised that "all these stories about *Haganah* and *Irgun* [Jewish defense organizations] . . . representing a certain strength were just stories. When the showdown came, they'd be a pushover . . . I thought of the Jews as eternal foreigners, city people who belonged behind a counter in some buying and selling game . . . [But then] . . . the incidents began to look more and more like real military victories . . . they suddenly had become respectable." Even the historian Arnold Toynbee, an otherwise unfriendly observer, in reviewing the Zionist achievement up to 1948, revised–if only for a short moment–his generalized opinion that Jewish ("Syriac") civilization was "fossil" and conceded that "the different response to a different challenge that had been made by the Zionist pioneers in Palestine . . . produced a striking differentiation of ethos and type . . ." After the Six Day War, the left-wing German weekly *Der_Spiegel* admitted in a lead article that "in a simple blitzkrieg the Israelis have conquered the Sinai Peninsula and the entire Federal Republic. With a single exemplary display of tough soldierly skill . . . they have entered into the hearts of the people in whose name once all the Jews were exterminated." In this country, the popular *Reader's Digest*, in contemplating the challenge with which the United States was confronted in the Middle East, concluded that "our aces in this highly dangerous game are the shining courage, the extraordinary and fully proven military proficiency of the Jews of Israel." Words of this kind had indeed a new ring. Within short decades, the Jews had been transformed from supplicants who needed protection into allies of a world power.

However, as it always goes, one attitude overlays, but rarely, if ever, replaces another attitude. The older attitude reasserts itself sooner or later. In this regard, the position taken by spokesmen of the Christian churches is significant because, as we know, some ingrained notions about the Jews are the result of persistent teaching of the Catholic Church as well as the Protestant denominations throughout the centuries that the Church is the "true Israel" and that the Jews were "rejected" and deprived of their land as a punishment for their supposed crime of deicide. To be sure, modern church leaders, such as the late Cardinal Spellman of New York, declared themselves "appalled" by the continued adherence to that notion on the part of many Christians, but the Second Vatican Council's Declaration on the Jews, had expressed itself with undue caution on the matter, "deploring" but not "condemning" hatred of the Jews; the stronger version of the first draft was abandoned. Also, the Second Vatican Council's Declaration had merely vaguely warned "not to impute to the Jews of our time that which was perpetrated in the Passion of Christ" rather than to remove the accusation of "deicide" from an entire people for all times. The reluctance of Church bodies and even of individual churchmen–with notable exceptions, such as Cardinal Cushing of Boston and the Protestant theologian Reinhold Niebuhr–to stand by the side of Israel in the anxious days preceding the Six Day War and the uneasiness at seeing Jerusalem in Jewish hands at the conclusion of the Six Day War and the may be understood as "a kind of unconscious hangover" from ages that otherwise may seem past and gone. Another liberal Protestant theologian expressed himself rather sharply on this issue when he explained that "Christian thinking has been unable, to date, to comprehend the Jew who is a winner." Fortunately, voices are raised inside the Christian churches that intend to promote a new understanding of the legitimacy of the Jewish position that the land of Israel, the people of Israel and the God of Israel are inseparable. This position need not necessarily be incompatible with the Christian belief that Jesus of Nazareth is Christ, the Redeemer.

If liberals have one thing in common with Christians it is that they, too, don't like a winner. It is comforting to rush to the verbal rescue of an underdog, and Israel is not an underdog in the contemporary Middle East. To be sure, many of the liberal spokesmen who, along with I. F. Stone, bewail the emergence of Israel as "a minuscule Prussia," are Jews; but when liberalism shades over into New Left radicalism and Third World enthusiasm, shriller voices are heard, accusing Israel of colonialism, fascism, and imperialism until the point is reached where "anti-Zionism" becomes a lightly veiled mask for old-fashioned anti-Semitism. It is not amazing, then, that both the Student Non-Violent Coordinating Committee (SNCC), which is a black racist and left-wing revolutionary organization, and the National States Rights Party (NSRP), a white racist, anti-Negro, anti-Jewish, neo-Nazi organization, have permitted themselves to become mouthpieces of militant Arab propaganda and are at one in denouncing Jews as "exploiters," "oppressors," "aggressors," "warmongers," and exponents of a Rothschild conspiracy. The accusation of aggressiveness is especially noteworthy in this context because it unites not only the radical left-wing and the radical right-wing, but a broad middle spectrum: it strikes an old chord. The medieval Jew was considered a man of overweening pride and an aggressive enemy of Christ. As against Christian "forgiveness" he was thought of being "revengeful." More recently, "aggressiveness" has been attributed to Jews in numerous attitudinal surveys. But while attributions of this kind in surveys are somewhat unsubstantiated, a leading churchman and past president of Union Theological Seminary, Henry P. van Dusen, was bluntly explicit, when he said shortly after the Six Day War: "All persons who seek to view the Middle East problems with honesty and objectivity stand aghast at Israel's onslaught, the most violent, ruthless and successful aggression since Hitler's blitzkrieg across western Europe in the summer of 1940, aiming not at victory but at annihilation–the very objective proclaimed by Nasser and his allies which had drawn support to Israel." Van Dusen went on to deplore Israel's "callous indifference" to the fate of the displaced Palestinian Arabs and to predict an "inescapable nemesis" in the future. Van Dusen's outburst was refuted by other theologians, but more recently Pope Paul opened a conversation with the visiting Israeli premier with the expression of regret that the Israelis had not been sufficiently "merciful" toward the Arabs. Whatever the merits of that observation, it is worthy of note that van Dusen finds it natural for Arabs to be enraged while the Pope expects the Jews to be compassionate. The measurement is with different yardsticks. With the stench from the gas ovens of Auschwitz and Treblinka still in our nostrils and the insensitivity of the world toward Jewish suffering in the death camps a matter of record, the tortured theme of Jewish callousness is being revived. The Reverend Billy Graham, the evangelist, in an interview in Washington, could not resist the temptation to compare the saturation bombing of Hanoi and Haiphong in December 1972 with Israeli retaliatory raids over Syrian territory, playing down the heavy civilian casualties in the populated centers of North Vietnam and playing up the fewer casualties that occurred in Syrian villages. In other words, while the emergence of Israel as a self-assertive state in the Middle East has changed the image of the Jew, that very self-assertiveness has reinforced attitudes of long standing at the same time.

The re-establishment of Jewish sovereignty after an interlude of two millennia is surely a new phenomenon. And yet, the question marks that accompanied the meteoric rise of political Zionism from the start have retained their validity. Is the enmity of the Arabs, which is embedded in their fear of the superiority of the Jews in all aspects of modernity, preferable to the jealousy of Christian competitors in the countries of the diaspora? How about the rage engendered by the military success of a people that seemed to be an easy target of aggressive impulse? Is sovereignty an effective protection for a small country? Does reliance on a great power offer a guarantee? Is Israel, situated as it is at the crossroads of East and West, not in the same perilous position as it once was when Pharaonic Egypt and Assyria or Babylonia strove for hegemony in the Middle East? Is political intermediacy less dangerously exposed than intermediacy in the social structure? Finally, and most importantly, has the problem of two peoples–Jews and Arabs–living in one country been faced seriously? These questions arrest our thoughts and prevent us from passing a final judgment.

We have carried our deliberations to the threshold of the present moment. The picture we have drawn has many facets, but one conclusion is sure; wherever we may look in the wide panorama of Jewish history which we have unfolded in Europe, saturated as it is with historical precedent, in confusedly groping America, in Israel which is placed between the desert and the Mediterranean Sea, everywhere–the Jew as the role of the mediator who transmits spiritual and material goods is assumed. The mediator, or intermediary, is an outsider who is looked upon with mistrust, but who is sought after on account of his presumed ability to be an impartial judge precisely because he is an outsider and an insider at the same time. The intermediacy between East and West, ruler and ruled, nobleman and commoner, producer and consumer, artist and the public (to mention just a few of the roles of which the entire complex role is composed) has been a cause of irritation and antagonism in many places but it also shows the appreciation with which Jews have been met at all times. Jews have been stimulators, advisers and friends, especially where wounds had to be healed and new life awakened amidst ruins. The Jews cannot escape that role. This being so, the hate of the haters must be taken in stride, if one intends to serve the cause of friendship among peoples and nations that unite all men and women of good will.

Bibliography

Chapter 1: Approach to the Subject

Adorno, T. W. et al. *The Authoritarian Personality*. New York: 1950.

Aly, Goetz. *"Endloesung." Voelkerverschiebung und der Mord an den europaeischen Juden*. Frankfurt am Main: Fischer Verlag, 1995.

Asch, Mitchell G., Soellner, Alfons, eds. *"Forced Migration and Scientific Change" Émigré German-Speaking Scientists and Scholars after 1933*. Washington, DC: Cambridge University Press, 1966.

Battenberg, Friedrich. *Das europaeische Zeitalter der Juden*. Darmstadt: Wissenschaftliche Buchgesellschaft, 1990.

Barkai, Avraham. "Wehr Dich!" Der Centralverein deutscher Staatsbuerger juedischen Glaubens 1893-1938. Munich: C.H. Beck Verlag, 2002.

Barkan, Elazar. *The Guilt of Nations. Restitution and Negotiating Historical Injustices*. New York: W.W. Norton, 2000.

Baron, Salo W. et al. *Great Ages and Ideas of the Jewish People*. New York: Random House, 1956.

Benz, Wolfgang, ed. *Antisemitismus in Deutschland. Zur Aktualitaet eines Vorurteils*. Munich: dtv, 1995.

Blasius D. and Diner, D. eds. *Zerbrochene Geschichte. Leben und Selbstverstaendnis der Juden in Deutschland*. Frankfurt: Fischer Verlag, 1991.

Boman, Thorleif. *Hebrew Thought Compared with Greek*. New York: W.W. Norton, 1970.

Boehm, Franz and Dirks, Walter, eds. *Judentum. Schicksal, Wesen und Gegenwart*. 2vols. Wiesbaden: Franz Steiner Verlag, 1965.

Brenner, Michael and Myers, David N. eds. *Juedische Geschichtsschreibung heute. Themen, Positionen, Kontroversen*. Munich: Verlag C.H. Beck, 2002.

Bronsen, David, ed. *Jews and Germans from 1860 to 1933. The Problematic Symbiosis*. Heidelberg: Winter, 1979.

Brumlik, Micha. *Deutscher Geist und Judenhass. Das Verhaeltnis des philosophischen Idealismus zum Judentum*. Munich: Luchterhand, 2000.

Cantor, Norman F. *The Sacred Chain. The History of the Jews*. New York: HarperCollins Publishers, 1995.

Christie, Richard and Jahoda, Marie, eds. *Studies in the Scope and Method of "The Authoritarian Personality." Continuities in Social Research.*, Glencoe, IL: The Free Press, 1954.

Claussen, Detlev. *Was heisst Rassismus*? Darmstadt: Wissenschaftliche Buchgesellschaft, 1994.

Doepp, Heinz-Martin. *Die Deutung der Zerstoerung Jerusalems und des zweiten Tempels im Jahre 70 in den ersten der Jahrhunderten n.Chr*. Tuebingen: Francke Verlag, 1998.

Douglas, Tom. *Scapegoats. Transferring Blame*. London: Routledge, 1995.

Duker, Abraham G. and Ben-Horin, Meir., eds. *Emancipation and Counter-Emancipation*. New York: KTAV Publishing House, 1974.

Dworkin, Andrea. *Scapegoat. The Jews, Israel and Women's Liberation.* New York: Simon and Schuster, 2000.

Encyclopedia Judaica (6 vols.), Jerusalem, 1971.

Enyedi, Zsolt and Eros, Ferenc, eds. *Authoritarianism and Prejudice. Central European Perspectives*. Budapest: Osiris, 1999.

Fackenheim, Emil L. *Encounters Between Judaism and Modern Philosophy*. New York: Basic Books, 1973.

Fleming, Donald and Bailyn, Bernard, eds. *The Intellectual Migration. Europe and America, 1930-1960*. Cambridge, MA. Harvard University Press, 1969.

Gabel, Joseph. *Reflexions sur l'avenir des juifs*. Paris: Meridiens Klincksieck, 1987.

Girard, Rene. *The Scapegoat*. Baltimore, MD: Johns Hopkins University Press, 1989.

Goodman-Thau, Evelyn and Schmied-Kowarzik, Wolfdietrich, eds. *Messianismus Zwischen Mythos und Macht: Juedisches Denken in der europaeischen Geistegeschichte*. Berlin: Akademie Verlag, 1994.

Greffrath, Mathias, ed. *Die Zerstoerung einer Zukunft. Gespraeche mit emigrierten Sozialwissenschaftlern*. Hamburg: Rowohlt, 1979.

Guttmann, Julius. *Philosophies of Judaism. A History of Jewish Philosophy from Biblical Times to Franz Rosenzweig*. New York: Schocken, 1973.

Hermand, Jost. *"Judentum und deutsche Kultur." Beispiele einer schmerzhaften Symbiose*. Cologne: Boehlau, 1996.

Herberg, Will. *Protestant, Catholic, Jew*. New York: Doubleday Anchor, 1960.

Horkheimer, Max and Adorno, Theodor W. *Dialektik der Aufklaerung*. Amsterdam: Querido Verlag, 1947.

Jaher, Frederic Cople. *A Scapegoat in the New Wilderness: the Origins and Rise of Antisemitism in America*. Cambridge, MA: Harvard University Press. 1994.

Kaplan, Mordecai M. *Judaism as a Civilization*. New York: Macmillan, 1934.

Katz, Jacob, ed. *Toward Modernity: The European Jewish Model*. New Brunswick, NJ: Transaction Publishers, 1987.

The Koran. Transl. N.J. Dawood. New York: Penguin Books, 1956.

Krinsky, Carol Herselle. *Synagogues of Europe. Architecture, History, Meaning*. Cambridge, MA: MIT Press, 1985.

Kueng, Hans. *Das Judentum*. Munich/Zurich: Piper, 1991.

Kuenzl, Hannelore. *Juedische Kunst. Von der biblischen Zeit bis in die Gegenwart.* Munich: Verlag C.H. Beck, 1992.

Landmann, Michael. *Juedische Miniaturen*. 2 vols. Bonn: Bouvier, 1982.

Landmann, Salcia. *Der juedische Witz*. Olten and Freiburg: Walter Verlag, 1960.

Levy, Ze'ev. *Between Yafeth and Shem. On the Relationship Between Jewish and General Philosophy*. New York: Peter Lang, 1987.

Lindemann, Albert S. *Anti-Semitism before the Holocaust*. Boston, MA: Addison-Wesley Pub. Co., 2000.

Maier, Johann. *Das Judentum. Von der biblischen Zeit bis zur Moderne*. Munich: Kindler Verlag, 1973.

Maier, Joseph B. and Waxman, Chaim I. *Ethnicity, Identity, and History. Essays in Memory of Werner J. Cahnman*. New Brunswick, NJ: Transaction Publishers, 1983.

McDonald, Kevin. *A People That Shall Dwell Alone*. Westport, CT: Praeger, 1998.

—. *Separation and Its Discontents*. Westport, CT: Praeger, 1998.

—. *The Culture of Critique: An Evolutionary Analysis of Jewish Involvement in Twentieth Century Intellectual and Political Movements*. Westport. CT: Praeger, 1998.

Meyer, Michael A. ed. *German-Jewish History in Modern Times*, 4 vols. New York: Columbia University Press, 1996.

Moses, Julius. *Die Loesung der Judenfrage. Eine Rundfrage*. Berlin-Leipzig: Modernes Verlagsbureau, 1907.

Niewyk, Donald and Nicosia, Francis. *The Columbia Guide to the Holocaust*. New York: Columbia University Press, 2000.

Reichmann, Eva. *Groesse und Verhangnis deutsch-judischer Existenz. Zeugnisse einer tragischen Begegnung*. Heidelberg: Lambert Schreider Verlag, 1974.

Rosen, Jonathan. *The Talmud and the Internet. A Journey Between Worlds*. New York: Farrar, Straus, and Giroux, 2000.

Roskies, David G. *Against the Apocalypse. Responses to Catastrophe in Modern Jewish Culture*. Cambridge, MA: Harvard University Press, 1984.

Roth, Cecil. *A History of the Jews*. New York: Schocken Books, 1989.

Schluchter, Wolfgang, ed. *Max Webers Studie ueber das antike Judentum*. Frankfurt am Main: Suhrkamp Verlag, 1981.

Schoeps, Julius H. and Schloer, Joachim, eds. *"Antisemitismus." Vorurteile und Mythen*. Munchen-Zurich: Piper Verlag, 1995.

Schubert, Kurt. *Christentum und Judentum im Wandel der Zeiten*. Vienna: Boehlau, 2003.

Schulte, Christoph. *Die juedische Aufklaerung. Philosophie, Religion, Geschichte*. Munich: C.H. Beck, 2002.

—. *.Deutschtum and Judentum. Ein Disput unter Juden aus Deutschland*. Ditzingen: Reclam, 2002

Shepherd, Naomi. *Ploughing the Sand: British Rule in Palestine 1917-1948*. London: John Murray, 1999.

Simon, H./Simon, M. *Geschichte der juedischen Philosophie*. Munich: Verlag C.H. Beck, 1984.

Srubar, Ilja, ed. *Exil, Wissenschaft, Identitaet*. Frankfurt am Main: Suhrkamp Verlag, 1988.

Stern, Fritz. *Gold and Iron and the Building of the German Empire*. New York: Vintage Books, 1979.

Thadden von, Rudolf, ed. *Die Krise des Liberalismus zwischen den Weltkriegen.* Goettingen: Sammlung Vandenhoeck, 1978.

Waldenegg, Georg Christoph Berger. *Antisemitismus: Eine gefaehrliche Vokabel. Diagnose eines Wortes.* Wien: Boehlau, 2003.

Werblowsky, Zwi R.J. and Wigoder. Geoffrey, Eds. *The Oxford Dictionary of the Jewish Religion.* Oxford: Oxford University Press, 1997.

Wiehn, Erhard et al. *Juden in der Soziologie.* Konstanz: Taschenbuch, 1989.

Zweig, Arnold. *Bilanz der deutschen Judenheit.* Cologne: Joseph Metzler Verlag, 1961.

Chapter 2: Theology as a Point of Departure

St. Augustine. *Civitas Dei.*

Babylonian Talmud, The. 35 vols. London: Soncino Press, 1935-1952.

Baron, S. W. *A Social and Religious History of the Jews.* 3 vols. New York: Columbia University Press, 1952.

___. *The Jewish Community: Its History and Structure to the American Revolution.* 3 vols. Philadelphia, PA: Jewish Publication Society, 1942.

Bernstein, F. *Der Antisemitismus als Gruppenerscheinung. Versuch einer Soziologie des Judenhasses.* Berlin: 1926.

Bickerman, Elias. *The Maccabees.* New York: Schocken Books, 1947.

Birnbaum, Philip. *Daily Prayer Book.* New York: Hebrew Publishing Co. 1949.

Brentano L. *Der wirtschaftende Mensch in der Geschichte.* Leipzig, 1923.

Cicero, *Oratio pro Flacco.*

Epstein, Abraham. R. *Moses ha-Darshan aus Narborme.* Vienna, 1891.

Graetz, Heinrich. *History of the Jews.* 6 vols. Philadelphia, PA: Jewish Publication Society, 1891-95.

Holy Scriptures, The, 2 vols. Philadelphia, PA: Jewish Publication Society, 1955.

Isaac, Jules. *Genèse de l'antisémitism.* Paris: Calmann Levy, 1956.

Koran, The. Translated by N. J. Dawood. New York: Penguin Books, 1956.

Marcus, Ralph. "Antisemitism in the Hellenistic-Roman World." In: Koppel S. Pinson, ed. *Essays on Antisemitism.* New York: Conference on Jewish Relations, 1946.

Mommsen, Theodor. *History of Rome*, 4.vols, 1854-56.

Moore, George Foote. *Judaism in the First Centuries of the Christian Era*, 3 vols. Cambridge, MA, Harvard University Press, 1927-30.

Murawski, Friedrich. *Die Juden bei den Kirchenvaetern und Scholastikern.* Berlin, 1925.

Pirenne, Henri. *Mohammed and Charlemagne.* Cleveland, OH: Meridian Books, 1957.

Poliakov, Leon. *A History of Antisemitism.* New York: Alfred A. Knopf, 1965.

Reinach, Theodore. *Texts d'auteurs Grecs et romains relatifs an Judaisme.* Paris, 1895.

Reinharz, Jehuda, ed. *Living With Antisemitism. Modern Jewish Responses.* Hannover, NH: University Press of New England, 1987.

Rengstonf and Kontzfleisch von, Siegfried. *Kiche und Synagoge. Handbuch zur Geschichte von Christen und Juden*, 2 vols. Stuttgart, 1968.

Seiferth, Wolfgang S. *Synagogue and Church in the Middle Ages. Two Symbols in Art and Literature*. New York: Frederick Ungar, 1970.
Stobbe, O. *Die Juden Deutschlands waehrend des Mittelalters in politischer, sozialer und rechtlicher Beziehung*, third ed. Berlin, 1923.
Tacitus. Histories V, chs. I and V.
Taubes, Jacob. *Die politische Theologie des Paulus*. Munich: Wilhelm Fink Verlag, 1995.
Toennies, Ferdinand. *Community and Society*, edited by Charles Loomis. New York: Harper and Row, 1957.
Weber, Max. *Ancient Judaism*. Translated and edited by H.H. Gerth and Don Martindale. New York: The Free Press, 1952.
___. *General Economic History*. New York: Collier Books, 1961.
Wischnitzer, Mark. *A History of Jewish Crafts and Guilds*. New York: Jonathan Davis, 1965.

Chapter 3: The Initial Position of the Jews in the Social Structure

Cabaniss, Allen. *Agobard of Lyon, Churchman and Critic*. Syracuse, NY: Syracuse University Press, 1953.
Goitein, S.D. *Jews and Arabs: Their Contacts through the Ages*. New York: Schocken Books, 1964.
Kisch, Guido. *The Jews in Medieval Germany: A Study of their Social and Legal Status*. Chicago: University of Chicago Press, 1949.
Margolis, Marx and Marx, Alexander. *A History of the Jewish People*. Philadelphia, PA: Jewish Publication Society of America, 1941.
Rabinowitz, L. *Jewish Merchant Adventurers*. London: Edward Goldston, 1948.
Roth, Cecil. *The Jewish Contribution to Civilization*. London: Macmillan, 1938.
___. *The History of the Jews of Italy*. Philadelphia, PA: Jewish Publication Society of America 1946
Strauss, Raphael. *Die Juden in Wirtschaft und Gesellschaft*. Frankfurt am Main, 1964.
Zuckermann, Arthur J. *A Jewish Princedom in Feudal France, 768-900*. New York: Columbia University Press, 1972.

Chapter 4: The Usury Privilege

Aquinas, Thomas. *Summa Theologica*. London: Burns, Oates, and Washburn, 1920-29.
Baron, Salo W. "The Economic Views of Maimonides," in: *Essays on Maimonides: An Octocentennial* volume, New York: Columbia University Press, 1941.
Bertholet, Alfred. *Die Stellung der Israeliten und der Juden zu den Fremden*. Freiburg und Leipzig, 1896.
Bloch, Joseph. *Israel und die Voelker nach juedischer Lehre*. Berlin-Wien, 1922.

Caro, G . *Sozial und Wirtschaftsgeschichte der Juden in Mittelalter und in der Neuzeit* Frankfurt am Main: Kaufmann Verlag, 1924.
Doellinger von, Ignaz. *Die Juden in Europa*. Berlin: Philo Verlag, 1924.
Guttman, Michael. *Das Judentum und seine Umwelt*. Berlin: Philo Verlag, 1927.
Nelson, Benjamin. *The Idea of Usury. From Tribal Brotherhood to Universal Otherhood*. 2nd ed. Chicago: University of Chicago Press, 1969.
Neuman, Abraham. *The Jews in Spain*. Philadelphia, PA: Jewish Publication Society, 1942.
Silberschmidt, W. *Die Kommenda in ihrer fruehesten Entwicklung bis zum 13. Jahrhundert*. Wuerzburg, 1884.
Strieder, Jakob. *Studien zur Geschichte kapitalistischer Organisationsformen: Monopole, Kartelle, und Aktiengesellschaften im Mittelalter und zu begin der Neuzeit*. Munich und Leipzig, 1925.
Trachtenberg, Joshua. *The Devil and the Jew*. New Haven, CT: Yale University Press, 1943.
Weber, Max. *Economy and Society*. 2 vols. Roth, Guenther and Wittich, Claus, eds. New York: Bedminster Press, 1968.
Wolfson, Harry A. *Philo: Foundations of Religious Philosophy in Judaism, Christianity and Islam*. Cambridge, MA: Harvard University Press, 1948.

Chapter 5: The Revolt of the Masses

Baschwitz, Kurt. *Du und die Masse. Studien zu einer exakten Massenpsychologie*. Leiden: Brill, 1951.
Bayer-Katte, Wanda. *Das Zerstoerende in der Politik*. Heidelberg, 1958.
Cohn, Norman. *The Pursuit of the Millenium*. New York: Oxford Press, 1970.
Freud, Sigmund. *Massenpsychologie und Ich-Analyse*. Leipzig: Internationaler Psychoanalitischer Verlag, 1923.
Goitein, S. D. *Jews and Arabs. Their Contacts Throughout the Ages*. New York: Schocken Books, 1967.
Hobsbawm, E.J. *Primitive Rebels. Archaic Forms of Social Movements in the 19th and 20th Centuries*. New York: W.W. Norton, 1959.
Parker, James W. *The Jew in the Medieval Community*. London, 1938.
Russel, Josiah, "Late Ancient and Medieval Population," *Transactions of the American Philosophical Society*, New Series, vol. 48, part 3, June 1958.
Straus, Raphael. *Regensburg und Augsburg*. Philadelphia, PA: Jewish Publication Society, 1939.
Synan Edward A. *The Popes and the Jews in the Middle Ages*. New York: Macmillan, 1965.

Chapter 6: The Jews and the Society of the High Middle Ages

Cambridge Medieval History. Vol. VII.
Chaucer, Geoffrey. *Canterbury Tales*.
Jacobs, Joseph. *The Jews of Angevin England*. New York-London, 1893.
Jones, Ernest. *On the Nightmare Part II: The Connection between the Nightmare and Certain Medieval Superstitions*. London: Hogarth Press, 1931.

Kisch, Guido. *The Jews in Medieval Germany. A Study of their Legal and Social Status*. Chicago: Chicago University Press, 1949.
Koehne, M. et al. *Politik und Bildung*. Braunschweig: Internationaler Arbeitskreis Sonnenberg, 1963.
Kracauer, J. *Geschichte der Juden in Frankfurt am M.* Frankfurt a. M.: Kaufmann Verlag, 1925
Park, Robert. *Race and Culture*. Glencoe, IL: The Free Press, 1950.
Roscher, Wilhelm. "Die Stellung der Juden in Mittelalter," in: *Aussicht der Volkswirtschaft aus dem geschichtlichen Standpunkte*, vol. II (1878).
Straus, Raphael. "Die Judengemeinde Regensburg im ausgehender Mittelalter." In: *Heidelberger Abhandlungen.*
Weber, Max. *The Religion of China.* Transl. H.H. Gerth. New York: The Free Press, 1951.
___. *The Religion of India.* Transl. H.H. Gerth and Don Martindale. New York: The Free Press, 1958.

Chapter 7: The Judeo-Arabic Symbiosis and The Splendor and Misery of the Jews of Spain

Baer, J. *Die Juden in christlichen Spanien.* Berlin, 1929-1936.
Becker, Howard and Barnes Harry Elmer. *Social Thought from Lore to Science.* Vol. I, New York, 1961.
Benech, Jose. *Essai d'explication d'un Melalh*, Paris, 1940.
Castro, Americo. *The Structure of Spanish History*. Princeton, NJ: Princeton University Press, 1954.
Chouraqui, Andre. *La Condition juridique de l'Israelite Maroccain*. Paris: Presses du Livre Français, 1950.
Coon, Carleton. *Measuring Ethiopia and Flight into Arabia*. Boston: Little, Brown,1935.
Fischel, W.J. "Jews in the Economic and Political Life of Medieval Islam," in: *Royal Asiatic Society Monographs*, vol. XXII, London, 1937.
Levy, Reuben. *The Social Structure of Islam*. Cambridge: Cambridge University Press, 1957.
Goitein, S.D. *Jews and Arabs. Their Contactsa Through the Ages*. New York: Schocken Books, 1964.
Menocal Maria Rosa. *The Ornament of the World*. Boston: Little, Brown, 2002.
Neuman, A.A. *The Jews in Spain. Their Social, Political and Cultural Life During the Middle Ages*. Vols. I & II, Philadelphia, PA: Jewish Publication Society, 1942.
Rosenstock, Morton, "Economic and Social Conditions among the Jews of Algeria 1790-1848," *Historia Judaica*, April 1956.

Chapter 8: The Jews of Eastern Europe

Aly, Goetz and Gerlach, Christian. *Das letzte Kapitel. Der Mord an den ungarischen Juden*. DVA 2002.

Balaban, Majer. *Skizzen und Studien zur Geschichte der Juden in Polen*. Berlin, 1911.

Bibo, Istvan. *Zur Judenfrage. Am Beispiel Ungarns nach 1944*. Transl. Bela Rasky, Frankfurt am Main: Verlag Neue Kritik, 1990.

Blue, Brian and Strom, Yale. *The Last Jews of Eastern Europe*. New York: Philosophical Library, 1986.

Braham, Randolph L., ed., *Hungarian Jewish Studies*. Vols. 1-3.New York: World Federation of Hungarian Jews, 1966-1973.

___. *The Holocaust in Hungary. A Selected and Annotated Bibliography, 1984-2000*. New York: Columbia University Press.

Braham, Randolph L. and Miller, Scott eds. *The Nazis' Last Victims: The Holocaust in Hungary*. Detroit, MI: Wayne State University Press, 1998.

Braham, Randolph L. and Pok, Attila, eds., *The Holocaust in Hungary: Fifty Years Later*. Boulder, CO: Social Science Monographs, 1997.

Dawidowicz, Lucy S., ed., *The Golden Tradition: Jewish Life and Thought in Eastern Europe*. Boston: Beacon Press, 1967.

Deak, Istvan. *Essays on Hitler's Europe*. New York: Columbia University Press.

___. Jan Gross, and Tony, Judt, eds., *Politics of Retribution in Europe: World War II And its Aftermath*. New York: Columbia University Press.

Denes, Bela. *Avos vilag Magyarorszagon. Egy cionista orvos emlekiratai*. Budapest: Kossuth kiado, 1991.

Deutscher, Isaac. *The Non-Jewish Jew and Other Essays*. New York: Hill and Wang, 1968.

Don, Yehuda and Karady, Victor, eds., *A Social and Economic History of Central European Jewry*. New Brunswick, NJ: Transaction Publishers, 1990.

Dubnow, S. M. *History of the Jews in Russia and Poland from the Earliest Times Until the Presentday*. 3 vols. Philadelphia, PA: Jewish Publication Society, 1916-1920.

___. *Weltgeschichte des juedischen Volkes von seinen Uranfaengen bis zur Gegenwart*. vol. 1-10, Berlin, 1925-1929.

Fejto, Ferenc. *Hongrois et Juifs. Histoire millenaire d'un couple singuler, 1000-1997* Paris, Balland, 1997.

Fischer, Rolf. *Entwicklungstufen des Antisemitismus in Ungarn 1867-1939. Die Zerstoerung der magyarisch-juedischen Symbiose*. Munich, 1988.

Frojimovics, K. et al. *Jewish Budapest*. Budapest: CEU Press, 1998.

Gati, Charles. *Hungary and the Soviet Bloc*. Durham, NC: Duke University Press, 1986.

Gazda, Aniko et al. *Magyarorszagi zsinagogak*, Budapest: Muszaki, 1989.

Goldman, Nahum. *Autobiography of Nahum Goldman*. New York: Holt, Rinehart, and Winston, 1969.

Gyurgyak, Janos. *A zsidokerdes Magyarorszagon*. Budapest: Osiris kiado, 2001.

Hahn, Hans Henning and Stueben, Jens, eds. *Juedische Autoren Ostmitteleuropas im 20. Jahrhundert*. Frankfurt am Main: Peter Lang, 2002.

Hanak, Peter. *Ungarn in der Donaumonarchie. Probleme der buergerlichen Umgestaltung eines Vielvoelkerstaates*. Munich: Oldenbourg Verlag, 1984.

Howe, Irving. *World of Our Fathers. The Jews of Eastern Europe*. New York: Harcourt Brace Jovanovich, 1976.

Jenks, William A. *Vienna and the Young Hitler*. New York: Columbia University Press, 1960.

Karady, Victor. *Gewalterfahrung und Utopie. Juden in der europaeischen Moderne*. Frankfurt a. M., 1999.

Kende, Peter. *Ropirat a zsidokerdesrol*. Budapest: Magveto, 1989.

Komlos, Aladar. *Magyar zsido szellemtortenet a reformkortol a Holocaustig*. (vol. 5), Budapest, 1997.

Kovacs, Andras. ed. *Zsidok es zsidosag a mai Magyarorszagon*. Budapest: Szombat, 2002.

Kubizek, A. *Young Hitler. The Story of our Friendship*. Boston: Houghton Mifflin, 1955.

Lendvai, L. Ferenc, Horvath Pal, Sohar, Aniko, eds. *Het evtized a hazai zsidosag eleteben*. 2 vols. Budapest: Magyar Filozofiai Intezet, 1990.

Levy, Robert. *Ana Pauker: The Rise and Fall of a Jewish Communist*. Berkeley: University of California Press, 2001.

Maimon, Salomon. *Geschichte des eigenen Lebens 1754-1800*. Berlin, 1935.

Marcus, Judith. *Georg Lukacs and Thomas Mann*. Atlantic Highlands, NJ: Humanities Press, 1987.

__, ed. *Surviving the Twentieth Century*. New Brunswick, NJ: Transaction Publishers, 1999

___. and Zoltan Tarr, eds. *Foundations of the Frankfurt School*. New Brunswick, NJ: Transaction Publishers, 1984.

McCagg, William O. Jr. *Jewish Nobles and Geniuses in Modern Hungary*. Boulder, CO: East European Quarterly, 1972.

___. *A History of Habsburg Jews 1670-1-1918*. Bloomington: University of Indiana Press, 1989.

Patai, Raphael. *The Jews of Hungary. History, Culture, Psychology*. Detroit, MI: Wayne State University Press, 1996.

Pok, Attila. "Scapegoats and Conspirators in 20th Century Hungary. Theoretical and Methodological Thoughts," in: *Kuzdelem az igazsagert. Tanulmanyok Randolph L. Braham 80. szuletesnapjara*, Budapest, 2002.

Poliakov, Leon. *The History of Antisemitism*. New York: Alfred A. Knopf, 1965.

Ranki, Vera. *The Politics of Inclusion and Exclusion: Jews and Nationalism in Hungary*. New York: Holmes and Meier, 1999.

Schulvass, Moses. *From East to West: The Westward Migration of Jews from Eastern Europe During the Seventeenth and Eighteenth Centuries*. Detroit, 1971.

Silber, Michael K. ed. *Jews in the Hungarian Economy 1760-1945*. Jerusalem: Magnes Press, 1992.

Simon, Robert, Ed. *Zsidokerdes Kelet- es Kozep-Europaban*. Budapest: ELTE, 1985.

Strauss, Herbert A., ed. *Hostages of Modernization. Studies on Modern Antisemitism 1870-1933. Austria-Hungary-Poland-Russia*. Berlin-New York: Walter de Gruyter, 1993.

Szabo, Robert. *A kommunista part es a zsidosag*. Budapest: Windsor kiado,

1995.
Tabor, Bela. *A zsidosag ket utja*. Budapest: Pesti Szalon Konyvkiado, 1990.
Marcus, Judith and Zoltan Tarr. "The Judaic Element in the Teachings of the Frankfurt School. In: *Leo Baeck Institute Year Book* XXXI (1986).
Tarr, Zoltan. *The Frankfurt School*. New York: Schocken Books, 1985.
Tarr, Zoltan. "Georg Lukacs zur Judenfrage," in: *Lukacs 2000. Jahrbuch der internationalen Georg-Lukacs Gesellschaft*. Bielefeld, 2000.
Ujvari, Peter, ed. *Magyar zsido lexikon*. Budapest: A Magyar zsido lexikon kiadasa, 1929.
Ungvari, Tamas. *Ahasverus es Shylock. A "zsidokerdes" Magyarorszagon*. Budapest: Akademiai, 1999.
Vago, Bela, ed. *Jewish Assimilation in Modern Times*. Boulder, CO: Westview Press, 1981.
Vago Bela and Mosse, George L. eds. *Jews and Non-Jews in Eastern Europe*. New York-Toronto, John Wiley & Sons, 1974.
Venetianer, Lajos. *A magyar zsidosag tortenete*. Budapest: Konyvertekesito vallalat, 1986.
Wistrich, Robert S. *Socialism and the Jews. The Dilemmas of Assimilation in Germany and Austria-Hungary*. London: Associated University Presses, 1982.
Yaron, Baruch, ed. *Jewish Assimilation and Radicalism in Hungary*. Jerusalem: Magnes Press, 1985.

Chapter 9: The Ghetto

Abbon, J.D. *Musulmans Andalons et Jude-Espagnols*. Casablanca, 1953.
Balaban, Majer. *Die Judenstaat von Lublin*. Berlin, 1919.
Benech, Jose. *Essai d'explication d'un Mellah*. Paris, 1940.
Cahnman, Werner J. "Ghetto," in: *Encyclopedia Britannica, Standard Jewish Encyclopedia Universal Jewish Encyclopedia.*
Goethe, J W. *Dichtung und Wahrheit*. Munchen: dtv, 1962, vol. 1, pp. 136ff.
Gregonovias, Ferdinand. *The Ghetto and the Jews of Rome*. New York, 1966.
Isaacs, Lionel A. *The Jews of Majorca*. London, 1936.
Lestschinky, Jacob, "Ghetto" in: *Encyclopedia of the Social Sciences.*
Levy, Robert. *Ana Pauker: The Rise and fall of a Jewish Communist*. Berkeley:University of California Press, 2001.
Philippson, David. *Old European Jewries*. Philadelphia, PA: Jewish Publication Society, 1894
Poliakoff, Leon. *Harvest of Hate*. London: Paul Elek, 1954.
Schnitt, Johann Jacob. *Juedische Merkwuerdigkeiten*. Frankfurt a. M. 1727.
Vorobeidnic, M. *The Ghetto Lane in Vilna*. Zurich und Leipzig, 1931.
Wirth Louis. *The Ghetto*. Chicago: University of Chicago Press, 1956.
Zborowski, Mark and Herzog, Elizabeth. *Life is with People: The Culture of the Shtetl*. New York: Schocken Books, 1969.
Zangwill, Israel. *Children of the Ghetto*. Philadelphia, PA: Jewish Publication Society, 1919.
___. *Dreamers of the Ghetto*. Philadelphia, PA: Jewish Publication Society, 1948.

Chapter 10: Court Jews and Bankers

Arendt, Hannah. *The Origins of Totalitarianism*. New York: Meridian, 1951.
Bloch, Josef Samuel. *Erinnerungen aus meinem Leben*. Wien-Leipzig: R. Lowit Verlag, 1923.
Cahman, Werner J. "Adolf Fischoff and his Jewish Followers." In: *Yearbook of the Leo Baeck Institute* (1959), pp. 111-139.
Cahnman, Werner. J. and Heberle, R. eds. *Ferdinand Toennies on Sociology*. Chicago: University of Chicago Press, 1971.
Conti, Egon Caesar Corti. *Der Aufstieg des Hauses Rotschild 1770-1830*. Leipzig: Insel Verlag, 1927.
___. *Das Haus Rotschild in der Zeit seiner Bluete 1830-1871*. Leipzig: Insel Verlag, 1928.
Ferguson, Niall. *The House of Rothschild. The World's Banker, 1849-1999*. New York: Viking-Penguin, 2000.
Fuchs, Eduard. *Juden in der Karikatur*. Munchen: A. Langen 1921.
Graeber, I. and Britl, S.A., eds. *Jews in a Gentile World*. New York: Macmillan, 1942.
Hertzberg, Arthur. *The French Enlightenment and the Jews*. New York: Columbia University Press, 1968.
___. *The Zionist Idea. A Historical Analysis and Reader*. New York: Athenaeum, 1959.
Hess, Moses. *Rom und Jerusalem*. Leipzig, 1862.
Marx-Engels Gesamtausgabe, vol I. Frankfurt a.M. und Moskau: Marx-Engels Verlag, 1927-1935.
Lueth, Erich. *Der Bankier und der Dichter*. Hamburg: Verlag "Der gute Tambour," 1964.
Parker, James. *The Jewish Problem in the Modern World*. London, 1939.
Patai, Raphael, ed. *The Complete Diaries of Theodor Herzl*. Vol. I, New York: Herzl Press, 1960.
Priebatsch, F. "Die Judenpolitik des furstlichen Absolutismus im 17. und 18. Jahrhundert," in: *Festschrift fur Dietrich Schaefer*, Jena, 1915.
Rengstoff, K.H. and Kontzfleisch, I. *Kirche und Synagoge*. Vol II, Stuttgart, 1970.
Silberner, Edmund. ed. *Moses Hess-Briefwecshel*. Gravenhage, 1959.
Simon, Leon. ed. *Selected Essays by Ahad Ha-am*. Philadelphia, PA: Jewish Publication Society 1936.
Sombart, Werner. *Der moderne Kapitalismus*. Leipzig: Duncker und Humblot, 1902.
___. *The Jews and Modern Capitalism*. New York: Burt Franklin, 1969.
Strieder, Jakob. *Jakob Fugger, der Reiche*. Leipzig, 1926.
Szajkowski, Zosa. *The Economic Status of the Jews in Alsace, Metz and Lorraine, 1648-1789*. New York, 1954.
Thomas, L. Alphonse. *Toussenel, socialiste national antisemite, 1803-1885*. Paris, 1941.
Tietze, Hans. *Die Juden Wiens*. Leipzig, 1933.

Toussenel, Alphonse de. *Les Juifs, rois de l'epoque: histoire de la feodalite nanciere*. Paris, 1846.

Weber, Max. *General Economic History*. Transl. Frank H. Knight, New York: Collier Books, 1961.

Chapter 11: *Galut* and Citizenship

Anchel, Robert. *Napoleon et les Juifs*. Paris: les presses universitaires de France, 1928.

Baron, Salo W. *Die Judenfrage und der Wiener Kongress*. Wien-Berlin: R. Lowit, 1920.

Dreifuss, E.M. *Die Familiennamen der Juden. Ein Beitrag zur Geschichte der Emanzipation*. Frankfurt a.M. 1927.

Graupe, Heinz. *Die Entsehung des modernen Judentums Geistesgeschichte der deutschen Juden 1650-1942*. Hamburg, 1969.

Katz, Jacob. *Die Entstehung der Judenassimilation in Deutschland und deren Ideologie*. Frankfurt a.M. 1935.

Kayserling, Meyer. *Moses Mendelsohn. Sein Leben und Wirken*. 1888.

Meyer, Michael. *The Origins of the Modern Jew*. Detroit, MI: Wayne State University Press, 1967.

Patai, Raphael. *The Tents of Jacob. Diaspora Yesterday and Today*. Englewood Cliffs, NJ: Prentice-Hall, 1971.

Stern, Selma. "The First Generation." In: *Leo Baeck Institute Yearbook*, vol. XV. 1970.

Stillschereig, Kurt. "Die Judenemanzipation im Licht des franzoesischen Nationalbegriffs" In: *Monatshefte fur. die Geschichte und Wissenschaft des Judentums*, vol. LXXXI (1927), pp. 457-478.

Sussman, Margaret. *Moses Mendelsohn-Gestalten und Kreise*. Zurich, 1959.

Szajkowszki, Zoja. *Jews and the French Revolutions of 1789, 1830 and 1848*. New York: KTAV, 1970.

Thompson, J.M. ed. *Napoleon Self-Revealed in Three Hundred Selected Letters* Boston: Houghton Mifflin, 1934.

Rost, L. and Leist F. eds. *Koenig Maximilian II von Bayern und Schelling*. Stuttgart, 1890.

Zinberg, Israel. *A History of Jewish Literature*. New York: KTAV, 1976.

Chapter 12: From Liberalism to Racism: The Dialectics of Catastrophe

Boehlich, Walter, ed. *Der Berliner Antisemitismusstreit*. Frankfurt a. Main: Insel Verlag, 1965.

Dohm, Christian Wilhelm. *Uber die buergerliche Verbesserung der Juden*. Berlin und Stettin, 1783.

Drumont, Edouard. *La France Juive. Essai d'histoire contemporaine*. Paris, 1886.

Ehrenberg, Richard. *Grosse Vermoegen. Ihre Entstehung und Bedeutung*. Jena, 1902.

Ferguson, Niall. *The House of Rotschild. The World's Banker, 1849-1999.* New York: Viking-Penguin, 2000.
Fichte, Johann Gottlieb. *Saemtliche Werke.* Berlin, 1845.
Fries, J.F. Uber die *Gefaehrdung d. Wohstandes und des Charakters der Deutschen durch die Juden.* Heidelberg, 1816.
Grunwald, Kurt. *Tuerkenhirsch: A Study of Baron Maurice de Hirsch, Entrepreneur and Philantropist.* Jerusalem: Israel Program for Scientific Translation, 1966.
Hobsbawm, E.J. *The Age of Revolution 1789-1848.* Cleveland, OH: World Publishing, 1962.
Huemmert, L. *Die finanziellen Beziehungen juedischer Bankiers und Heereslieferanten zum bayerischen Staat.* Munich, 1927.
Joehlinger, O. *Bismarck und die Juden.* Berlin: C. Reimer, 1921.
Lips, A. *Ueber die kuenftige Stellung der Juden in den Bundesstaaten.* Erlangen. 1819.
Mannheim, Karl. *Ideology and Utopia.* New York: Harcourt, Brace, and World, 1936.
Ruchs, F. *Ueber die Anspruche der Juden an das deutsche Buergerrecht.* Berlin, 1816.
Silberner, Edmund. *Sozialisten zur Judenfrage.* Berlin: Colloquium Verlag, 1962.
Smulheimer, Paul. *Die finanziellen Beziehungen der Juden zum bayerischen Staat im 18. Jahrhundert.*
Sterling, Eleanore. *Er ist wie Du. Fruehgeschichte des Antisemitismus.* Munich: Kaiser Verlag, 1956
Stern, Selma. *The Court Jew.* Philadelphia, PA: Jewish Publication Society, 1950.
Treitschke, Heinrich von. "Ein Wort ueber unser Judentum," *Preussische Jahrbuecher*, 15. Nov. 1879.

Chapter 13: The Actual Jew and the Mythical Jew

Barkai, Avraham. *"Wehr Dich!" Der Centralverein deutscher Staatsbuerger juedischen Glaubens. (C.V.)*, Munich: C. H. Beck Verlag, 2002.
Beller, Steven. *Vienna and the Jews.* New York: Cambridge University Press,
Bettelheim, Anton. *Berthold Auerbach. Der Mann, sein Werk, sein Nachlass.* Stuttgart and Berlin, 1907.
Cahnman, Werner J. "Friedrich Wilhelm Schelling ueber die Judenemanzipation," In: *Zeitschrift fuer bayerische Landesgeschichte*, vol. 37 (1974) pp. 614-623.
Erckmann-Chatrian. *L'Ami Fritz.* Paris, 1865.
Fichte, Johann Gottlieb. *Berliner Vorlesungen ueber die Bestimmung des Gelehrten*, 1841.
___. *Reden an die deutsche Nation,* 1808.
Freytag, Gustav, *Soll und haben.* Leipzig, 1888.
Jeggle, Utz. *Judendoerfer in Wuerttemberg.* Tuebingen: Verlag .f. Volksde. 1969.
Klemm, Gustav. *Allgemeine Culturgeschichte der Menscheit.* 10 vols. Leipzig, 1843-52.

Mayer, Sigmund. *Die Wiener Juden 1700-1900.* Vienna: K. Lowith Verlag, 1917.

Oppenheimer, Moritz. *Erinnerungen.* Frankfurt a.Main, 1924.

Rosenstock, Morton. "Economic and Social Conditions Among the Jews of Algeria," In: *Historia Judaica.* Vol. XVIII, April 1956.

Tietz, Georg and Tietz, Hermann. *Geschichte einer Familie und ihrer Warenhaeuser* Stuttgart, 1966.

Vogelin, Eric. *Rasse und Staat*, Tuebingen, 1933.

Wagner, Richard. *Das Judentum in der Musik.* Leipzig, 1869.

Wasserman, Jakob. *Mein Weg als Deutscher und Jude.* Berlin: Fischer Verlag, 1921.

Chapter 14: A Comment about the Soviet Union

Borschtschagowski, Alexander. *Orden fuer einen Mord. Die Judenvefolgung unter Stalin.* Berlin: Propylaen Verlag, 1997.

Dubnow, Simon. *History of Jews in Russia and Poland.* New York: KTAV Publishing House, 1975.

Ehrenburg, Ilya, and Vasily Grossman, eds. *The Complete Black Book of Russian Jewry.* New Brunswick, NJ: Transaction Publishers, 2001.

Gessen, Iurii. Istoriia evreiskogo naroda v Rossii (History of the Jewish People in Russia) 2 vols., 1925-27.

Luks, Leonid. *Der Spaetstalinismus und die "juedische" Frage.* Vienna: Boehlau, 1998.

Lumer, Hyman, ed. *Lenin On the Jewish Question.* New York: International Publishers, 1974.

Nedava, Joseph. *Trotsky and the Jews.* Philadelphia, PA: Jewish Publication Society, 1972.

Shapiro, Leo. *Soviet Jewry Since the Death of Stalin.* New York: The American Jewish Committee, 1978.

Solzhenitsyn, Alexander. *Dvesti let vmeste* (Two Hundred Years Together). Moscow: Russkii Put, 2001.

Vetter, Matthias. *Antisemiten und Bolschewiki. Zum Verhaeltnis von Sowjetsystem und Judenfeindschaft 1917-1939.* Berlin: Metropol Verlag, 1995.

Chapters 15 & 16: Is Americas Different?; Varieties of Pluralism in America

The American Jewish Yearbook. New York: The American Jewish Committee.

Bayme, Steven, ed. *Facing the Future. Essays on Contemporary Jewish Life.* New York: KTAV, 1989.

Birmingham, Stephen. *Our Crowd. The Great Jewish Families of New York.* New York: Harper & Row, 1967.

Cahnman, Werner J., ed. *Intermarriage and Jewish Life. A Symposium.* New York: Herzl Press, 1963.

Cohen, Rich. *Tough Jews: Fathers, Sons and Gangster Dreams.* New York: Simon & Schuster, 1998.

Cohen, Naomi W. *Jacob H. Schiff: A Study in American Jewish Leadership*. Hannover, NH: Brandeis University Press, 1999.
Fein, Leonard. *Where are We? The Inner Life of America's Jews*. New York: Harper & Row, 1988.
Glazer, Nathan. *American Judaism*. Chicago: University of Chicago Press, 1972.
Hertzberg, Arthur. *A Jew in America: My Life and a People's Struggle for Identity*. San Francisco, CA: HarperSanfrancisco, 2003.
Novick, Peter. *The Holocaust in American Life*. Boston: Houghton Mifflin Company, 1999.
Shafir, Shlomo. *Ambiguous Relations. The American Jewish Community and Germany Since 1945*. Detroit, MI: Wayne State University Press, 1999.
Sklare, Marshall. *America's Jews*. New York: Random House, 1971.

Chapter 17: Jews and Blacks

Berman, Paul, ed. *Blacks and Jews: Alliances and Arguments*. New York: Delacorte, 1994..
Davis, Lenwood G., *Black-Jewish Relations in the United States, 1752-1984*. Westport, CT: Greenwood, 1984.
Geltman, Max. *The Confrontation: Black Power, Anti-Semitism, and the Myth of Integration*. Englewood Cliffs, NJ: Prentice-Hall, 1970.
Halpern, Ben. *Blacks and Jews*. New York: Herder & Herder, 1971.
Harris, Louis. *Black-Jewish Relations in New York City*. New York: Praeger, 1970.
Lerner, Michael and West, Cornel, eds. *Jews & Blacks: A Dialogue on Race, Religion, and Culture in America*. New York: Putnam, 1995.

Chapter 18: The State of Israel

Brenner, Michael. *Zionism: A Brief History*. Princeton, NJ: Markus Wiener, 2003.
Evron, Boaz. *Jewish State or Israeli Nation*. Bloomington: Indiana University Press, 1995.
Ezrachi, Yaron. *Gewalt und Gewissen. Israels langer Weg in die Moderne*. Berlin: Alexander Fest Verlag, 1998.
Freedman, Samuel G. *Jew vs. Jew: Struggle for the Soul of American Jewry*. New York: Simon & Schuster, 2000.
Karmi, Ghada and Cotran, Eugene, eds. *The Palestinian Exodus 1948 bis 1999*. Reading, PA: Ithaca Press, 1999.
Rabinovich, Itamar. *Waging Peace. Israel and the Arabs at the End of the Century*. New York: Farrar, Straus & Giroux, 1999.
Robertson, Ritchie. *Theodor Herzl and the Origins of Zionism*. New York: Columbia University Press, 1997.
Rogan, Eugene L. and Shlaim, Avi , eds. *The War for Palestine: Rewriting the History of 1948*. Cambridge: Cambridge University Press, 2001.
Samuel, Edwin. *The Structure of Society in Israel*. New York: Random House, 1969.
Schoeps, Julius H. *Theodor Herzl 1860-1904*. Vienna: Brandstatter, 1995.

Shepherd, Naomi. *Ploughing Sand: British Rule in Palestine 1917-1948*. London: John Murray, 1999.

Shlaim, Avi. *The Iron Wall: Israel and the Arab World.* New York: W.W. Norton, 1999.

Sternhell, Zeev. *The Founding Myths of Israel: Natonalism, Socialism, and the Making of the Jewish State*. Princeton, NJ: Princeton University Press, 1998.

Halpern, Ben. *The Idea of the Jewish State.* Cambridge, MA: Harvard University Press, 1961.

Talmon, Yonina. *Family and Community in the Kibbutz.* Harvard University Press, 1974.

Wolffsohn, Michael. *Die unbeliebten Juden. Israel—Legenden und Geschichte*. Munchen und Zurich: Diana Verlag, 1998.

Zimmerman, Moshe. *Wende in Israel. Zwischen Nation und Religion*. Berlin, 1996.

Selected Bibliography of Werner J. Cahnman

Books

Co-author (with Jean Comhair): *How Cities Grew: The Historical Sociology of Cities* (Madison, NH: Florham Park Press, 1959).

Editor: *Intermarriage and Jewish Life: A Symposium* (New York: The Herzl Press and the Jewish Reconstructionist Press, 1963).

Co-editor. (with Alvin Boskoff): *Sociology and History: Theory and Research* (New York: The Free Press, 1964).

Co-editor (with Rudolf Heberle): *Ferdinand Toennies on Sociology: Pure, Applied, and Empirical* (Chicago: University of Chicago Press, 1971).

Editor: *Ferdinand Toennies: A New Evaluation* (Leiden: E.J. Brill, 1973).

Weber and Toennies: Comparative Sociology in Historical Perspective, editors: Joseph B. Maier, Judith Marcus, and Zoltan Tarr. (New Brunswick, NJ: Transaction Publishers, 1995).

Articles

1937

"Warum hebräisch lernen?" in *Frankfurter Israelitisches Gemeindeblatt* (March 1937).

1941

"The Decline of the Munich Jewish Community 1933-38," in *Jewish Social Studies* Vol. III, No. 3 (1941), p. 285.

1942

"Jewish Morale in Our Time," in *Social Forces,* Vol. 20, No. 4 (May 1942), pp. 491-496.

"Methods of Geopolitics," in *Social Forces*, Vol. 21, No. 2 (December 1941), pp. 147-154.

"Stefan Zweig in Salzburg," in *Menorah Journal*, Vol. XXX, No. 2, pp. 195-198.

1943

"An Ethical Will and A Memorial Tribute," in *Reconstructionist*, Vol. IX, No. 10 (June 25, 1943), pp. 29-32.

"Concepts of Geopolitics," in *American Sociological Review*, Vol. VIII, No. 1 (Feb. 1943), pp. 55-59.
"The Mediterranean and Caribbean Regions – A Comparison in Race and Culture Contacts," in *Social Forces,* Vol. 22, No. 2 (Dec. 1943), pp. 209-214.
"A New Learning," by Franz Rosenzweig, in *Chicago Jewish Forum*, Vol. 1, No. 3 (Spring 1943), pp. 55-61.
"Reflections on the Sociology of the Jews," in *Jewish Frontier*, Vol. X, No. 4 (99) (April 1943), pp. 13-17.
"A Regional Approach to German Jewish History," in *Jewish Social Studies*, Vol. V, No. 3, pp. 211-224.
"Two Maps on German-Jewish History," in *Chicago Jewish Forum*, Vol. 2, No. 1 (Fall 1943), pp. 58-65.

1944

"An American Dilemma," in *Chicago Jewish Forum*, Vol. 3, No. 2 (Winter 1994-45), pp. 92-96.
"The Concept of *Raum* and the Theory of Regionalism," in *American Sociological Review*, Vol. IX, No. 5 (Oct. 1944), pp. 455-462.
"Ethiopia and Palestine," in *Jewish Frontier*, Vol. XI, No. 9 (116) (Sept. 1944), pp. 12-16.
(with Wayland J. Hayes) "Foreign Area Study (ASTP) as an Educational Experiment in the Social Sciences," in *Social Forces*, Vol. 23, No. 2 (Dec. 1944), pp. 160-164.

1945

"Conflict Patterns in the Near East," in *Chicago Jewish Forum*, Vol. 4, No. 2 (Winter 1945-46), pp. 81-85.
"France in Algeria, in *Review of Politics*, Vol. 7, No. 3 (July 1945), pp. 343-357.
"Negroes and the Jews," in *Youth and Nation*, Vol. XIII, No. 9 (June 1945), pp. 11-13.

1946

"The Arabs and the Zionist Policy," in *Youth and Nation*, Vol. XIV, No. 7 (May 1946), pp. 6-8.
"Ein Deutscher Jude an einer Neger-Universität," in *Aufbau* (April 19, 1946), pp. 19-20.
"The Emergence of Negro Consciousness," in *Jewish Frontier*, Vol. XIII, No. 4 (134) (April 1946), pp. 14-17.
"The Italians in America," in *Jewish Frontier*, Vol. XIII, No. 2 (132) (Feb. 1946), pp. 8-10.
"Life History of the Norwegian Americans," in *Jewish Frontier*, Vol. XIII, No. 1 (131) (Jan. 1946), pp. 16-19.

1948

"Communication and Opinion," in *American Sociological Review*, Vol. XIII, No. 1 (Feb. 1948), p. 96.
"Intercultural Education and Jewish Content," in *Reconstructionist*, Vol. XIV, No. 6 (April 29, 1948), pp. 9-15.

"Outline of a Theory of Area Studies," in *Annals of the Association of American Geographers*, Vol. XXXVIII, No. 4 (Dec. 1948), pp. 233-243.

"Principles for Jewish Centers," in *Chicago Jewish Forum*, Vol. 7, No. 1 (Fall 1948), pp. 43-47.

1949

"Attitudes of Minority Youth: A Methodological Introduction," in *American Sociological Review*, Vol. XIV, No. 4 (Aug. 1949), pp. 543-548.

"Frontiers Between East and West in Europe," in *Geographical Society*, Vol. XXXIX, No. 4 (1949), pp. 605-624. (Reprinted in the Bobbs-Merrill *Reprint Series in Geography*.)

"Theories of Anti-Semitism" in *Chicago Jewish Forum*, Vol. 8, No. 1 (Fall 1949), pp. 50-53.

1950

"The Jewish Scene in the United States," in *Midwest Journal*, Vol. 3, No. 1 (Winter 1950-51), pp. 24-30.

1952

(with H. Mendelsohn) "Communist Broadcasts to Italy," in *Public Opinion Quarterly*, Vol. 16, No. 4 (Winter 1952-53), pp. 671-680.

1953

"The MacIver Report Recommendations and Philosophy," in *Chicago Jewish Forum*, Vol. 11, No. 1 (Fall 1953), pp. 1-5.

1954

(with Alice Taylor) "Spain" in *Focus*, Vol. V, No. 3 (Nov. 1954), pp. 1-6.

1955

"The Story of North Africa," in *Chicago Jewish Forum*, Vol. 14, No. 1 (Fall 1955), pp. 37-39.

"Suspended Alienation and Apathetic Identification, in *Conference on Jewish Social Studies*, Vol. XVII, No. 3, pp. 223-228.

"The Tercentenary Conference on American Jewish Sociology," in *Reconstructionist*, Vol. XX, No. 19 (Jan. 2, 1955), pp. 24-28.

"The UN Territory in Jerusalem: A Proposal" in *Congress Weekly*, Vol. 25, No. 18 (Nov. 24).

1956

"Religion in Israel" in *Reconstructionist*, Vol. XXI, No. 18 (Jan. 13, 1956), pp. 17-22.

"The Weiner Library," in *Chicago Jewish Forum*, Vol. 14, No. 4 (Summer 1956), pp. 235-237.

1957

"Socio-Economic Causes of Antisemitism," in *Social Problems*, Vol. V, No. 1 (July 1957), pp. 21-29.

1958

"A Program for the Refugees," in *New Outlook*, Vol. II, No. 3-4 (Nov./Dec. 1958), pp. 17-22.

"The Frustrated Escapist," in *Reconstructionist*, Vol. XXIV, No. 2 (March 7, 1958), pp. 15-20.

"Scholar and Visionary," in *Herzl Year Book*, Vol. I, ed. Raphael Patai (Herzl Press, New York, 1958), pp. 165-179.

1959

"Adolph Fischhof and his Jewish Followers," in *Year Book IV of the Leo Baeck Institute of Jews From Germany* (London, 1959), pp. 111-139.

"Reconstruction in the Wirondacks," in *Reconstructionist,* Vol. XXV, No. 17 (Dec. 25, 1959), pp. 12-14.

1960

"Race-Individual and Collective Behavior," in *Chicago Jewish Forum*, Vol. 18, No. 3 (Spring 1960), pp. 229-232.

1962

"Culture, Civilization, and Social Change," in *Sociological Quarterly*, Vol. III, No. 2 (April 1962), pp. 93-106.

1964

"In the Dachau Concentration Camp," in *Chicago Jewish Forum*, Vol. 23, No. 1 (Fall 1964), pp. 18-23.

"The Life of Clementine Kraemer," in *Year Book IX of the Leo Baeck Institute* (London, 1964), pp. 267-292.

1965

"Attitudes of German Youth," in *Reconstructionist*, Vol. XXXI, No. 5 (April 16, 1965), pp. 14-17.

"Ideal Type Theory: Max Weber's Concept and Some of its Derivations," in *Sociological Quarterly*, Vol. 6 (Summer 1965), pp. 268-280.

"Martin Buber: A Reminiscence," in *Reconstuctionist*, Vol. XXXI, No. 12 (Oct. 15, 1965), pp. 7-11.

"Role and Significance of the Jewish Artisan Class," in *Jewish Journal of Sociology*, Vol. VII, No. 2 (Dec. 1965), pp. 207-220.

1966

"The Historical Sociology of Cities: A Critical Review," in *Social Forces,* Vol. 45, No. 2 (Dec. 1966), pp. 156-162.

1967

"Ghetto," in *Encyclopedia Britannica* (1967), p. 389.

"The Interracial Jewish Children," in *Reconstructionist*, Vol. XXXIII, No. 8 (June 9, 1967), pp. 7-11.

"New Intermarriage Studies: A Critical Survey," in *Reconstructionist*, Vol. XXXIII, No. 2 (March 17, 1967), pp. 7-12.

1968

"The Stigma of Obesity," in *Sociological Quarterly*, Vol. 9, No. 3 (Summer 1968), pp. 283-299.

1969

"A Comment on My Son the Doctor," in *American Sociological Review*, Vol. 34, No. 6 (Dec. 1969), pp. 935-936.

1970

"Germany in 1970," in *Reconstructionist*, Vol. XXXVI, No. 13 (Dec. 25, 1970), pp. 14-18.

"Tönnies and Durkheim: Eine dokumentarische Gegenüberstellung," in *ARSP* Vol. 1970, LVI/2, pp. 189-208.

1971

"Eine Geschichte der Soziologie," in *ARSP*, Vol. 1971, LVII/1, pp. 129-138.

"Sociology," in *Encyclopaedia Judaica*, Vol. 15, SM-UN, columns 62-69.

1972

"Adolf Fischhof's jüdische Persönlichkeit," in *Zeitschrift für Religionswissenschaft und Theologie* (Neue Folge, XIV, Jahrgang 1972), pp. 110-120.

"Rolle und Bedeutung der Jüdischen Handwerkerklasse," in *Archiv. Europ. Sociology*, Vol. XIII (1972), pp. 111-125.

"Soziologie und Geschichte," in Hans-Ulrich Weber, ed. (Kiepenheuer & Witsch, Köln, 1972), pp. 157-186.

1973

"Jews and Blacks: An Overview," in *Reconstructionist*, Vol. XXXVIII, No. 10 (Jan. 1973), pp. 7-14.

"Werner Cahnman at Seventy," in *Reconstructionist*, Vol. XXXIX, No. 5 (June 1973), pp. 24-32.

1974

"Adolf Fischhof als Verfechter der Nationalität und seine Auswirkung auf das jüdisch–politische Denken in Österreich," in *Studia Judaica Austriaca* (Wien, 1974), pp. 78-91.

"Der Dorf und Kleinstadtjude als Typus," in *Zeitschrift für Volkskunde*, Vol. II (1974), pp. 169-193.

"Friedrich Wilhelm Schelling über die Judenemanzipation," in *Zeitschrift für bayerische Landesgeschichte* (Bd. 37, Heft 2, 1974), pp. 614-625.

"Der Pariah und der Fremde: Eine begriffliche Klärung," in *Archiv. Europ. Sociology*, Vol. XV (1974), pp. 166-167.

"Pariahs, Strangers, and Court-Jews: A Conceptual Clarification," in *Sociological Analysis*, Vol. 35, No. 3 (Fall 1974), pp. 155-166.

"Village and Small Town Jews in Germany: A Typological Study," in *Year Book XIX of the Leo Baeck Institute* (London, 1974), pp. 107-130.

1976

"Historical Sociology: What It Is and What It Is Not," in Baydia N.Varma, *New Social Sciences* (Westport, CT., Greenwood Press, 1976), pp. 107-122.

"Tönnies, Durkheim and Weber," in *Social Science Information*, Vol. 15, No. 6 (1976), pp. 839-853.

"Vico and Historical Sociology," in *Social Research*, Vol. 43, No. 4 (Winter 1976), pp. 826-836.

1977

"Agenda für das Studieren des Landjudentums," in *Vereinigte Zeitschrif-schrift über Israel und Judentum* (Heft Nr. 5-6, 1977), pp. 5-10.

"Tönnies in America," in *History and Theory*, Vol. XVI, No. 2 (1977), pp. 147-167.

1979

"Adolf Fischhof and the Problem of the Reconciliation of Nationalities," in *East European Quarterly*, Vol. XII, No. 1 (1979), pp. 43-56.

(with C.M. Schmitt) "The Concept of Social Policy," in *Journal of Social Policy*, Vol. 8, Part 1 (Jan. 1979), pp. 47-59.

1980

"Nature and Varieties of Ethnicity," in Parmatma Saran and Edwin Eames, eds. *The New Ethics: Asian Indians in the United States* (New York: Praeger, 1980), pp. 5-28.

1989

"The Three Regions of German-Jewish History," in *German Jewry: Its History and Sociology* (Oxford, U.K.: Transaction Publishers, 1989), pp. 3-14.

"The Role and Significance of the Jewish Artisan Class," Ibid., pp. 29-42.

"The Jews of Munich: 1918-43" (annotated and translated from the German by Judith Marcus), Ibid., pp. 97-150.

"Martin Buber: A Reminiscence," Ibid., pp. 201-206.

"Friedrich Wilhelm Schelling and the New Thinking of Judaism," Ibid., pp. 209-248.

Reviews

1943

Baron, *The Jewish Community*. Reviewed in *Social Forces,* Vol. 22, No. 1 (October 1943), pp. 111-113..

Dropalen, Andreas, *The World of General Haushofer: Geopolitics in Action* (New York: Farrar & Rinehart, Inc., 1942). Reviewed in *Journal of Political Economy*, Vol. LI, No. 3 (June 1943), pp. 268-272.

Weigert, H.W., *Generals and Geography: The Twilight of Geopolitics* (New York: Oxford University Press, 1942). Reviewed in *Journal of Political Economy,* Vol. LI, No. 3 (June 1943), pp. 268-272.

Whittlesey, Derwent, with collaboration of Colby, C.C. and Hartshorne, R., *German Strategy of World Conquest* (New York: Farrar & Rinehart, Inc., 1942). Reviewed in *Journal of Political Economy,* Vol. LI, No. 3 (June 1943), pp. 268-272.

1944

Elbogen, Ismer, *A Century of Jewish Life,* translated from the German by Moses Hadas, with an appreciation of the author by Prof. Alexander Marx (Philadelphia: The Jewish Publication Society of America, 1944). Reviewed in *Social Forces,* Vol 23, No. 2 (October 1944), pp. 229-230.

Johnson, Charles S. and associates, *To Stem This Tide: A Survey of Racial Tension Areas* (Boston and Chicago: Pilgrim Press, 1943). Reviewed in *Jewish Social Studies*, Vol. VI, No. 3 (July 1944), pp. 286-288.

Kulischer, *The Displacement of Population in Europe*. Reviewed in *Social Forces,* Vol. 22, No. 4 (May 1944), pp. 457-458.

1945

Bienfeld, F.R. *The Germans and the Jews*, translated by Herdman Pender (New York: Frederick Ungar, 1939). Reviewed in *Jewish Social Studies*, Vol. VII, No. 2 (April 1945), pp. 161-164.

1946

Nathan, R., Gass, O., Creamer, D. *Palestine, Problem and Promise: An Economic Study* (Washington, D.C.: Public Affairs Press, American Council on Public Relation, 1946). Reviewed in *Social Forces,* Vol. 25, No. 2 (December 1946), pp.230-231.

1948

Hugelmann, K.G., Boehm, M.H., Hasselblatt, W., eds., "Volksehre und Nationalitaetenrecht in Geschichte und Gegenwart," Ser., 3, Vol. I (Essen: Essener Verlagsanstalt, 1940). Reviewed in *American Journal of Sociology,* LIII, No. 4 (July 1947-May 1948), pp. 309-311.

Kloss, Heinz, *Das Volksgruppenrecht in den Vereingten Staaten von Amerika*, Erster Band: *Die Erstsiedlergruppen* ("The Right of Ethnic Groups in the U.S.A., Vol. 1: "The First Settlers"). Reviewed in *American Journal of Sociology*, LIII, No. 4 (July 1947-May 1948), pp. 309-311.

Roth, Cecil, *The History of the Jews of Italy* (Philadelphia 5706-1946: The Jewish Publication Society of America). Reviewed in *Menorah Journal*, Vol. XXXVI, No. 1 (Winter 1948), pp. 102-114.

Simey, T.S., *Welfare and Planning in the West Indies* (Oxford: Clarendon Press, 1946). Reviewed in *American Journal of Sociology*, Vol. LIII, No. 4 (July 1947-May 1948), pp. 309-311.

1949

Linton, Ralph, ed., *Most of the World: The Peoples of Africa, Latin America and the East Today* (New York: Columbia University Press, 1949). Reviewed in *American Journal of Sociology,* Vol. LV, No. 1 (July 1949), pp. 106-108.

1952

Chonraqui, André, *La Condition Juridique de l'Israélite Marocain* (Paris: Alliance Israélite Universelle: Presses du Livre Français, 1950). Reviewed in *Jewish Social Studies,* Vol. XVI, No. 3 (July 1954), pp. 275-276.

Chonraqui, André, *Marche vers l'Occident-Les Juifs d'Afrique du Nord* (Paris, Presses Universitaires de France, 1952). Reviewed in *Jewish Social Studies,* Vol. XVI, No. 3 (July 1954), pp. 275-276.

Chonraqui, André, *The Social and Legal Status of the Jews of French Morocco* (New York: The American Jewish Committee, 1952). Reviewed in *Jewish Social Studies*, Vol. XVI, No. 3 (July 1954), pp. 275-276.

Zborowski, Mark and Herzog, Elizabeth, *Life Is With people: The Jewish Little-Town of Eastern Europe* (New York: International Universities Press Inc., 1952). Reviewed in *American Sociology Review*, Vol. 17, No. 5 (October 1952), pp. 655-656.

1954

Mead, M. and Metraux, R., eds., *The Study of Culture at a Distance* (Chicago: The University of Chicago Press, 1953). Reviewed in *American Sociological Review*, Vol. 19, No. 6 (December 1954), pp. 792-793.

Sraffa, *The Works and Correspondence of David Ricardo*. Reviewed in *Social Forces*, Vol. 32, No. 4 (May 1954), pp. 379-380.

1957

Eisenstadt, S.N., *The Absorption of Immigrants: A Comparative Study Based Mainly on the Jewish Community in Palestine and the State of Israel* (Glencoe, Ill.: The Free Press 1955). Reviewed in *Jewish Social Studies*, Vol. XIX, No. 3-4 (July-October 1957), pp. 156-157.

Hughes, E.C. and Hughes, H.M., *Where People Meet: Racial and Ethnical Frontiers* (Glencoe: The Free Press, 1952). Reviewed in *Jewish Social Studies*, Vol. XVII No. 1 (January 1955), pp. 74-75.

1958

Zwiedinek, Otto von, *Mensch und Wirtschaft: Aufsaetze und Abhandlungen zur Wirtschaftstheorie und Wirtschaftspolitik* ("Man and Economy: Essays and Discussions of the Economic Theory and Policy") (Berlin: Duncker and Humblot, 1955). Reviewed in *American Journal of Sociology*, Vol. LXIV (July 1958-May 1959), pp. 329-331.

1960

Antoni, Carlos, *From History to Sociology: The Transition in German Historical Thinking*, translated by Hayden V. White (Detroit: Wayne State University Press, 1959). Reviewed in *American Sociological Review*, Vol. 25, No. 1 (February 1960), pp. 120-121.

1961

Siddur, de Sola Pool, *The Traditional Prayerbook for Sabbath and Festivals,* ed. and translated by David de Sola Pool (New Hyde Park: New York

University Books, 1960). Reviewed in *Social Forces*, Vol. 39, No. 4 (May 1961), p. 356.

1966

Schwarz, Stefan, *Die Juden in Bayern im Wandel der Zeiten* (München und Wien: Gunter Olsog Verlag, 1963). Reviewed in *Jewish Social Studies*, Vol. XXVIII, No. 1 (January 1966), pp. 43-46.

1968

Ringer, B., Vol. II: *The Edge of Friendliness: A Study of Jewish-Gentile Relations* (New York and London, 1967). Reviewed in *American Jewish Historical Quarterly*, Vol. LVIII, No. 2 (December 1968), pp. 287-291.

Sklare, M. and Greenblum, J., *The Lakeville Studies: Vol. I: Jewish Identity on the Suburban Frontier. A Study of Group Survival in the Open Society*. Reviewed in *American Jewish Historical Quarterly*, Vol. LVIII, No. 2 (December 1968), pp. 287-291.

1969

Glock, Charles Y. and Stark, Rodney, *Christian Beliefs and Anti-Semitism*. Reviewed in *Social Forces*, Vol. 47, No. 3 (March 1969), pp. 349-350.

Symmons-Symonolewicz, Konstantin, *Modern Nationalism: Towards a Consensus in Theory* (New York: The Polish Institute of Arts and Sciences in American, 1968). Reviewed in *Journal of Social History*, Vol. 2, No. 4 (1969), pp. 280-282.

Weber, Max, *Economy and Society*, ed. Gunter Roth and Claus Wittich. Reviewed in *Social Forces*, Vol. 48, No. 2 (December 1969), pp. 269-270.

1970

Aron, Raymond, Main Currents in Sociological Thought, Vol. 1: *Montesquieu, Comte, Marx, Tocqueville, The Sociologists and the Revolution of 1848* (New York: Basic Books, 1965). Reviewed in *Journal of the History of the Behavioral Sciences*, Vol. VI, No. 4 (October 1970), pp. 368-370.

Aron, Raymond, Main Currents in Sociological Thought, Vol. II: *Durkheim, Pareto, Weber* (New York: Basic Books, 1967). Reviewed in *Journal of the History of the Behavioral Sciences*, Vol. VI, No. 4 (October 1979), pp. 368-370.

Erikson, Kai T., *Wayward Puritans: A Study in The Sociology of Deviance* (New York: John Wiley & Sons, 1966). Reviewed in *Journal of the History of the Behavioral Sciences*, Vol. VI, No. 4 (October 1970), pp. 367-368.

Lipset, S. M. and Hofstadter, R., eds., *Sociology and History: Methods* (New York: Basic Books, 1968). Reviewed in *Journal of the History of the Behavioral Sciences* Vol. VI, No. 4 (October 1970), pp. 373-375.

Mitzman, Arthur, *The Iron Cage: An Historical Interpretation of Max Weber* (New York: Alfred A. Knopf, 1970). Reviewed in *Journal of the History of the Behavioral Sciences*, Vol. VI, No. 4 (October 1970), pp. 373-375.

Nisbet, R.A., *Social Change and History: Aspects of the Western Theory of Development* (New York: Oxford University Press, 1969). Reviewed in *Journal of Social History*, Vol. 4, No. 2 (Winter 1970-71), pp. 190-192.

1971

Banton, Michael, *Race Relations* (New York: Basic Books, 1967). Reviewed in *Journal of the History of the Behavioral Sciences*, Vol. VII, No. 1 (January 1971), pp. 109-111.

1972

Ben-Sasson, H.H. and Ettinger, S., *Jewish Society Through the Ages* (New York: Schocken Books, 1972). Reviewed in *Americn Jewish Historical Quarterly*, Vol. LXII, No. 2 (December 1972), pp. 220-222.

Itzkoff, Seymour, *Ernst Cassier: Scientific Knowledge and the Concept of Man* (Notre Dame/London: University of Notre Dame Press, 1971). Reviewed in *ISIS* 63, 3, 218 (1972), pp. 425-427.

1973

Hummell, H.J. and Opp, K.D., *Die Reduzierbarkeit von Soziologie auf Psychologie: Eine These, ihr Test und ihre Theoretische Bedeutung* (Braunschweig: Friedrich Vieweg & Sohn, 1971). Reviewed in *American Journal of Sociology*, Vol. 78, No. 6 (May 1973), pp. 1559-63.

Pollack, Herman, *Jewish Folkways in Germanic Lands (1648-1806): Studies in Aspects of Daily Life* (Cambridge, Mass.: The M.I.T. Press, 1971). Reviewed in *Journal of Social History* (Fall 1973), pp. 104-105.

1975

Medick, Hans, *Naturzustand und Naturgeschichte der bürgerlichen Gesellschaft: Die Ursprünge der bürgerlichen Sozialtheorie als Geschichtspilosophie und Sozialwisssenschaft bei Samuel Pufendorf, John Locke und Adam Smith* (Kritische Studien zur Rupprecht, Göttingen, 1973). Reviewed in *Archiv für Rechts und Sozialphilosophie*, Bd. LXI, 1 (1975), pp. 151-154.

Index